Buddhism in Japan

With an Outline of Its Origins in India

*Bodhidharma, by Soga Jasoku. From the Daruma Triptych,
late fifteenth century. Height 87 cm. Yōtoku-in Temple,
Kyoto.*

Buddhism in Japan

With an Outline of Its Origins in India

By

E. Dale Saunders

Philadelphia
University of Pennsylvania Press

A mon maître
Monsieur Charles Haguenauer
professeur à la Sorbonne
en témoignage de ma respectueuse gratitude

Buddhism -- Japan - History

Foreword

THE FOLLOWING HISTORY of Japanese Buddhist Doctrine is neither exhaustive nor detailed. If anything, it may be called "selective." My aim has been to provide an historical framework, based on the noteworthy points of Buddhist Doctrine, which the reader may use as a point of departure for further reading. Although the following pages focus on the evolution of the Doctrine in Japan, it is, of course, impossible to limit a study of what is, after all, a "foreign" religion for the Japanese to Japan alone. Therefore, the history has been divided into two parts: Part I, giving the general outlines of the Doctrine as it evolved in India; and Part II, presenting a more detailed treatment, according to sects, of Buddhism in the Japanese islands from earliest times until the twentieth century. The evolution of Buddhism in China, certainly pertinent to Japanese religious history, has been omitted, though I have made specific reference to the Chinese phase under the various Japanese sects whenever I felt that such information served to fill out the history of a sect in Japan. Chinese Zen, for example, has been accorded considerably more space than the continental antecedents of other sects.

In general, the Sanskrit names of elements of the Buddhist *Tripitaka* have been preserved in Part I, while Japanese transcriptions have regularly been used in Part II. When necessary, in Part II, the Sanskrit title has been given in parentheses after the Japanese. It will be noted that each sūtra title is followed by the letter T and a numeral. The T refers to the Taishō edition of the Chinese *Tripitaka* and the numerals to the listing in the Taishō edition as given in the tables of the *Hōbō-girin, Dictionnaire encyclopédique du bouddhisme d'après les sources chinoises et japonaises.* Sūtra readings have also been based on this source.

Since, as was noted above, the present history is meant to provide a point of departure for further reading, a bibliography has been appended. Here too, the bibliography is not exhaustive but selective in nature. It will be noted that sections on Chinese and Tibetan Buddhism have been included for the benefit of those wishing to read on these subjects, even though they have not been treated extensively in the text. Quotations and references in the text have been kept to a minimum. They may be consulted in an appendix.

Quite a number of Sanskrit and Japanese names are used in the following pages. Sanskrit being to Buddhism what Latin is to Christianity, it has been impossible to avoid the basic technical terms in their original language, as well as in Japanese. A note concerning the treatment and pronunciation of these words may be of assistance.

In general, both Sanskrit and Japanese words have been italicized in the main body of the text only on first usage. In Japanese words the macron has been omitted from common place names, i.e., Tokyo and Kobe. With the exception of the macron, diacritical marks have been omitted in Sanskrit words whose transliteration, although not technically exact, has been changed to comply with English pronunciation. This holds true of sūtra titles also.

Generally speaking, Sanskrit vowels have long and short forms, all pronounced roughly as in Italian. An exception is the short *a*, which sounds like the *u* in *but* (long *a*, correctly written *ā*, sounds like the *a* in *father*). Long syllables contain a long vowel written with a macron [$\bar{a}$], *e*, or *o*; a dipthong; or a vowel followed by two consonants, except *h*. The presence of *h* indicates aspiration, and *th* sounds always like the *th* in *fathead*. Accent falls on the penult if it is long; if it is short, accent shifts to the first long syllable toward the beginning of the word : tathāgata, úpanishad.

Pronunciation of Japanese words should present no difficulty. Generally speaking, there is no tonic stress; consonants are as in English, vowels as in Italian.

Lastly, 1 should like to express my sincere appreciation to those of my friends who have helped me in the preparation of this text: to Schuyler Cammann, Chimyō Horioka, and Bernard Frank who gave me the benefit of numerous suggestions, and to William McGuire who did much for the technical preparation of the manuscript. I am indebted to all of them.

E.D.S.

Castello San Peyre
Opio (A.M.)
August, 1960

Contents

Foreword   5

Part I : The Indian Background   13
Pre-Buddhist Notions   15
Life of the Buddha   18
Sources   31
Buddhism in India   45
Doctrine   51
Mahāyāna   70
Tantrism   75
Extension of Buddhism   82

Part II : Japanese Buddhism   89
The Introduction of Buddhism to Japan   91
Nara Period (710–784)   101
Heian Period (794–1185)   134
Kamakura Period (1185–1333)   185
Post-Nichiren Period (1300–1600)   238
Tokugawa Period (1600–1868)   246
Meiji Period (1868–1912)   255
Survey of Japanese Buddhism   261
New Religions   265

Notes   287
A Selected Bibliography   289
Statistics on Religions   297
Chronologies   301
Glossary of Indian Terms with Their Japanese
     Equivalents   307
Index   321

List of Illustrations

(with Credits)

Bodhidharma, by Soga Jasoku. (Courtesy Bollingen Foundation.) *Frontispiece*

The nativity of the Buddha. (Courtesy Mrs. A. K. Coomaraswamy) 21

Prince Shōtoku by Enkai. (Courtesy Bollingen Foundation.) 95

The Golden Hall of the Hōryūji. (Courtesy Consulate General of Japan, New York.) 120

A kaidan – Mt. Kōya. (Courtesy Kōya-san Publishing Company.) 126

Procession of Shingon priests—Mt. Kōya. (Courtesy Kōya-san Publishing Company.) 151

The *homa* fire on the inner altar of the Great Stūpa, Mt. Kōya. (Courtesy Kōya-san Publishing Company.) 164

Dainichi (Vairochana) in the Great Stūpa, Mt. Kōya. (Courtesy Japanese Foreign Ministry.) 167

Amida with two attendant bodhisattvas. (Courtesy Bollingen Foundation.) 169

Shaka, with the bodhisattvas of medicine, Yakuō and
Yakujō. (Courtesy Bollingen Foundation.)   171

Kannon (Avalokiteshvara) with the Wishing Jewel.
(Courtesy Bollingen Foundation.)   173

Jizō (kshitigharba). Statue in wood, dated 1365, in
the Hōkaiji, Kamakura. (Courtesy Yasuda Sa-
burō.)   175

The monk Shinran (1173–1262). (Courtesy Bollingen
Foundation.)   198

Buddhist nuns meditating (Koide-machi, Niigata
Prefecture). (Courtesy Consulate General of
Japan, New York.)   215

Lin-chi (Rinzai), by Soga Jasoku. (Courtesy Bollingen Foundation.)   217

Takuan, the Zen master. (Courtesy Bollingen
Foundation.)   219

The Ryōanji garden, Kyoto. (Courtesy Consulate
General of Japan, New York.)   227

Nichiren.   229

Hakuin's portrait, by one of his disciples. (Courtesy
Bollingen Foundation.)   251

Tenrikyō dance. (Courtesy H. van Straelen.)   269

PART I

The Indian Background

Pre-Buddhist Notions

THE SIXTH CENTURY B.C. IN INDIA, during the lifetime of
Gautama Buddha, was an age of great intellectual ferment.
Speculation as to the nature of the universe took varied forms.
Intellectual positions, then as now, were seldom considered
absolute but rather as aspects of the universal truth. Such
tolerance made it possible for numerous philosophic "schools"
to develop and coexist. These schools, as a whole, constituted
a common fund of Indian thought, providing in a sense a
repository for the numerous religious systems that flourished
in India, a common philosophic well from which religions
could draw their main tenets, thereafter to develop in the light
of their own ideals. This means that religions in India share a
surprising number of resemblances, their differences being in
the realm of systems and interpretations.

BRĀHMANISM, SANKHYA, AND YOGA

Generally speaking, Brāhmanism conceives of a universal
order, or *dharma,* to explain the workings of the cosmos. There
is a god-entity (Brahman), a metaphysical concept. Brahman
can be worshiped as a divinity; but, to put it more precisely,
he is a kind of super-order, tending to be of an impersonal
nature. He was existent in man and indeed formed what we
call the Self (*ātman*). The actual functioning of things among
themselves depends on the proper coexistence or harmony of
the parts. A priestly class of individuals, called Brāhmans,
insured the operation of the universe by means of rituals. Since

the Brāhmans alone were conversant with the proper rites for assuring the existence, or better, the coexistence of things, they held a religious monopoly and, to a certain extent, a temporal one as well. Brāhmanism used speculation to transform man into a god-entity.

Along with Brāhmanism, there were other speculative systems common to the schools of Indian thought in general, among the most important being Sānkhya and Yoga. Sānkhya was largely a system of classification and enumeration. The world of phenomena—that is, of things—was held to be composed of a number of basic elements (*guna*); the same was held to be true of abstract concepts. Existence could thus be explained by enumerating the component parts of any given object or concept. Thought itself, being so compounded, could be analyzed in much the same fashion as things. The spiritual principle (*purusha*) is counterbalanced by matter (*prakriti*), or Nature, between which exists a varying equilibrium. Any act of creation comes from the association of these two fundamental elements conceived as a male (*purusha*)–female (*prakriti*) duality. The basic ideas of classification and enumeration developed so highly in the Sānkhya system were to have considerable influence on subsequent Indian philosophical thinking. Whereas Sānkhya concentrated largely on material classifications and on the dissecting of the material world, its companion system, Yoga, devoted itself to the acquiring and perfecting of a kind of psychic control by which it aimed to rise above the phenomenal world. Its goal was an extrasensory state, a kind of mystical union with the absolute forces of the universe. Its methods combined body control (breathing, posturing, etc.) and concentration of the mind, for both of which Yoga offered strict disciplines. Of course, concepts of classification and psychic control permeate Indian thinking and, like the concept of dharma, or universal order, are fundamental ideas taken up again and again by religious thinkers and fitted into different and sometimes conflicting religious systems.

THE DHARMA

In a sense, Buddhism began not only as a protest against the monopoly held by the Brāhmans—against the running of the universe by a few who, by virtue of belonging to a certain social class, assumed religious leadership—but also against the Brāhmanic concept of Self (*ātman*). As a consequence, since Brāhmanism claimed to be based on the concept of dharma (lit., law), Buddhism established its greater universality by proclaiming its True Law (*saddharma*). If the Brāhmanic Law is the cosmic order, the Buddhist True Law is above the cosmic order. Moreover, Buddhism offered the possession of this True Law to all, not simply to a priestly clique as the Brāhmans were. In contrast to Brāhmanism, Buddhism promised salvation not by observing the rites but by neglecting them, in fact by neglecting the world itself. And finally Buddhism refused the idea of Self (*ātman*) by calling existence illusory and self nonexistent (*anātman*). Hence, Buddhist speculation has as its goal the suppression of existence, or rather the suppression of the succession of existences, rather than the establishment of a single, absolute existence. It was with such a task before him as this that a religious leader was born, one Siddhārtha, who was later to become the Buddha.

Life of the Buddha

ALTHOUGH THE EARLY SOURCES relating to the life of the Buddha are confused and at times contradictory, the general outline of the life of a real, historical man does emerge. Obviously, the texts relating his life are a mixture of veracity, exaggeration, and contradiction, and one must make reservations concerning the reliability of such "historical" details. Although Western scholars have entertained a number of divergent theories relative to the Buddha's life story, present-day opinion tends to support the euhemeristic interpretation, according to which it is assumed that a real man existed on whose life and works subsequent generations have built up traditionalized versions. Certain Pāli texts seem to encourage this point of view. So numerous and detailed are the descriptions they give of the daily acts of the historical Buddha, as well as of his last sickness and death, that it is difficult not to glimpse the lineaments of a human character. It is not unreasonable to suppose, in the light of these Pāli texts, that the Buddha was a man who lived and died in northeastern India in the sixth and fifth centuries B.C. The tradition is in fact very old and would seem to go back to a common source for all schools. Actually, apotheosis is a common phenomenon even now in India, and it is possible that the legendary characteristics of the Buddha began to evolve even before his death. The elements of the extraordinary are probably very old; they abound in the sources containing the most ancient outlines.

18

Attributions of extraordinary qualities are common in India, where every important figure has from time immemorial been so endowed. It is not excessive to suppose that at least a part of the miracles that the Buddha is said to have performed may have been attributed to him during his lifetime. The Buddha as presented in these texts is of course a mythical figure, the Hero, or Great Man (*mahāpurusha*), a type represented universally: in India by Vishnu, Rāma, and Krishna, for example; elsewhere by such figures as Christ, Mohammed, etc.

CONCEPTION OF THE HISTORICAL BUDDHA

The historical Buddha was born into a warrior (*kshatriya*) clan called the Shākya, at the head of the small confederation of Uttarakosala, whose capital was Kapilavastu, a small town in northeast India, near the Nepalese border. His father, Shuddhodana ("Pure Food"), was a Gautama, a family line considered to be Brāhmanic. His mother, the first wife of his father, was Māyā.

Shortly before his earthly birth, the *Bodhisattva*—that is, the "person to be awakened," he who will be Buddha, "the Awakened One"—is making retribution for past existences in the Heaven of the Satisfied (*tushita*). Possessing the power to observe his future life, he chooses Shuddhodana and Māyā as his parents in the coming existence, which is to be his last, for he will leave it as a Buddha, never to be reborn. This last existence is made possible by the merits which the Bodhisattva had accumulated in his previous lives. Therefore, he chooses the state which he judges to be the most propitious to his ultimate awakening, that is, a human (rather than animal) body and the masculine sex. The decision made, he descends in unborn form into the womb of Māyā, at which point the texts report a somewhat excessive and unrealistic exaltation throughout the country. This idea of exaltation, apparently a con-

sistent element of the legend from the first, would seem to
have been included to emphasize the fact that the country of
his birth was the perfect place. This detail has two motivations.
First, it corrects the lowliness of a birth which must necessarily have appeared too real; and, second, it refutes the fact
that the land of the Buddha's birth does not stand among those
traditionally considered pure by Brāhmanism.

The texts point out that, for some time before the Bodhisattva's birth, the king and queen, presaging their future
role as mother and father of a Buddha, had for a certain
period observed chastity in the marriage relationship, thereby
establishing the purity necessary for the coming Buddha's
conception. The method of conception itself varies and hence
cannot be thought of as stemming from a common tradition.
The Bodhisattva is usually represented as entering the right
side of his sleeping mother, sometimes in the form of a six-
tusked elephant, sometimes in that of a six-month-old child.
In older versions, Māyā merely dreams of the event. According to one system of calculation, the conception is to be placed
in June–July 559 B.C.,[1] although different traditions support
other dates—the Chinese reckoning puts the death date in
947 B.C., and for Ceylon, Burma, Thailand, and Cambodia it
is 543 B.C.

During the gestation, Māyā sees the Bodhisattva in her
womb as through a kind of transparent stone. Hence, any
contact between the mother and the unborn child is obviated,
thus carrying on the idea of the pureness of the conception.
The tradition evades the obvious question by noting that the
child is nourished by a drop of elixir taken from an open lotus
at the time of his conception. The gestation lasts ten lunar
months, the usual count in old India. During this time the
mother is free from any physical imperfection; she herself
entertains no impure desires and, moreover, inspires none in
those who see her, specifically in her husband Shuddhodana.

The nativity of the Buddha.

BIRTH

The birth itself takes place outside Kapilavastu, in the Lumbinī gardens, where the mother is walking. In Buddhist iconography, Māyā is represented standing, holding the branch of a *shāla* tree in her right hand, and delivering from her right side. The newborn child is, appropriately, received by the two Brāhmanic gods Indra and Brahmā. Soon after his birth, the boy is given the name Siddhārtha ("Goal Reached"), and upon examination he is found to bear the thirty-two principal and the eighty secondary signs characteristic of a Great Man (*mahāpurusha*), or archetypal male. The prophecy is made that there are two ways open to him : if he continues in the footsteps of his father he will become a great universal monarch (*chakravartin*); if he renounces the world and follows a religious path, he will ultimately be awakened, that is, he will become a Buddha.

Seven days after the birth of Siddhārtha, his mother, Māyā, dies. The sources do not concur on the cause of her death. Perhaps tradition ruled that the mother identified with this unsullied conception and gestation should not risk future pollution by bearing other children. Be that as it may, the explanations seem to show the embarrassment of the tradition before a worrisome but ever-present fact for which the Bodhisattva is nowhere held responsible. From the time of his mother's death until the age of seventeen, the future Buddha is brought up by his father's second wife, who is also a maternal aunt, Mahāprajāpatī Gautamī.

Youth of the Buddha

Siddhārtha's education includes a thorough training in the knowledge, techniques, and sports of his time, collectively known as the sixty-four arts (*kalājnāna*). And it is not surprising to learn that his distinction in them is exceptional. The tradition tells of his teacher, who, questioning the child on the kinds of writing, is startled to hear the future Buddha enumerate sixty-four varieties, most of which are unknown to the master himself. Among the miracles told of the child's youth is the one in which he is left in the shade of a tree for some hours by his attendants. The sun is sinking in the west when they return to his side. Although the position of the sun has changed, the shadow of the tree, mindful of the marvelous child's presence, has not moved.

MARRIAGE OF THE BUDDHA

At the age of sixteen (543 B.C.), the Bodhisattva, like former Buddhas, resolves to marry. The tradition notes that he is reticent about taking this step but is finally persuaded to do so, doubtless in consideration of the conventional desire for progeny. The traditions vary concerning the wife, or wives, of the Bodhisattva. Actually he may have had three. The principal ones are Gopā ("Shepherdess of the Earth") and Yashodharā ("Carrier of Glory"), although both of these may originally have been the same woman. Great importance was accorded the winning of a suitable mate for so august a personage. In a series of contests, the Bodhisattva, in competition with other worthies, shows himself superior to all. The entire problem of the marriage seems to be a cause of embarrassment in the monastic texts, and the fact that the chroniclers are at such pains to explain it would seem to constitute a kind of proof of the authenticity of a worrisome realistic detail.

THE FOUR MEETINGS

Surrounded by the luxury of the royal palace, the Bodhisattva, on the order of his father, is protected from all contact with the outside world. On four occasions, however, the Bodhisattva does succeed in leaving the royal quarters, each time in the company of his chariot driver. Each excursion is in the direction of a different cardinal point, and each is marked by an encounter : these are known collectively as the Four Meetings. On the first outing, the Bodhisattva sees a decrepit old man. On questioning his driver, he learns that everyone, even the Bodhisattva, must inescapably become old.

On the second and third, he sees a sick person and a dead man respectively. From these three encounters he realizes that nothing that lives can escape old age, sickness, and death. On the fourth excursion, the Bodhisattva meets a religious man and is struck by the obvious sincerity of his bearing. He realizes that the inescapable sufferings witnessed in the three preceding meetings do have a remedy—that is, the remedy to suffering lies in religious sincerity.

As a result of the Four Meetings, the Bodhisattva is repulsed by the world he has seen and manifests a desire to leave it. Just at this time, a son, Rāhula, is born to him, whom the Bodhisattva considers but one more attachment to the world. Nevertheless, this birth in a sense frees the way for the Bodhisattva's departure, for, by assuring the continuation of his line, he has satisfied the fundamental belief in the importance of succession that obtained in India at that time, as it does now.

Departure and Wanderings

The Great Departure (*mahābhinishkramana*), which marks the Bodhisattva's taking leave of his home, occurred on his twenty-ninth birthday (529 B.C.). Despite the objections of his father and with the help of the gods, who assist by putting everyone in the palace to sleep by opening the barred doors, and by muffling the hoofs of the Bodhisattva's horse, he sets out mounted on his favorite steed, Kanthaka, and accompanied by his equerry, Chandaka. Traveling toward the southeast, the Bodhisattva pauses at the edge of a forest. Here he cuts his hair and exchanges clothes with a hunter whom he meets. He then dispatches his horse and equerry back to the palace and sets forth alone on the great search which will eventually lead to his Awakening.

His first stop is Vaishālī, where for some time he devotes himself to study under the Brāhmanic teacher Ārāda Kālāma.

The Bodhisattva easily comprehends the teachings of his master, but he is aware that they do not offer a solution to the problems of existence and of suffering to which he was introduced at the time of the Four Meetings and which he is bound to solve. He goes then to Rājagriha, the capital of Magadha, ruled at that time by the charitable king Bimbisāra. Struck by the demeanor of the Bodhisattva, Bimbisāra offers to serve him by begging his food and finally presents him with half of his entire kingdom. This the Bodhisattva refuses, knowing that riches and power, unlike a service, will be a hindrance to him. But because of the king's devotion, the Bodhisattva promises to return with the Truth when he has come to the end of his search, a promise which he is ultimately to keep.

ASCETICISM

Under another teacher, Udraka Rāmaputra, the Bodhisattva rapidly masters the advanced methods of meditation—chiefly the Yoga practices so much esteemed in India. Still dissatisfied, he again abandons his master. At this point the Bodhisattva is followed by five disciples, known as Those of the Happy Group (*bhadravargīya*), and with them he proceeds to a place near Gayā, a calm site propitious for religious exercises. For six years the Bodhisattva and his disciples practice asceticism. By this action he is following in the tradition of all Indian wisemen (*muni*), and he acquires the epithet of Shākyamuni, "wiseman of the Shākyas" (his clan), now used universally throughout the Far East. So successful is the Bodhisattva in the practice of asceticism that at the end of the six years he clings to life by a single thread; his strength is reduced to one-thousandth of its former degree, and he has the look of death. Even his mother, worried lest he should die, comes down from the heavens to plead with him to give up such vain practices. And so the Bodhisattva, realizing its ultimate uselessness, abandons asceticism. He asks alms, which he receives in the form of boiled rice. This he divides into forty-nine parts for the seven following weeks, and the tradition notes at the first helping he miraculously regains his beauty. The disciples, disappointed in the Bodhisattva's lack of perseverance in the path they consider right, desert him.

At this juncture, the Bodhisattva has a dream which announces the approaching moment of his Awakening. He proceeds to a shāla wood, where he chooses a pīpal tree as the site of his ultimate meditation. He circumambulates this tree seven times, considering the world from the various points of the compass, and finally chooses to establish himself in the east, which he judges to be the only unshakeable point. He now begins his final meditation, during which he is continually tempted by the demon Māra, but in vain, for the Bodhisattva is advanced too far on the way to the Awakening to regress.

THE AWAKENING

The final and complete act of Awakening (*abhisambodhana*) takes place at the end of a night in the full moon of Vaishākha (April–May, 523 B.C.). During the first watch, the Bodhisattva goes through the four degrees of meditation, freeing the spirit from all psychic operations attached to the senses; during the second, he recapitulates all his previous existences and notes the inescapable return to misery concomitant with rebirth; and, during the third watch, he becomes fully "conscious," that is, he is completely Awakened.

THE FOUR TRUTHS

Just what the Bodhisattva is "conscious" of, just what his state of being Awakened is, constitutes the fundamental truth of Buddhism. It may be summed up by saying that the Bodhisattva is at last aware of the causes and effects of existence and how to make them cease. He is in possession of what is known in Buddhism as the Four Noble Truths : all existence is suffering; there is a cause of this suffering; this cause may be stopped; there is a way to the stopping. The final Truth the Bodhisattva will later develop into a discipline known as the Eightfold Path. From this point on, the Bodhisattva is a Buddha : he is an "Awakened One." European and American scholars have often called the Buddha "enlightened," but "awakened" is perhaps a better designation, for his consciousness (of the Four Noble Truths), or *bodhi,* exists by virtue of an opening of the mind rather than through any exterior light coming into it.

The Buddha remains on the throne of his Awakening for seven days, as did all preceding Buddhas. This act would seem to reflect the custom in India of kings remaining in the place of their coronation for a week afterward. He then moves to the northeast of the tree, and from this point he sits contemplating the world for the second week. He changes his situation during each succeeding week, until on the sixth he goes to Lake Muchalinda to continue his meditation there. He is overtaken by a seven-day rain, and in Buddhist iconography he is shown protected by the serpentlike deity (*nāga*) of the lake—also called Muchalinda—who in cobra form spreads his head as a canopy and wraps his body as a cloak around the meditating Buddha.

THE OFFERING OF TRAPUSHA AND BHALLIKA

The end of the seven weeks is marked by the arrival of the merchants Trapusha and Bhallika. The caravan in which they are traveling stops of its own accord as it draws near to the place where the Buddha sits, and the two men realize that this is due to some marvelous reason. They investigate and, finding the Buddha, offer him honey and sugar cane, which he accepts. However, wishing to set an example for monks, he takes alms only in a bowl to be used for that purpose. According to the tradition, the guardians of the four cardinal points offer him four bowls, each made of a precious stone. The Buddha refuses them, and each guardian then offers a bowl made of common stone. The Buddha accepts the four and fuses them into a single bowl, so that each guardian may have the pleasure of making an offering. The Buddha then takes the food which the merchants offer and for their pains gives them relics (hair and nail clippings). These the merchants place in *stūpas,* or reliquary mounds (*see* below) which they construct in their country on returning.

The Buddha returns to the ajapāla tree, where he considers the advisability of preaching the Doctrine, which he considers too difficult for average beings to understand. However, he is besought to do so by the god Brahmā. His final decision is an affirmative one, largely because he envisions sentient beings as being like so many lotuses. Some have risen to the surface of the water, where they are in bloom; some are almost at the surface of the water and appear to need but little assistance to come forth; others are deeply immersed and will doubtless never rise to the light. It is especially for the second category, who seem near to rising to the Light, that the Buddha decides to disseminate his doctrine.

SETTING THE WHEEL OF THE LAW IN MOTION

Judging his former disciples to be, of all beings, the most capable of understanding his exposition, the Buddha sets out to find Those of the Happy Group. He joins them in the present-day city of Sārnāth, and in a Deer Perk (near Benares) he announces to them that he has "thus come" (*tathāgata*), as his predecessors before him—so that Tathāgata becomes henceforth one of the important epithets of the Buddha. He announces to the disciples that he brings them the Truth which they by their ascetic practices could not find. He teaches them the Four Noble Truths. This first sermon, or predication, on the fundamentals of Buddhist doctrine is called "setting in motion the Wheel of the Law" (*dharmachakrapravartana*). It is represented in Buddhist iconography either by a wheel alone or by a wheel inscribed on the Buddha's throne. The five disciples are converted; thus is formed the Community (*Sangha*). The disciples go their separate ways to teach the Law (523 B.C.), as does the Buddha himself, proceeding to Rāja-griha to keep his promise to King Bimbisāra.

The period of the Buddha's ministry continues with his visit to Kapilavastu, where he converts his father and the rest of the Shākyas, despite the resistance of some of them. He admits into the orders the first woman, his aunt Mahāprajāpatī Gautamī (c. 519 B.C.). The Buddha had at first refused to admit women into the Community, and his reticence even concerning his aunt is apparent in his observation that a religion in which men alone take part in monastic life would last a thousand years; when women take part, it will last five hundred.

DEATH

The Buddha travels over India, preaching and converting. Finally he comes to rest in a sanctuary at Chāpāla, weary from his travels. He tells his disciple Ānanda three times that it is possible for him to prolong his life to the end of the cosmic period. But, for some reason, Ānanda fails to request him to do so. As a result, the Buddha realizes his end is near. Besides, he has earlier promised his adversary Māra that, after the establishment of the Community, he would die. The Buddha and Ānanda go to Pāpā, where they are invited to dinner by the son of a smith, an admirer of the Buddha. The meal includes a pork delicacy or pig's food (e.g., truffles?), and after eating of it the Buddha is gravely stricken with diarrhea. Despite his illness he sets out for Kushinagara, where he arrives exhausted. Realizing that the end is at hand, he lies down fully conscious, facing the west, his head to the north, on his right side, his left leg reposing upon the right. It is in this position that he is regularly represented in Buddhist iconography as attaining the state of "great total extinction" (*mahāparinirvāna*). This occurred in the present-day village of Kasia, some thirty miles east of Gorakhpur. For the last time the Buddha gathers the faithful around him and exhorts them, his last words being : "All composite things must pass away. Strive onward vigilantly." And so, in the third watch on the full moon of *Kārttika* (November), 478 B.C., he enters into the final and supreme meditation.

It is not surprising that, after so human a fatal illness, the tradition saw to it that the funeral has its portion of marvelous happenings. There is lamentation, and all the Malla come from the city to view the deceased. The body is washed, clothed, and placed on a funeral pyre worthy of a king. For seven days there are music and dancing, at the end of which the body of the Buddha is cremated and the relics of bone are divided among the mourners.

Sources

WHAT SOURCES CAN WE RELY ON to tell us of the earliest history of Buddhism? From the archaeological standpoint, nothing has survived from the time of its founding. Apart from the remains of the Indus Valley civilization the most ancient Indian monuments are chiefly Buddhist dating from the period of the expansion of the religion—that is, from around the third and second century B.C. Almost no artifacts survive from the Vedic period.

PILLARS

The oldest monuments we know are Buddhist pillars with inscriptions, dating from the time of the emperor Ashoka (c. 250 B.C.), who devoted his royal efforts to the encouragement of Buddhism. Some are free standing and others form an integral part of buildings. Some of them give the six Ashokan edicts and call for the observing of the Order, and often they allude to the efforts of the emperor to assist the Order.

STŪPAS

Along with the pillars, we should consider the stūpas, or mound-shaped funerary shrines, of which those at Sānchī are perhaps the best known today. They were regally decorated with elaborately carved reliefs. Literary tradition tells of stūpas even before Ashoka, and they do in fact antedate the organization of Buddhism as an independent religion. Briefly,

31

stūpas are reliquaries meant to hold the remains of the deceased and the funeral bier; they may be commemorative in nature and, although frequently Buddhist, they are not necessarily so. The oldest examples extant today are the balustrade of Stūpa II at Sānchī, various parts of Stūpa III on the same site, and the Stūpa of Bhārhut in Central India. In the carvings of these early shrines, the presence of the Buddha is represented only by symbols, but numerous legends *(jātakas)* relating to him are depicted in more or less detail constituting an important source of textual information. In the south, the famous Stūpa of Amarāvatī is evidence of the widespread occurrence of this form of architecture : it dates from around the beginning of the Christian era (70 B.C.–200 A.D.). Many stūpa ruins are to be found also in the northwest and nearby territories, where they are called *topes*. They are especially numerous on the route to Gandhāra, located on the upper Indus, in the area of present-day Panjab. In Ceylon, stūpas are called *dagoba*, from the Sanskrit *dhātu-garbha*, relic-container.

Stūpas are intimately connected with the pre-Buddhist cult of *chaityas*. A chaitya was a sacred spot, perhaps a grove of trees, or even a single tree, perhaps tumuli, particularly those of chieftains. These chaityas were believed to be the abode of earth spirits and as such appealed to the popular imagination more than did the austere gods of the high cult. The Buddha himself is said to have respected these shrines. Pilgrimages to such holy spots were common, and Buddhism simply took over the chaitya cult, making the stūpa with its relic into a sacred spot, which henceforth becomes a specifically Buddhist object of worship.

EARLY IMAGES

In the early period of Buddhism, it was considered incorrect to represent the actual form of the historical Buddha. Rather, the Buddha was represented by means of symbols for his metaphysical attributes and the big events of his life, such as the tree, the throne, the wheel, and the stūpa. Buddhist images do not make their appearance until around the beginning of the Christian era, when the human form of the Buddha evolved under Graeco-Roman impetus in northwest India. Some scholars (e.g., Coomaraswamy) maintain that the early Buddha figure came from the purely Indian school of Mathurā, but it appears in the light of more recent research that Graeco-Roman influences are definite. The Buddha image as we first know it seems to take its inspiration in large part from the familiar figure of "Apollo the Orator," which must have been known in the northwest from the time of Alexander the Great, around the end of the fourth century B.C.

INSCRIPTIONS

Inscriptions are the surest check on texts: the inscriptions of Ashoka, for example, not only show the attitude of this famous king toward Buddhism, but they shed considerable light on the status of the religion in the third century B.C. They reveal the existence of a cult of holy places, of past Buddhas, as well as of texts close to the Pāli canon—the tradition set down around 100 B.C. by the monks of Ceylon in the Pāli language (related to Sanskrit). Inscriptions at Bhārhut show that legends were already fixed in the second century B.C.; these inscriptions reveal the popularity of certain types of texts.

TEXTS

The primary sources of Buddhism are, of course, the texts themselves, as set down in manuscripts. They are to be found not only in India but in temples and monasteries of a large part of the Asian continent, including Tibet and China, where the respective canons are of the utmost value in the reconstruction of the history of Buddhism. Generally speaking, these writings may be divided into two main groups: the canonical, which consist traditionally of the words of the Buddha; and the noncanonical, which are composed of such sundry items as commentaries, chronicles, diaries, technical manuals, ritual manuals, and iconographical works.

Soon after the cremation of the Buddha, a council (about which more will be said later) was called in order to establish the Buddhist canon, for during the Buddha's lifetime the teachings had been passed on orally. The first council was that of Rājagriha. According to one tradition, this and later councils established the three parts, or baskets (Tripitaka), of the Pāli canon: the *Sūtranta* written in Sindhi, the *Pāramitā* in Sanskrit, and the *Mantra* (and *Tantra*) in Sanskrit and others. Actually such a division corresponds quite well with reality. Pāli literature dominates in present-day Burma, Thailand, Cambodia, and Laos and Ceylon, whence it penetrated to the Indo-Chinese countries. It forms the canon of a large part of southeast Asia, being the textual basis of what is known commonly as Southern Buddhism. This form of Buddhism is also called Theravāda (Skt. Sthaviravāda), "those who follow the elders." *Thera* (Skt. *sthavira*), "elder," is a generic term for any respected religious man, but here it is used specifically for those wise men who first set down the Buddha's word and thus formally established the Buddhist canon. Theravādins are also called Vibhajjavādins, that is, "those who make distinctions."

CANON

The Tripitaka, or "Three Baskets"—the canon in its entirety —is composed of the *Vinaya-pitaka*, the *Sūtra-pitaka*, and the *Abhidharma-pitaka*. The numerous texts forming the Vinaya, or "discipline," section are chiefly practical admonitions for the working of the Community. These texts include rules for monks and nuns, recommendations for good actions, rules for hygiene, historical and legendary accounts, and a number of writings largely in catechistic or question-and-answer form that are in fact recapitulations of the above.

Sūtra

The *Sūtras* are texts claiming to report the discourses of the Buddha or of his immediate disciples. Sūtra means "thread," and the allusion is doubtless to the threads of words woven together to form the fabric of the Doctrine. Each sūtra, complete in itself, usually takes the form of a dialogue in which a personage comes to visit the Buddha and interrogates him on specific questions. Typical of the sūtra is the interpolation, between the prose passages, of *gāthā,* "songs," which regularly begin with the words *tatth evam vuccati,* "concerning this it is said. . . ." In style the sūtras are characterized by the constant repetition of stereotyped sentences. A man decides to send something to the Buddha; a discourse is made concerning this decision. The discourse is repeated for the messenger and again by him. It is further repeated by the messenger upon delivering it to the Buddha and then by the Buddha. Each time the discourse is fully reproduced. Like the gāthā, each sūtra begins with a characteristic phrase: *evam me sutam,* "thus have I heard. . . ." The sūtras are divided into four general categories (*nikāya*): long (*dīghanikāya*), medium (*majjhimaikāya*), "gathered" (*samyuttanikāya*), and "numbered" (*anguttaranikāya*). Altogether these categories are known as the "tradition," or *āgama* in Sanskrit.

There are thirty-four principal long sūtras. A well-known example is the *Brahmājālāsūtra, Text of Brahmā's Net,* in which men caught in this world, of which Brahmā is the great god, are compared to fish caught in a net. The Buddha is portrayed as going from Rājagriha to Nālandā. An ascetic and a disciple take the same route. The first blames the Buddha, and the second praises him. The Buddha, questioned on the wisdom of such praise or blame, teaches the disciples to lay great store on neither. The sūtra then proclaims the essential goal of Buddhism, that is, of deliverance.

The medium sūtras, somewhat shorter, are divided into three books (50, 50, 52), containing in all 152 texts divided according to subject (e.g., flowers, saints, sin, etc.) of which there are twenty-six in all. An example of this type is the famous *Dharmapada,* or *Verses on the Law,* which as its title implies are lines with four feet (*pada*) each on edifying subjects pertaining to the Doctrine. These verses are considered to be of high literary value.

ABHIDHARMA

The third division of the Tripitaka is called the *Abhidharma-pitaka.* This "basket" contains technical expositions of the Law in the form of metaphysical, or better, scholastic texts treating systematically the teachings of the sūtras. The exposition regularly proceeds by analytical questions and enumerative responses. In these texts, the universe is seen not as an exterior object, but rather as man's idea of it : that is, the universe is the ensemble of psychic ideas, a detailed psychological inventory of man's mind. The central theme is that all things are "composed" of coexisting parts. This coexistence is at best temporary, and hence things are subject to decomposition. All is impermanent, because everything is made up of dissociable components. The only exception to this order is the state of *nirvāna,* which alone is "noncomposed" and hence not subject to decomposition and therefore stable, lasting, permanent. The goal "is not the knowledge of the spirit for itself, but the demonstration, by means of the evidence of name and class, of the composed character of every thing, including thought, which must be abandoned for nirvāna, toward which Buddhist conduct leads."[2] The *Abhidharma* texts set forth a psychology with an ethical goal.

VINAYA AND ABHIDHARMA

Buddhist tradition holds that both the *Vinaya* and the sūtras were collected at the council of Rājagriha, but this thesis is rejected by most scholars in view of the fact that the texts seem to date from different times. According to the theory widely accepted at present, it is probable that the *Vinaya* texts were the first to be established. Obviously the practical, disciplinary rules were easy to fix, and they were probably edited at the same time, relatively, as the *Vinaya*. The sūtras, on the other hand, were not necessarily composed at the same period, and their similarity of style indicates a secondary editing, as well as a common base. The *Abhidharma* is certainly the most recent of the three parts of the Tripitaka. In the first place, it reflects a scholastic point of view. Moreover, the *Abhidharma* of different schools varies, a fact which tends to show that its formation took place along with the creation of diverse schools. Finally, the *Abhidharma* expounds the other two sections of the Tripitaka, largely the sūtras, from a metaphysical point of view, and it is at once apparent that it is later.

COMMENTARIES

In addition to the canonical texts, there is copious non-canonical literature, composed chiefly of commentaries. Many of the early commentaries are lost. Perhaps the oldest commentator is Mahinda, who is reported to have introduced Buddhism to Ceylon in the third century B.C. and to have translated a number of existing commentaries into Singhalese. There is a group of classical commentaries, mostly in prose, a few in verse, devoted to the explanation of grammar and technical terms. Some commentaries are in turn commented upon.

Three important later commentators may be mentioned: Buddhadatta, Buddhaghosa, and Dhammapala (Dharmapāla). Buddhadatta, a Tamil, was born at the end of the fourth century A.D. at Uragapura, the capital of the Chōla kingdom. He became a monk at the monastery of Kailāsa, near Uragapura, and later went to Ceylon. At the beginning of the fifth century he returned to India, where he wrote his commentaries founded on Singhalese works and on Buddhaghosa. His chief commentaries on the *Vinaya* are the *Vinayavinicchaya,* a work in 3183 verses, and the *Uttaravinicchaya,* or *Later Decision,* in 969 verses. Concerning the *Abhidharma,* he composed the *Abhidammāvatāra,* or *Descent into the Abhidharma.*

The most famous of the Pāli commentators was Buddhaghosa. Born of a Brāhman family from Magadha, near the place where the Buddha attained bodhi, and early versed in the *Vedas,* he was converted to Buddhism by Thera Revata. At the beginning of the fifth century A.D. he went to Ceylon to study the Singhalese commentary of Mahinda, at the great cloister of Mahāvihāra. It was he who translated all of Mahinda's writings. Also attributed to him, perhaps falsely, is a commentary called the *Jātakatthavannanā* (*Description of the Meaning of the Jātakas*), a work dealing with the *Jātaka* stories of the previous lives of the Buddha, which show the ensemble of good acts by which the Bodhisattva is reborn as the Buddha and emphasize his detachment from existence. The Buddha himself tells these stories, for he is capable of seeing his preceding lives. The accounts are frequently depicted in art and through the centuries have been universally popular. Not only have the jātaka been instrumental in the edification of the faithful, but they are extremely rich in folklore, reflecting the simple, folk attitudes toward the religion. They date in large part from around the fifth century A.D. The classic recension contains 547 texts.

Like Buddhaghosa, Dhammapala studied at the Mahāvihāra in Ceylon. A Tamil, he lived at the end of the fifth century. Some thirteen commentaries are credited to him; they contain introductions to texts and glosses pertaining to them.

SANSKRIT LITERATURE

Besides the Pāli canon treated above, there exists a considerable literature in Sanskrit, sporadically preserved, which in view of the fragmentary nature of the original texts, must be completed by recourse to Tibetan and Chinese sources. The three principal sources are Central Asia, Kashmir, and Nepal. In the mid-seventh century A.D., for example, the Chinese monk traveler Hsüan-tsang notes a number of Sarvāstivādin texts from the oases of the Tarim basin, in far western reaches of China. This Sanskrit literature contains numerous texts accepted as canonical in many parts of northern India (Gandhāra, Kashmir), Central Asia, China, and Japan. Since it is related mainly to the Buddhism of these "northern" countries, it stands in opposition to the Southern Buddhist canon, written in Pāli.

AVADĀNASĀTAKA AND THE STORY OF MAITRAKANYAKA

Among the examples of Sanskrit literature is the *Avadānashataka, The Hundred Exploits,* which presents ten decades of exemplary acts leading to Buddhahood. Some scenes are prophetic, some reminiscent of *Jātaka* tales. This text contains some of the most celebrated legends of Buddhism, notably the story of Maitrakanyaka. Maitrakanyaka was the orphan son of a sea merchant. Unacquainted with his father's work, he busied himself with various jobs in order to support his mother. One day he learned of his father's calling and at once conceived the desire to go to sea. When his mother tried to stop him, he struck her and despite her admonitions set forth. At length he came to an island inhabited by nymphs (*apsaras*): evidentally a reward for the good he had done for his mother. However, he is subjected to torture in which a red-hot iron wheel again and again cuts off his head, which constantly regains its place on his body: apparently punishment for striking his mother. Maitrakanyaka resolved to endure this excruciation until mankind was saved, whereupon he was immediately transformed into a Bodhisattva and was thus delivered. The Buddha reveals that he himself was once Maitrakanyaka.

Mahāvastu

The *Mahāvastu* or *Great Subject,* preserved in Nepāl, is perhaps the most important text of the Mahāsānghika school, of which it constitutes a part of the *Vinaya.* However, it does not treat of discipline but is rather the complete history of the Buddha, beginning with his previous existences. Here the Buddha's lives exemplify the basic ideals of the Community. Though classified as *Vinaya,* the *Mahāvastu* contains numerous sūtra excerpts and jātakas juxtaposed, as well as a great quantity of legendary material. Certain passages are relatively late, although the work in general is accepted as dating from the first centuries of the Christian era. In its entirety it has not been rendered either in Tibetan or Chinese although many separate elements have been translated.

Sanskrit Texts

Sanskrit literature includes many texts of the Mahāyāna, or "Greater Vehicle," as Northern Buddhism is called. They fall

into three divisions : (1) the *Mahāyāna-sūtras,* (2) the *Dhāraṇī,*
or magical formulas, and (3) the *Vaipulya-sūtras,* which are
Mahāyāna-sūtras greatly amplified. Among the principal of
the sūtras is the *Lalitavistara* (*Development of the Game*—
"game" referring to the human manifestation of the Buddha),
which presents the legend of the Buddha from his next to last
existence to the sermon at Benares. The text itself, which is
actually intermediate between Hīnayāna and Mahāyāna, re-
poses on old traditions common to pre-Mahāyāna schools. It
is written mainly in Sanskrit prose, although occasional poetic
stanzas repeat the ideas of the prose passages : it may be noted
that these stanzas show numerous correspondences with Pāli
sūtras. The original text was perhaps in mixed Sanskrit, and it
was doubtless rendered in purer language at the time it was
adopted by Mahāyāna schools. The Sarvāstivādins (Hīnayāna), who accept this text as their life of the Buddha, were
perhaps responsible for the Sanskritization. The *Lalitavistara*
contains many elements going back to a common, very early
base. It was translated into Chinese in 308 A.D., but the
Chinese translation does not correspond to the text as we know
it today.

LOTUS OF THE GOOD LAW

Perhaps the most famous of the Sanskrit sūtras is the
Saddharmapuṇḍarīka-sūtra, or *The Sūtra on the Lotus of the
Good Law.* Moreover, it is of utmost importance, for it gives
invaluable information of the Mahāyāna cult of Buddhas and
Bodhisattvas. It was the first sūtra to be translated into a European language : French, by Eugene Burnouf, in 1852. The
Lotus of the Good Law is a predication in twenty-seven chapters (twenty-eight chapters in the Chinese version), the theme
being the nature of the manifestations of the Buddha. It
opposes the Great Means to the Lesser Means : the absolute

Truth to the transcendence of the Tathāgata. In the *Lotus,* the Tathāgata takes on human form in order to preach, and this sūtra contains some of the most famous parables of Buddhist literature. Two may serve as examples. In the parable of the burning house, a number of children are trapped in a flaming dwelling. But they are not alarmed, despite the imminent danger. Their father's first thought is to leap into the fire, gather up the children in his arms, and carry them to safety. But he reflects that in their ignorance they will doubtless bolt and so be destroyed by the fire. Instead, the father lures them out by promising them their toys, carts drawn by bullocks, goats, and deer, and the children promptly leave the house in safety. Once on the outside they ask for their promised playthings, but the father gives them bullock carts only. It should not be thought that the Buddha is here supporting a lie on the part of the father; rather, he is emphasizing the validity of the "clever means" by which the children are saved in accordance with their tastes in spite of themselves. In like manner, the Buddha entices mankind to forsake the world and by his mediation attain nirvāna. In Buddhist terms, the three vehicles represent (1) the *shravaka,* those who listen to the Buddha's words; (2) the *pratyekabuddhas,* those who become Buddha by and for themselves; (3) and the Bodhisattvas, those who attain to salvation but who devote themselves to the deliverance of mankind as well. In another parable a lost child grows up and at length meets with his father, who has become a powerful king. The father recognizes his son, but the son does not recognize his father. The king makes the young man perform all sorts of lowly chores, which he does faithfully, gradually becoming more and more expert. When he judges the moment propitious, the king reveals his identity and accepts his son. In like fashion, the Buddha helps mankind to Awakening.

The *Lankāvatāra-sūtra,* or *Descent to Ceylon* is one of the most important Sanskrit sūtras because of its doctrinal content. In nine chapters of prose mixed with gāthā, it presents the teaching given to Lankā (Ceylon) by the Buddha, through 108 questions of the Bodhisattva Mahāmati concerning error, liberation, and the like.

AMIDA AND WISDOM SŪTRAS

Two other groups close the list of Sanskrit writings: the *Amilūbha-* and the *Prajnaparamitā-sūtras.* The former (*Amitāyurbuddhānusmriti*), of which the original texts have been lost, are preserved in Chinese translation. Their main theme is that meditation on the Buddha Amitābha ("Limitless Light") or Amitāyus ("Long Life") makes rebirth possible in his Western Paradise (*Sukhāvatī*). Somewhat later are the *Kārandavyūha* (*Development on the Cap*), which exalts Avalokiteshvara, and the *Gunakārandavyūha* (*Development on the Cap of Qualities*). Both these sūtras relate the adventures of Avalokiteshvara in quest of the salvation of beings, in the course of which the Bodhisattva enters Hell in order to help the suffering. He takes the form of a flying horse (*balāla*) to save Simhala who has been shipwrecked on the island of man-eating demons (*rākshasī*). Included in this group is the *Karunā-pundarīka,* or *Lotus of Compassion,* which describes the continent of Padma, divided into five *parivarta,* and contains explanations by the Buddha made at the request of Maitreya. The *Prajnāpāramitā* group, or *Perfection of Intelligence,* expound the doctrine of the Void and are the basis of the *Mādhyamika,* or "Middle Path."

MAGICAL FORMULAS

Mention must also be made of a group of texts composed largely of magical formulas (*dhārani*). These "charms" (against

serpents, demons, etc.), which occur sometimes in the form of
sūtras, are intermediate between the sūtras and Tantric literature; they are named according to the Buddha to whom they
are related, e.g., *Aksobhyanāmadhāranī*. Of the same intermediate nature are the texts under the name of *Manjusrīmu-
lakalpa*. Composed before the tenth century A.D., they are in
fifty-five chapters of an encyclopedic nature, containing notices
on ritual, images, astrology, history, and the like. They are
composed in classical Sanskrit prose and verse, the latter pre-
dominating. Much mention is made of Brāhmanic divinities
and formulas.

Finally a voluminous literature exists composed largely of
tantra, types of manuals in which the symbolism of the sexual
union plays an important role and which present in great
detail ritual practices and iconographic elaborations. In such
texts, metaphysical speculation is perhaps secondary to practical, cultic guidance. Tantrism, which is the body of beliefs
based on these texts, is both Hindu and Buddhist. Buddhist
Tantrism, about which more will be said later, was doubtless
influenced by Hindu Tantrism, but the two are distinct and in
some ways represent opposite poles of thought. The Hindu
Tantras honor most especially Shiva conceived as static and
unmoving. With him is closely associated a feminine counterpart, his *shakti*. Her name is Pārvatī, and she is in every way
his opposite : active, moving, dynamic. She constitutes, as it
were, his power, and it is she who, with him, creates. All
Tantric divinities have their active feminine counterparts, and
their sexual polarity plays an important role in defining the
area of their activity.

Buddhism in India

THE EARLY COMMUNITY

IT IS NOTABLE THAT AT HIS DEATH the Buddha left no instructions concerning the propagation of the religion he had preached. After him there remained only the Dharma, the Law, as he conceived it, and the Sangha, or Community (of monks). The monks had the custom of gathering together, especially during the rainy season, for the purpose of holding discussions on religious matters. They formed numerous, often widely scattered groups rather than anything one could think of as an organized "church." Moreover, during the Buddha's lifetime and soon after his death, the teachings were transmitted largely by word of mouth. It is thus not surprising that interpretations of doctrine tended to differ from one community to another and that schisms sprang up within these early groups. Such a state of affairs made it essential to establish the Law in a recorded form that would perform the function of an established canon. It was for this purpose, then, that in the rainy season of 477 B.C. (the dates differ) the leading monk Kāshyapa called a council (*samgīti*) in the city of Rājagriha.. It lasted for about seven months, and during the course of it the disciples questioned one another on the sense they considered that the Buddha had attached to his teachings. Ānanda, although he had been the almost constant and greatly esteemed companion of the Buddha for the last twenty-five years of his life, enjoyed little prestige among the disciples.

Actually, the council had been called by Kāshyapa for the purpose of declaring against Ānanda. Ānanda is questioned by Kāshyapa concerning the discourses made by the Buddha, and his answers constitute the Sūtras. In like manner, Upāli, who is examined concerning the more practical matters of the Community, by his answers constitutes the *Vinaya*. After the Council, curiously enough, Ānanda becomes a most important personage, while Kāshyapa retires into the shadow.

COUNCIL OF VAISHĀLĪ

Other councils were held, among which perhaps the most important was that of Vaishālī, which took place exactly one hundred years after the nirvāna, in 377 B.C. Here the issue was that the monks of Vaishālī had engaged in a number of practices considered to be nonorthodox, such as storing salt in a horn, accepting food after noon, and so forth. They had been reproved by Yashas, a disciple of Ānanda, who as a result was expelled by the Vaishālī monks. Yashas then convened at Vaishālī a council, consisting of some 700 monks from various parts of India, the final sense of which was a condemnation of Vaishālī practices.

ASHOKA

Other schisms occurred subsequent to the Vaishālī council, but it is apparent that by around the middle of the third century B.C., Buddhism had considerably expanded and by this time commanded a sizable following. Rock edicts dating from around this time show the great piety of the famous Ashoka (274–236 B.C.), sometimes called "the Constantine of Buddhism." From Pāli texts, we may surmise that the king's conversion took place soon after 260 B.C., the date of his crowning, for he is supposed to have given his son and daughter to the community six years thereafter (c. 254). He made great efforts to propagate the new religion, and despite his zeal Buddhism of this period gave proof of considerable tolerance. Buddhist missions are said to have been sent out to Kashmīr, to northwest India under Greek conquest, to Burma, and to Ceylon. In Ceylon, in fact, Buddhism is said to have been introduced around 242 B.C. by Mahinda, the supposed son, or younger brother, of Ashoka, where it took root at once and, despite the Tamil invasions, flourished.

EXTENSION OF BUDDHISM

By the second century B.C. in India, there was a marked revival of Brāhmanism, with the result that Buddhism was sporadically persecuted. It continued to develop, however, in central and western India, while in the northwest and beyond it flourished. In the northwest, despite the Greek invasions, the religion was to witness a noteworthy further evolution. In fact, rather than being hindered by the Greek invasions, Buddhism made use of a kind of propaganda (e.g., the *Milindapanha*) directed especially toward the Greek colonists. The presence of Buddhists in Bactria is attested in the first century B.C. by Alexander Polyhistor (80–60 B.C.), and there were important nuclei at Amarāvatī, Andhra. Information concerning the period of the Kushāna—a Buddhist people living about the second century A.D.—is slight. The Kushānas were physically a Turkish type, but doubtless had their origins in eastern Central Asia on the Chinese frontier. They were called "moon people" by the Chinese, and their displacement westward had doubtless been caused by the warlike Huns. By the middle of the first century A.D., they had gained control of northwestern India. The best known of the Kushāna rulers is Kanishka (c. first half of second century A.D.), an ardent believer in Buddhism. This period marks, especially, the extension of Buddhism abroad, a continuation of the movement begun under Ashoka. This extension was encouraged by the Greek invasions. Greek coins bearing Buddhist symbols were struck, and the afore-mentioned *Milindapanha, Questions of Menander,* a kind of manual for the propagation of the religion among the Greeks, gives evidence of the conversion of the Greek King Menander. With the Shaka (Scythian) invasions, Buddhism spread into Central Asia, and some time before the beginning of the Christian era it had expanded as far as China.

The Indo-Scythian empire in fact straddled India and Central Asia and was hence in a position to facilitate exchanges between these two regions. It is from the north-western reaches of India, that is, from Kashmīr, that the traditions concerning the famous Kanishka, king of Gandhāra, come. Distressed by the diversity of opinions concerning the doctrine, he called the Council of Kashmīr, which was pre-sided by Vasumitra. The reign of this monarch, like Ashoka, is noted for the impetus given to Buddhism. The religion experienced a period of unremitting growth in the northwest and was to continue to expand under the later Kushāna until about 450. The Chinese pilgrim Hsüan-tsang in the seventh century notes persecutions by the invading Kidarites, but local suffering left the ensemble of the community largely un-affected, especially as concerns its expansion toward Central Asia. Even in southern Tamil territory (Chōla), the existence of monasteries is attested in the fourth and fifth centuries.

DECLINE OF COMMUNITY

Under the Gupta dynasty (300–650 A.D.), Buddhism flourished. Kumaragupta I, in the first half of the fifth century, founded the famous intellectual center of Nālandā. However, in the northwest the persecutions by the Huns were ultimately disastrous, and, along with doctrinary changes, the importance of the Community substantially declined. This diminishing of the Community's importance was less characteristic of Mahāyāna and Tantric Buddhism than of Hīnayāna, for the former two, rather than insisting on the disciplinary training of the monks, which was typical of Hīnayāna centers, rather emphasized rites and magical practices and was actually nearer the Brāhmanic idea of the *guru* ("director") and his fluctuating group of followers.

Hsüan-tsang's memoirs in the seventh century provide a number of exact details concerning the state of Buddhism during his visit to India from 629 to 645 A.D., under the reign of Harsha (d. 647). This was a time which, while marking the decadence of Buddhism in many areas, constituted the last golden era of the religion in India. At this time there was a general trend toward the abandoning of monasteries, and yet there was substantial literary activity. The northwest, after a hundred years of Hunnic devastation, was a desert. Udyāna still maintained an active Buddhist cult, though of Mahāyānic inspiration, largely devoted to formulas and magical practices. In sum, one notes a general abandonment of the old centers (Vaishālī, Shrāvastī), although the decadence was not uniform everywhere. Mahāyāna and Hīnayāna existed side by side, along with Tantric practices. This latter form had developed especially in Udyāna, Bihar, Orīssā, Bengal, and Nepāl. Even Nālandā, the stronghold of Buddhist dialecticism, had by the seventh century become progressively given to Tantric teachings.

FINAL DISINTEGRATION

The history of Buddhism, after about the fifth century A.D. is one of progressive decline. Buddhist monasteries survived in many parts until the Muslim invasions at the end of the twelfth century (1192), e.g., the monasteries of Bihar and

Bengal. Inscriptions and archaeological evidence show fairly prosperous Buddhist monasteries at Sārnāth (site of the first sermon) and at Shrāvastī (where the Buddha spent much of his actual life). In the Deccan and Dravidian south, there are few evidences of Buddhism after the tenth century. There is no doubt but that monastery life had become estranged from that of the people, restricted as it was to small circles of initiates. Alongside the evolution of Hīnayāna to Mahāyāna and Tantrism, with the concomitant changes in doctrine, went the abandonment of communities. The Buddha himself came to be accepted as a kind of fantasy, an illusion, and the Bodhisattvas tended to merge with the Brāhmanic gods, with the result that Buddhism came closer and closer in feeling to Brāhmanism. In Gupta times, in fact, the Buddha was worshipped in his shrines as a Hindu divinity with acts of homage (pūjā), that is, offerings of lights, flowers, food, etc., and it is notable that the Buddhist Pāla kings observed the rules of Hindu dharma. Thus the Buddha became just one of many gods, and after the twelfth century Buddhism was completely assimilated to Hinduism.

Doctrine

Pre-Buddhist Elements

BUDDHISM AROSE IN THE EAST OF INDIA, a more recently,
although, at the time of the Buddha, completely Brāhmanized
part of the subcontinent, which may still have maintained
some non-Aryan elements. It was nevertheless at a lively
period of Brāhmanic philosophical activity. Buddhism drew on
both Aryan and non-Aryan factors. For example, the *Upani-
shads,* among the basic Brāhmanic texts, had already expressed
such ideas as karma and rebirth (samsāra), both of which were
to be developed in Buddhism. And Brāhmanic thought had
engaged in general speculation on other elements that were to
reappear in Buddhism : the eternity of Self (*ātman*); the acquisition of transcendental powers by psychic discipline; eternity
as opposed to noneternity (Brahman is eternal : beings are
impermanent); the identification of Self with body and hence
of Self with impermanence; and so forth. Indeed, "Buddha
replaced the soul by the theory of a mind-continuum, by a
series of psychical states rigorously conditioned as to their
nature by the causal law governing them. . . . According to
him this alone provides for progress . . . and continuity . . . as
each succeeding state (good or bad) is the result of the previous
state."[3] The Buddha himself, it will be remembered, had
studied with Brāhmanic masters. Ārāda Kālāma and Rudraka
had taught him the so-called "domain of nothingness," which
was in reality a psychic exercise of "equalization" (*samāpatti*)
which embraced the five Yogic methods: faith (*shraddhā*),

51

energy (*vīrya*), presence in mind (*smriti*), the governing of the psyche (*samādhi*), and understanding (*prajnā*). Ajita had taught that everything was composed of elements; at death the body returned to these elements, just as the faculties returned to space (considered the fifth element). There were, of course, other Brāhmanic teachers whose influence on Buddhism is notable. Buddhist attitudes towards the gods were indeed inherited from the pre-Buddhist tradition. Brahmā himself was adopted into the Buddhist pantheon, though in the early texts, with greatly reduced prestige.

The systematic presentaticn of Buddhist doctrine which follows does not, it should be noted, serve as an account of early Buddhism as it actually was. The Buddha himself never expounded the Law in a sequential or logical manner; his teachings rather took the form of unrelated pronouncements on certain theological points; answers to specific questions put by his followers; short, almost epigrammatical, discourses; and the like. The systematization which follows, therefore, is arbitrary; it is based largely on the Theravādin (Hīnayāna) Pāli canon.

THE FOUR TRUTHS

The crux of the whole Buddhist doctrine is embodied in the Four Noble Truths, and the rest of the Doctrine is simply an amplification of these four general principles. The first Truth posits the existence of suffering (*duhkha*), which afflicts both material and spiritual being. Every act of life involves suffering : birth, sickness, death, separation, frustration, are its forms. It is inescapable. But suffering is not inherent; it exists only in respect to desire. Desire is self-defeating, of course, for we can never possess what is not ourself. Love, for example, carries in it the seeds of its own downfall, for the ultimate possession of the loved one is impossible, and love exists only so long as the illusion of progressive possession obtains. If this is pessimistic, it must be considered so only for non-Buddhists, for Buddhism offers an escape from this state by positing a second Truth : suffering has an origin.

The second Truth teaches that all suffering stems from what we may call thirst (*trishnā*), that is, from appetites which nourish our desires. These are of three types : thirst for an "object of desire" (*kāma*), for existence (*bhava*), and for nonexistence (*vibhava*). Desires cause suffering because they cannot be satisfied perpetually, particularly when it is a question of an "object of desire." Yet even the blind will to live, the very desire to exist can itself become an "object of desire" and as such cause suffering. Those who overcome the desire for existence may believe that they have cleared away the last obstacle to the complete suppression of trishnā. But they confuse lack of desire with desire for nonexistence, which, of course, is simply another kind of desire, even though a negative one. Suicide, for example, is wrong, because it is in fact a desire for nothingness, or rather, for nonexistence.

Romantic love and passion in the Western sense, for example are condemned by Buddhism, not because they are impure but simply because, as forms of desire, they attach one even more to an unattainable object of desire. They are disapproved because they are a form of attachment, and only as such does Buddhism strive to suppress them. Hence, in Buddhism disapproval of the sexual act contains none of the sense of guilt that has attached to it under the Judaeo-Christian system of thought.

Love leads inevitably to suffering, for the object of one's love can never be totally possessed. There is always the inevitable separation and the consequent frustration of desire.

The third and fourth Truths teach the stopping of suffering : that is, (3) the stopping of desire for rebirth, a longing linked with pleasure and passion; and (4) the positing of a way leading to the stopping of suffering. This fourth

Truth is what is known as the Eightfold Path, a discipline aiming at a disillusioned vision of the Absolute Truth and emphasizing psychological rectitude.

THE EIGHTFOLD PATH

The Eightfold Path consists of the following grades or phases :

1. *Right Vision,* that is, observing the phenomenal world as it really is and not as the illusions which usually dominate our vision of things dictate. Right Vision means recognizing objects for what they are, impermanent unities of parts, not for what they seem to be in their worldly forms. Such corrected vision leads inevitably to—

2. *Right Representation.* Having observed things as they are, it is important to represent them correctly, for, if objects are misrepresented, they in turn falsify subsequent vision, create illusions, and nullify all attempts to escape suffering. An important element of correct representation, of course, is—

3. *Right Word,* that is, a correct externalization of the right concept as it has been perceived with respect to the above two points. This phase is obviously a reflection of pre-Buddhist, Hindu beliefs in the extreme importance of word and form (*nāma-rūpa*), the two being interdependent. Right Word leads to—

4. *Right Activity,* which is a result of the previous word-form rectification. It is the act that stems from the Word, the physical from the mental, with which the first three items have been concerned. Act leads to—

5. *Right Means of Subsistence,* that is, by correct action rectified livelihood is established in which all areas combine to make a good life. A good life, of course, implies—

6. *Right Application* of this means of subsistence. In Buddhist terms this means the observance of the Communal regulations, the Discipline, the Law, for without Right Application

life is misguided, no matter how good our intentions. Right Application in turn leads to—

7. *Right Presence of Mind* (smriti), in other words, a right attitude to or understanding of Self, of Reality, of the Absolute. It is a psychic state dependent on the preceding four physical states and itself the basis of the eighth and final rectitude—

8. *Right Positioning of the Psyche* (samādhi), that "interior" state, often described as a kind of mystic raptness attained during profoundly concentrated meditation.

Thus the Eightfold Path is, so to speak, a mental and physical discipline aiming at an absolute conditioning of the psyche. Indeed, if Buddhism seems overladen with methods and disciplines, it should be remembered that the final goal is the complete transformation of being, toward which such procedures are indispensable. For sentient beings the Four Truths, with the Eightfold Path, form a progression leading from the beginning of Buddhist discipline to final extinction— nirvāna. They constitute an essentially optimistic view of the course to be run, for, despite the emphasis on suffering, they lead to ultimate liberty. As such they contain the kernel of Buddhist teaching.

CHARACTER OF THINGS

If the Four Truths and the Eightfold Path deal particularly with being, Buddhists are no less concerned with the "things" which make up the phenomenal world in which we live and with which we are obliged to deal. Things have no being of themselves because they are impermanent. That is, they are compounded of various, separable parts, which for varying lengths of time exist together to form what we think of as a unity, an object. But because these unities are really groups of parts, because they are "compounded," they are subject to decomposition. This "compounded" state is characteristic of the phenomenal world. For Buddhism there is only one condition which is not "compounded," hence which is not subject to disintegration. That is the state of nirvāna. Not being a temporary union of parts, it is permanent.

AGGREGATES

There are five categories of "compounded" things. These categories, or Aggregates (*skandha*), may be said to constitute a definition of phenomena. First, there is *form* (*rūpa*), a category which includes all material things. The five kinds of form stand always in relation to sense organs through which they are registered : hence, the eye (visible form), the ear (sound), the nose (odor), the tongue (taste), and the body (touch). Form is dependent on various temporary combinations of the four elements (earth, water, fire, and wind); everything is a combination of these. Sometimes a fifth element (space) is added, but it was not a part of the early theory.

The second Aggregate is *sensation* (*vedanā*), which arises from the contacts of the sense organs. These contacts produce various results, agreeable, disagreeable, or indifferent, some lists carrying the number to over a hundred.

The third Aggregate is *perception* (*samjnā*), comprising thought phenomena—cogitative phenomena, as against the affective phenomena which typify the preceding (sensation).

The fourth Aggregate is *predisposition* (*samskāra*), that which makes up the psyche. Filliozat calls this "psychic construction," of which the principle aspects are contact, sensation, memory or mentalizing, energy, and intelligence, but the list is by no means complete. This predisposition, or "psychic construction," is what we may commonly term the complex of character traits that make up our personality, that which typifies the individual, that temporary unity which we call our self.

The fifth and final Aggregate is *practical knowledge*

(*vijñāna*), those ideas which result from other psychic phenomena, the practical knowledge gained through the sensory faculties, especially the mind. Knowledge is established in the heart, which serves as a centralizer and establishes such divisions as good, bad, nondefined, and so on. The total sum comes to eighty-nine different distinctions of kind.

COSMOLOGY

Buddhist cosmology posits an infinity of worlds, which are conceived as disks on an axial mountain (Sumeru). This mountain is surrounded by seven circular chains of mountains which in turn are separated by seven oceans. Around all these worlds there is a peripheral ring of mountains and in the interval a great ocean. At the cardinal points are located the great continents (*dvīpa*). Each world has its universe of nine planets and the main stars, and each exists on three levels: desire (*kāma*), form (*rūpa*), absence of form (*arūpa*). Men inhabit the desire level but can perceive the levels of form and absence-of-form by the exercise of their faculties.

The *kāmadhātu*, or level of desire, contains men, animals, and certain divinities. It is provided with heavens, earth, and hells. The hells are divided into two series of eight, the hot hells and the cold hells. The latter are mainly styled according to the type of blister the cold produces: hence such names as the "superficial blister" (first) hell, "broken blister" (second) hell, and "great lotus" (eighth) hell, the last so called because of the likeness of its cold blister to the lotus flower. The heavens are subjected to similar divisions, beginning with the heaven of the Guardian Kings, that of the thirty-three gods on Mount Sumeru, of Yāma, of the "satisfied" (*tushita*), and so forth. Above Mount Sumeru, the divinities reside in aerial palaces.

The *rūpadhātu*, or form level, is inhabited by gods who have the notion of form. Its four main stages correspond to

four meditations : exclusion of desires, appeasement of intellectual activities (i.e., serenity), suppression of passion (i.e.
imperturbable meditation), and destruction of happiness.
There are various subdivisions.

The *arūpadhātu,* or level of formlessness, excludes all
material things having form. It cannot be localized. It also has
four subdivisions, or dominions, which are related to psychic
states : dominions of the infinity of space, of the infinity of
knowledge, of nothingness, and of no-ideas and not no-ideas.

Matter is conceived of according to a kind of atomic theory,
in which the ultimate atom is always missing. Matter is composed of the four elements (water, fire, earth, metal), and their
cohesion is assured by wind, the fifth element. This theory of
the elements was to explain not only the constitution of matter
but also its proper functioning. It therefore occupies an important position in Buddhist medical theories.

TIME

Time, in the Pāli canon at least, was accorded but slight
attention. Rather than a category of being, it was merely an
aspect of predisposition or "psychic construction," that is, the
personality or "self," which could be considered in relation to
past, present, or future. Subsequently, however, time measurement was to become finely graded : snap of the fingers or a
wink, which constituted an instant (*acchara*). Ten instants
equal one moment (*khana*), ten moments one *laya,* and so on.
There are twelve months of thirty solar days in each year, six
days being subtracted, one every two months, plus the insertion
of an intercalary month in order to conform with the solar
year. The largest measurement of time is the *kalpa,* which is
of incomprehensible, astronomic length and is divided into
four incalculable periods (*asamkhyeyakalpa*), each containing
twenty interim periods (*antarakalpa*), each of which in turn

contains eight worldly ages (*yuga*). An asamkhyeyakalpa is further divided into successive periods of involution and evolution. In the former, beings cease to be born and those that are alive die, and, according to their karma, are reborn in other worlds in a state of evolution. Worlds in evolution progress gradually toward destruction by fire, water, or wind. Certain periods are called "fortunate" or "empty" according to whether or not there is a Buddha. The present period, in view of the existence of the historical Buddha, is known as a "fortunate period" (*bhadrakalpa*).

BEINGS

Beings are divided into five or six categories, according to their "destinations" (*gati*), which are good or bad depending on previous acts. The bad destinations are the hells, animal incarnations, world of the dead or hungry ghosts (*preta*), and world of the titans (*asura*), while the good are the worlds of the gods (*deva*) and of men. Those who are condemned to the hells, the animal state, or the world of the dead are so dealt with in retribution for previous acts. Such condemnation is never eternal. The dead (*preta*) have been reborn in this miserable condition because of previous sins. They inhabit the intervals of the worlds or haunt the worlds, and they are depicted with "needle-eye" mouths through which they vainly try to satisfy their hunger by devouring foul things. The asura titans are rivals of the gods, having an ambivalent character, sometimes being classified with the preta, sometimes with the gods, sometimes being considered good, sometimes bad. Their major faults are pride and jealousy, although it is not unknown for them to practice both the Law and almsgiving. The asura live in cities at the bottom of the sea and sometimes in caves on land, and principal among them is Rāhu, agent of the eclipse.

GODS

The lower orders of divinities are in general inherited from Brāhmanism. The higher orders of the Law are psychological conditions and these are more characteristically Buddhist. The humblest gods live on earth. They haunt cities, forests, deserts, etc. Others circulate in the atmosphere. Among the higher gods are the four Guardian Kings (*lokapāla*): Dhritarāshtra to the east, Virūdhaka to the south, Virūpāksha to the west, and Vaishravana to the north. There are also the *apsarases,* angelic messengers of the gods; *yakshas,* protective or dangerous divinities often living in trees; *rākshasas,* man-eating divinities of human form, living in the forests and in the sea; *kinnaras,* half man, half bird; and others of lesser importance. The so-called gods of meditation exist in the world of form and formlessness above the realm of desire and are in reality psychological states. They are therefore less and less attached to the lower world. They occupy four main stages. The first, of human meditation, is characterized by the Brāhmans ruled by the Great Brahman (*Mahābrahman*), omnipotent, omniscient, creative. But Mahābrahman secretly confesses to error, thereby admitting the supremacy of the Buddhist Law. It is the error of the Brāhmans, who are always the first to be born in the periods of evolution and the first to die in the periods of involution. The Brāhmans are absorbed in meditation on their error. The second and third stages of human meditation are represented by gods more and more remote from thought processes. The fourth stage is represented by divinities who have suspended all ideation.

BUDDHAS AND BODHISATTVAS

At the top of the hierarchic ladder stand the Bodhisattvas and the Buddhas. The Bodhisattvas are beings (*sattva*) ready to attain awakening (*bodhi*), and the Buddhas are those who have attained it, thus having advanced to the supreme point on the path toward the stopping of pain. They are the "Awakened Ones." The Buddhas are of two kinds : those who have attained Enlightenment through their own efforts and for themselves : they are hence called Buddhas-for-self (*pratyekabuddha*), and their wisdom is not passed on to others; and the perfectly Awakened Buddha (*samyaksambuddha*), of which the historical Buddha is an example. In Buddhist legend, a number of Brāhmanic wisemen (*rishi*) are considered to be Buddhas for self. As for the Buddhas, the tradition varies. The older Pāli tradition lists seven Buddhas in succession, that is, the historical Buddha and six preceding, while later Pāli texts list some twenty-four, the career of each being almost the same. To be added to either list is Maitreya, the Buddha of the future, who is at present residing in the Heaven of the Satisfied (tushita). Tradition has it that Maitreya will be born into a Brāhman family when human life has reached some eighty thousand years of age. His career will be like those of his predecessors. Maitreya is perhaps related to the Iranian deity Mithra. Both are saviors, both are "unconquered" : Mithra is the "sol invictus" and Maitreya is "ajita," the unconquered. This Buddhist idea of a savior is completely in keeping with the cyclic idea of time described above.

CAUSE AND EFFECT

Buddhism analyzes man in order to understand and thereby to stop the process of his attachment to life. It is hence an investigation of his psychic being by means of the elements of its composition and of their functions. It is a study of the interrelations of things, with special emphasis on psychological conceptions inherited from the pre-Buddhist milieu. Indeed, in the older passages of the canon, the Buddha refused to speculate on self. Rather, he preferred to find a way of stopping pain. Such an orientation naturally led to the practical study of the psychic being in an effort to uncover a cause, or rather a series of causes, through the suppression of which an enduring nirvānic state could be attained. Such a background provided the essential impetus for the establishment of the theory known as the Chain of Cause and Effect.

The Chain of Cause and Effect is actually a series of interrelated conditions, each element of which is at once a cause or an effect depending on how it is considered. In view of the many variations it has in the Pāli canon, apparently this concept was not set forth by the Buddha himself. The most common chain is the twelvefold one of the Pāli *Vinaya,* which we will consider in some detail.

It will be helpful to visualize the Chain of Cause and Effect as a circle or wheel, in the way Buddhists often do. The explanation of the wheel can start at any place on its rim, for there is no single element of the Chain that marks a beginning or an end. The Chain, like a wheel, goes on perpetually. Usually, however, to facilitate explanation, an arbitrary point is chosen, namely, *Blindness (avidyā* : ignorance), which is the kernel of existence that remains after death and which leads to a blind *Will to Live,* the second link in the Chain. Blindness is therefore the cause of this motivation toward life, which in turn is the effect of Blindness. These are called the two causes of the past. Although Will to Live is, from the standpoint of Blindness, an effect, it is nevertheless a cause of *Knowledge (vijñāna).* Knowledge is the first constituent of the newly conceived embryo. From it arises the conception of *Name-Form* (nāma-rūpa), which corresponds to the evolution of young children. Name-Form implies the existence of *Sense Organs* (meaning in this instance the six sense domains) and corresponds to the prenatal development of the child's body. The Sense Organs establish *Contact (sparsha),* that is, they become active. This is a stage which corresponds to the first few years after the birth of the child, a time when touch pre-

dominates. From the Contact of the sense organs arises *Sensation*. This state corresponds to the child of about five years. The faculty of perception becomes apparent.
apparent.

The preceding five stages are known as the five effects of the present, that is, they are the effects of the two causes of the past. Sensation then produces *Desire*, the thirst to possess what the sense faculties report, a state which corresponds to the mature adult. Desire in turn leads to *Appropriation*, that is, the appropriation for self of the object of desire. Sexual attraction and love are often used to exemplify this stage. Desire leads in turn to *Existence* (bhava), which is the realization of life. The preceding three stages are called the three causes of the present; along with the five effects of the present, they constitute present time in its entirety. The two future effects stemming from Existence are *Birth* and—its inevitable effect—*Death*. As we noted above, in Death the kernel of ignorance persists and the Chain of Cause and Effect begins anew. Thus movement in the cycle can be in either direction, but no end is possible until it is broken through the exercise of knowledge.

TRANSMIGRATION

Closely connected with the above concept is that of transmigration (*samsāra*), an idea taken over from Brāhmanism. Samsāra is closely associated with the concept of act. Acts are threefold—of body, of word, and of mind—and their performance corresponds to a sort of "conceptualizing" (*chetanā*). This leaves an imprint on the fundamental psychic phenomena which constitute the being. This "impression" (*vāsanā*) is the result of past deeds and experiences on the personality. Impressions are perishable, in theory at least, though in actuality they are extremely long lasting. They do not die with the body but exist after its death and tend to drive the discarnate being to resume a body. They do this by virtue of their characteristic tendency toward "joining" (*pratisamdhi*). These impressions are exhausted throughout a series of lives by means of rectification of wrong attitudes, but they may be renewed, or replaced by new ones, so that in practice they become almost endless.

Acts, it may be noted, relate specifically to human life; in early Buddhism, psychic phenomena are not characteristic of animals or inanimate objects. Human life then leads in one of two directions: by virtue of accumulated merits, the "impressions" which tend toward rebirth are suppressed and an interruption in the chain of transmigrations comes about; or these impressions are renewed or new impressions established which inevitably cause the cycle of births and deaths to continue. There is actually a kind of intermediate existence between two births, but little attention is paid to this interval in the Pāli canon. Later Sanskrit texts describe it in more detail, noting that the psychic phenomena which endure after death are united with the embryo at the time of the sexual act. At this juncture the new being is drawn either to the male or to the female element. Hence it became a common belief that the last thought at the moment of death was crucial for the destiny of the transmigrating being. Certain schools (*pudgala-vādin*) believe that the "person" (*pudgala*) is the same in various lives, while others (*Skandhavādin*) believe that there is no real stability, no permanent self, the "person" is only an ever-changing group of aggregates (*skandha*).

The stopping of pain, which is the crux of the fourth Noble Truth, involves, then, the arrestment of the continuous succession of existences, the breaking of the chain of death and rebirth by the rectification of acts and their corresponding "impressions" which cause this chain to continue. But the interruption or arrestment of acts is in itself insufficient, for abstention from an act is itself an act of the will and hence a continuation of activity. Suspension of acts leads inevitably to death and hence to willful suicide, an act of the will which bears its own consequences or effects and therefore leads to rebirth. Suppression of acts then involves great lengths of time, long successions of births and deaths, until all "impressions" are exhausted. For this suppression certain conditions must be met, and early Buddhism is at pains to set them forth in terms of a practical discipline. These conditions are threefold: moral, psychic, and intellectual.

SOCIAL AND MORAL CONDITIONS

The moral conditions are essentially admonitions (*shīla*), of which there are five basic ones: admonitions against killing, stealing, fornication, lying, and inebriety. To them are sometimes added another group of five: admonitions against eating at the wrong time, dancing and singing, ostentatious dress, sensuousness, and covetousness. The moral conditions thus are addressed to social living, first in the Community and, by extension, among laymen as well. However, in the observance of these commandments Buddhism stresses not so much their social importance as the fact that infringement leads toward eventual rebirth and hence to a continuation of the Chain of Cause and Effect.

These psychophysiological and intellectual conditions are closely identified with the systematic training of mind and body, largely by Yoga methods—that is, rendering the mind "completely disposed" (*samāhita*), or in other words disciplining the psyche through meditation. Closely linked with this psychic training is the element of intelligence (*prajñā*), which the Buddha explained as being the discernment of things, the faculty of being conscious of realities through thinking. The ultimate goal of this intelligence is the comprehension of the Four Truths.

NIRVANA

The state toward which all this psychophysiological training leads is nirvāna. The way toward nirvāna is sometimes considered an aspiration toward "nothingness," a negative idea. Or it is sometimes, as in Brāhmanism, considered to be the attainment of the Absolute. For the Pudgalavādin, or those who believe in the transmigrating body, it is a stable state arising from the cessation of transmigration; for the Skandhavādin, or those who believe that things are but a temporary association of aggregates (*skandha*), it is variable. For other schools (Theravādin) it is an "un-made-up," and hence imperishable, state. Or again, it is thought of in largely negative terms, characterized merely by "absence" (Sautrāntika). There are, however, some generalities which may validly be applied in describing the nature of nirvāna. Traditionally the nirvānic state is compared with a fire which has gone out, and hence *nirvāna* is frequently translated "extinction." However, this extinction does not imply annihilation. Rather it is a state of absence, in much the same way that immortality is the absence of death, health the absence of sickness, darkness the absence of light. Psychologically, nirvāna is the cessation of psychic complexes. It is the state of a person reposing on himself, withdrawn from the stress and movement of phenomena. The nirvānic state is of two types: "with a remainder of acquisitions" and "without a remainder of acquisitions." In the former, there is an extinction of all desire attaching to existence. It is the state of the arhat, or sage, of the Buddhas and Bodhisattvas who continue to devote their enlightenment to the general good of sentient beings. In the state "without a remainder of acquisitions," everything acquired is liquidated, and there is no longer any connection with the world of sentient beings.

CONDUCT AND TRAINING

The path of psychic conduct and training which leads to the stopping of pain attains the nirvānic state in four ways, corresponding respectively to those of the convert entering the right path (i.e., Buddhism), the monk who has only one more existence to live, the monk who is now in his last existence, and the sage (arhat) who draws near to nirvāna. The path comprises five kinds of exercises: (1) rules of morality, education, dress, etc., in sum, the regulations set down in the *Vinaya* texts covering the functioning of the Community; (2) psychic techniques, including meditation, training of the psyche, and recitation of sacred texts; (3) psychic creations (*bhāvanā*), in which meditation leads to an imitation of reality so perfect that it is indistinguishable from the phenomenal; (4) meditation (*dhyāna*), which consists in large measure of Yoga practices, a training toward the emptying of the consciousness (it is further subdivided into four stages: exclusion of desires, appeasement, suppression of passion, and destruction of happiness and pain alike); (5) ecstatic meditation (*samādhi*), sometimes known as "positioning of the psyche," resembling meditation but more restricted, being a series of exercises which bring the individual into a determined psychological attitude. In this deep, meditative state, the essential oneness of all things, of Self with the universe, achieves realization. Samādhi is a condition of profound concentration, of absorption, when consciousness of separate subject and object ceases to exist and all blends indistinguishably into the One. It is a state of psychic oneness brought about by the suppression of all intellectual activity.

SCHOOLS OF BUDDHISM

It is impossible to reconstruct to any precise degree the schools of early Buddhism, concerning which there is still considerable confusion. Tradition notes eighteen, and in all probability there were many more; the number eighteen very likely was borrowed from the traditional eighteen *Purāna,* ancient texts of Brāhmanism. The original school is known as that of the Elders (*Sthavira*), supposedly those who received the teaching directly from the Buddha or his disciples. It was continued by the Theravādin of the Pāli tradition.

The first sect to break away is known as the Mahishāsaka, which maintained, among other doctrinal tenets, the impossibility of retrogression on the part of an arhat and denied the existence of a transmigrating "person." This school is known only as opposing the Sarvāstivādin idea of "all exists." The Sarvāstivādin sect, which broke away in the third century after the Buddha's nirvāna, was one of the most important schools of north and northwest India. It played a great role in the expansion of Buddhism into Central Asia. Its doctrine, which will be discussed later under the Japanese sects which reflect it, is based on the concept that "all exists" (*sarva-asti*). "All" signifies in this instance both an un-made-up and made-up things. The adherents of this school accepted the existence of past, present, and future as aspects of a single unity, in the same way a female is at the same time woman, daughter, and mother. They denied the existence of any transmigrating entity of a permanent nature. The Sarvāstivādin sect depended most particularly on the *Abhidharma* section of the canon (*see* p. 36).

The Sautrāntika, on the other hand, reacted against this dependence on the *Abhidharma* and, basing themselves on the *Sūtras,* accepted Ānanda as their patron. By the first century after the Buddha's nirvāna, there were groups in existence that ultimately became the Sautrāntika sect, which was officially formed three centuries later. The Sautrāntika, which will be treated in more detail below, believed in the instantaneous existence of things (i.e., made-up things), which they maintained disappeared with each moment, to be immediately reborn. Wind is the "prime mover." Phenomena are illusory. We are an ever-changing, constantly reborn series of temporary arrangements of parts. Act is also momentary, but it leaves a trace on the psyche, which itself is both cause and effect, like the fruit which is both seed and flower. This school posits a sort of "subtle psyche" existing in the subconscious, preserving the germs of "impression" which in turn serve to produce other phenomena. This "subtle psyche" is an absolute person lasting through various transmigrations and stands in contrast to the empirical, evanescent person. It may be thought of as a "grouping of a unique kind" proceeding from one existence to the next.

Mahāyāna

BY THE FIRST OR SECOND CENTURY A.D., i.e., about six hundred years after the Buddha's nirvāna, a new movement in Buddhism had begun to evolve. In order to distinguish itself from the type of belief that had preceded it and on which in fact it was founded, the new persuasion took the name of Greater Vehicle (Mahāyāna) and accordingly began to refer to earlier Buddhism as the Inferior Vehicle (Hīnayāna). "Vehicle" refers here to the respectively greater or lesser means of progress. The development of the Mahāyāna is attributed to the writer Nāgārjuna (2d century A.D.?). It adopts the psychological methods of older Buddhism, which it develops but colors differently. It opens up the way to religious fervor and speculation, and therefore, rather than a reform, it constitutes an enrichment of existing concepts, particularly those of the Bodhisattva and the impermanence of things.

Mahāyāna Buddhism is generally characterized by the growth of speculation concerning the Bodhisattvas and the Buddhas, and what in the older Hīnayāna had been a stress on the destruction of pain became a call for salvation. For the arhat arduously working by himself toward nirvāna, Mahāyāna substitutes as the central ideal the compassionate Bodhisattva who works for universal salvation throughout numberless lives. Religious ardor replaces rigorous discipline and leads inevitably to the multiplication of Buddhas and Bodhisattvas. Emphasis is placed on the compassion (*karunā*) of these divinities and on the fact that it is transferable to beings. Hīnayāna had already admitted the existence of numerous Buddhas, but Mahāyāna developed them on both a mythological and philosophical plane. Metaphysically, Mahāyāna emphasizes the distinction between a "truth of experience" and the "Absolute Truth" already noted by the Theravādin.

THREE BODIES

Typical of the Mahāyāna is the doctrine of the Three Bodies (*Trikāya*). Theravāda Buddhism had already implicitly posited three bodies for the Buddha : (1) the body made of the four elements, that is, his corruptible, human body; (2) the body made up of the mind, that is, the idea (or "ideal") body of the Buddha, the one in which he visits the world of Brahmā; and (3) the Body of the Law, which is that of the holy writings. The Sarvāstivādin assumed two bodies which had corresponded roughly to the above-mentioned material and the mental bodies, while Hinduism also had a threefold concept which admitted : (1) a transcendent Principle (*Brahman-ātman*); (2) Lord of the universe (*īshvara*); and (3) historical incarnation (*avatāra*). Against such a background the Mahāyāna evolved a threefold theory, which was to be transmitted with the spread of Buddhism throughout the whole Far East. It is present in Japanese Buddhism today. Asanga—for the theory supposedly dates from him (says Suzuki)—posited (1) a *dharmakāya,* or Law Body, which was the real essence of the Buddha, the equivalent of Void, of Suchness, of divine knowledge, and of wisdom; (2) a *sambhogakāya,* or Body of Bliss, which is the Buddha-essence as it is manifest in heaven and to the Bodhisattvas; and (3) a *nirmānakāya,* or Transformation Body, which is the form of the historical Buddha as he is manifested on earth. The latter is an emanation, or projection, of the sambhogakāya. It is interesting to note that despite the transcendence of the dharmakāya, this essence-body is active in nature and therefore permits the reappearance of Buddhas after their nirvāna.

The three body system then is simply a threefold description of godhead, not unlike the Christian description of the Father, Son, and Holy Ghost. The Law Body is in reality the essence of the godhead, while the Bliss Body is the godhead conceived of as divinity, and the Transformation Body is this divinity in a specific form (Jesus, the Buddha, etc.).

VOID

Another theory developed by the Mahāyāna is that of the Void (*shūnyatā*). It is expounded largely in the group of texts known as the *Prajñāpāramitā-sūtras* (see p. 43). The doctrine of the Void is a method of rejecting all attachment. It maintains that things have no Self, that is, that they are "empty." The state of shūnyatā, or Void, is one in which all polarity, all subject-object differentiation has ceased to exist. But it must be borne in mind that for Mahāyānists this is a positive concept: Void is not a nothingness conceived in negative terms. This positive concept of Void is often compared with the emptiness inside a vase. Without this interior nothingness, the vase would not exist as such—it would be useless. It is precisely the nothingness of the vase that is its very essence and that renders it useful. The same holds true for the Mahāyāna Void when it is said that the Self is empty. The voidness of self is that state of being devoid of all subjectivity and all objectivity, of any notion of polarity.

MIDDLE PATH

Closely related to the idea of Void was Nāgārjuna's concept of the so-called Medianist (*Mādhyamika*). The Middle Path is a characterless state in which there is neither affirmation nor negation of things. Imagine a point on a straight line, for example, at which there is no longer any idea of left or right, up or down. Thus the Middle Path is essentially Void. The goal is not to affirm but to dissolve mundane illusions; and just as Void is not a form of nonexistence, the Middle Path is not a form of nihilism but a method of underlining the fundamental unreality of phenomenal appearances, although it accepts, or rather does not deny, the reality of illusion itself.

The foregoing theories led to the formation of one of the principal schools of Mahāyāna, that of the Vijnānavādin, "those who follow the way of thought." For this school, things are reduced to "only thought"; they are simply psychic representations, thought (*vijnāna*) being the only absolute reality. Existence itself has no more reality than the texture of a dream. Hence, existence may be likened to visions perceived in mental concentration but representing no object. The main idea of this school is that thought can know and that hence there is a knowable (*jneya*) which is not necessarily exterior. In fact, the "support of the knowable" (*jñeyāshraya*) is the inner psyche, which is not a simple consciousness but rather a fundamental vijnāna. Things, then, are purely psychic. They are differently based, however, and this school posits three different types : (1) things totally imagined (e.g., the horns of a hare or a squared circle); (2) things of dependent nature, that is, phenomena related by the Chain of Cause and Effect, like dreams or echoes, which have no reality in themselves but which depend for their existence on a cause; and (3) things entirely of a self-nature, that is, existing completely within themselves, such as abstractions. This last state is absolute being, nondual, permanent, despite the multiplicity of illusory, phenomenal forms. Of course, such a state is indescribable, and one is obliged to refer to it by such paraphrases as the "thing as it is," the state "such as it is" or "suchness" (Skt. *tathatā;* Jap. *shinnyo*).

Suchness

Suchness is the ultimate foundation of Buddhist thought and concerns the "real state of all that exists." It is the unchanging fact amid the constant evolution of the phenomenal world. It defies definition, and the Buddha when questioned concerning the first cause, or life principle, said that it was "the true state . . . without any special condition." By this he meant that reality has no specific character or nature, that it has no "substance." Inaction in action, action in inaction, immobility in motion, motion in immobility, calm in wave, wave in calm, Suchness is none of these individually, neither one nor the other of them. It is all of them, it is the Middle Path, and as such, the true state of all things.

Tantrism

IT MUST BE BORNE IN MIND that Buddhism never wholly supplanted other cults and systems. Hinduism, for example, continued to develop even during the periods in which Buddhism showed its greatest strength. Outside of the monks, purely Buddhist laymen were doubtless few, for the majority of the people tended to patronise Hinduism and Buddhism at the same time. From the fourth century A.D., however, Buddhism had begun to lose ground. The Guptas (fourth to seventh centuries), who ruled all of northern India, were followers of Vishnu. In the fifth century, the Chinese monk Fa-hsien (in India, 405–411), noted the flourishing of Buddhist monasteries, but at the same time he observed that both Buddhists and Hindus joined in the same processions, to the extent that Buddhism seemed but a branch of Hinduism. Other Chinese pilgrims (Hsüan-tsang [602–664] and I-ching [635–713]) reported the decline of Buddhism in the seventh century, after which time the chief stronghold of the religion lay in Bihar and Bengal, in eastern India. By this time, Hīnayāna had almost completely disappeared from eastern India, and the Buddhism that remained was largely Mahāyāna or branches thereof, such as Vajrayāna. Buddhism flourished in the east until the twelfth century, with the support of the Pāla dynasty, and it was from this region that it spread to Nepal and Tibet in the eighth century.

MAGICAL PRACTICES

From the fifth century on, with the decline of the Guptas, interest in feminine divinities and magical rites, which had their foundation in ancient indigenous practices, became more pronounced. Such religious observances had as their goal salvation through the attainment of superhuman power, and they often included what some would call licentious features. These features were not new; they may be traced back to the *Vedas*. They owe their survival to their continuous practice among the lower orders of society. Earlier Buddhism, of course, had never rejected the supernatural, and monks who had advanced far along the path of Buddhist discipline into the higher stages of concentraction were known to possess supranormal cognition. Although the Buddha had cautioned against the use of such powers, magical practices grew, doubtless under the influence of hermit monks, who grafted such practices onto traditional Buddhism. This magical Buddhism in its later development is known as Buddhist Tantrism, being based on the group of texts known as *Tantras*. Tantras are essentially texts which describe spells, formulas, iconography, and rites. They are manuals, so to say, which emphasize the practical effects of magic, as it is worked by rites, to the detriment of profound metaphysical speculation. Although Buddhist Tantrism did not appear in an organized form much before the seventh century, its influence must have been evolving for some time previously. Hsüan-tsang, for example, notes that at the time of his visit to India (629–645) whole communities were devoted to the practice of magic.

LEFT- AND RIGHT-HANDED TANTRISM

Buddhist Tantrism is divided into two types, known as Left-handed and Right-handed. Right-handed Tantrism emphasizes devotion to masculine divinities. Although it has left little surviving literature in Sanskrit, it became influential in both China and Japan, where it will be considered in connection with the Shingon school. Left-handed Tantrism, to which the title Vajrayāna, "Thunderbolt Vehicle," is chiefly applied, postulates feminine counterparts of the Buddhas, Bodhisattvas, and other divinities. These counterparts are called Tārās, "savioresses," and Left-handed Tantrism worships them chiefly as the "personified, active aspects" of the deities in question. The lore of this type of Tantrism, as to a certain extent of the Right-handed form as well, was imparted to the initiate only through the words of a "spiritual preceptor," hence the term *Esoteric Buddhism* for the Tantric school

Magical Formulas

The Tantric ritual stresses the use of mystical syllables and phrases (*mantra* and *dhāranī*). On the psychological plane these phrases, which are chiefly formed with a vowel and a nasal (*hrīm, ham, hūm, phat,* etc.), tend to produce through continuous pronunciation a resonance in the head, a kind of profound inner echo, leading to a mystical rapture wherein the practicioner is aware of the vast overtones of the universe and the laws inherent in the nature of things. On the symbolic plane, these formulas apply variously to religious or sexual ideas. The often quoted *om mani padme hūm* ("Ah! The jewel is in the lotus!") stands at the same time for the existence of the Buddhist Law in the World (lotus) and for the union of the Bodhisattva with his Tārā, the lotus being frequently a feminine symbol in Tantrism. Yoga postures and meditation are practiced. At a certain degree of spiritual attainment, normal rules are no longer valid; rather, their breach spurs the adept on his way, and such excesses as drunkenness and even ritual murder are known to have been practised.

Sex in Tantrism

Vajrayāna adopts the essential principles of the Mahāyāna, those of the Void and the Middle Path, and accepts the ultimate emptiness of all things. It does not, however, disparage the phenomenal world, which, in fact, it believes to be fundamentally the same as Void. Thus the adept is encouraged to use this world of phenomena as a kind of "means" (*upāya*). Of course, the full consciousness of the emptiness of all things is Supreme Wisdom (*prajñā*), and in the Vajrayāna system this Wisdom is personified as a goddess. Final bliss is the union of the two, a union of phenomenal Means with noumenal Wisdom. The symbol of this mystic fusion is the sexual act. The system was eventually to establish a philosophical basis for erotic practices and images depicting them.

By the third century A.D. two important feminine divinities had made their appearance : Prajñāpāramitā, the creation of metaphysicians as the incarnation of Supreme Wisdom; and Tārā, the manifestation of the "Great Goddess" of aboriginal India. In these two divinities, the mystery of woman was rediscovered. Every woman becomes representative of the secret of fecundity and generation. In her remoteness, she incarnates the mystery of creation and being. "The process of Enlightenment is therefore represented by the most obvious, the most human and at the same time the most universal symbol imaginable : the union of male and female in the ecstasy of love—in which the active element (*upāya*) is represented as a male, and the passive (*prajñā*) by a female figure. . . ."[4] The ultimate union of these two forces, often represented in the iconography of Tibet and called in Tibetan (*yab-yum*), is essentially a pure, metaphysical act, which, as performed by the divinities, stands for the ultimate and supreme fusion of multiplicity into the oneness of an absolute state.

TANTRIC IMAGES

Tantrism is antiascetic and antispeculative. For the Tantrist, liberation is pure spontaneity, the satisfaction of all desires.

The ideal is to transform oneself into a "Being of Diamond" (*vajrasattva*), that is, into an ultimate, unchangeable, permanent Void. For this purpose, Tantrism places great importance on iconographic paraphernalia. Images are "supports" for meditation, and the whole iconographic universe must be entered and assimilated, first by transporting oneself onto the cosmic plane inhabited by the divinity and by assuming the "powers" of the divinity in question. The interiorization of iconography depends on Yogic disciplines of meditation and concentration whereby the image is, so to speak, cast on a mental screen by an act of creative imagination, after which it is "realized" by the person meditating. In the same way as the images, the mantra and dhāranī (mystic phrases and formulas) serve as "supports" for meditation; and, though meaningless to the uninitiated, they are of profound mystic significance and force to the initiate, who through these sounds "assimilates" the god.

MANDALA

Another iconographic device is the *mandala,* a graphic representation of the cosmos or a "cosmogram"[5]—a "receptacle" for the gods, who descend to this privileged place, the center of which is the mystic center of the world. Literally *mandala* means "circle," "center," "that which surrounds." In its simplest graphic form, it is composed of two superimposed triangles (*yantra*). The triangle pointing down stands for the feminine principle (*yoni*), the one pointing up for the male principle, and a central dot represents the undifferentiated Brahman. The mandala may take the form of a circle traced on the ground, or it may be simply any ritual arrangement of images. Whatever its form, there is no doubt that the mandala is connected with the symbolism of royalty, and that its use, or entry into it, implies the gift of special status. The adept indeed becomes a sovereign, because by his entry into the sacred precincts of the mandala he rises above the play of the cosmic forces obtaining in the phenomenal world. The center of the mandala is the sacred place, the magical place, toward which the adept directs his efforts. For him it is the place which on a psychic plane symbolizes the complete integration of his personality, just as the outer sections and the exterior represent its fragmentation. Hence, from the religious stand-point the mandala symbolizes the unification, the fusion, of the devotee with the central divinity and his identification with the mystical Absolute. This takes place subsequent to his gradual identification with the intervening multiple gods. Psychologically the mandala stands for the integration of all psychic phenomena which compose what we call the person, as against the destructive forces which characterize the world of phenomena.

Typical of Yoga, as well as of Tantrism, is the practice of the mandala and its projection within one's own body. The body then becomes a kind of divine ground, an instrument for the conquest of death rather than a source of pain. The person is, in other words, transformed into a microcosm in which the breath is identified with the cosmic winds and the spinal column with the cosmic axis. The Yogic aspirant "realizes" this microcosm through his meditations. The spinal column becomes Mount Meru, the four limbs the four continents, the head the world of the devas, the eyes the sun and moon, etc. The goal of this projection is the awakening of the *kundalini*, of an energy which must be drawn upward from its dwelling place at the midpoint of the body.

TANTRIC SEXUAL UNION

Tantrism of the Left-handed variant engages in consider-able mystical erotism not usually present in the Right-handed type. It is known that in pre-Tantric India orgiastic union had been practiced for the purpose of obtaining universal fecundity (rain, harvests, animal and human birth) or for creating a "magical defense." The woman was a sacred, pure place for sacrifice, and indeed the female organ was identified with the sacred fire. The sexual act was in a psychophysiological sense devitalized, and emphasis was placed on it as a ritual. It was a "conjunction of opposites" filled with profound metaphysical meaning. Thus, every woman incarnates the universal woman, or prakriti. She is a goddess, and the adept must hence become a god, or universal male (*purusha*). But the god is immobile, activity being rather on the side of his feminine counterpart (*shakti*). Thus the human couple becomes a divine couple, and the sexual union becomes the means of obtaining "Supreme Bliss." Decadence set in only with the diminishing of the symbolical meaning of bodily activities.

Extension of Buddhism

AFTER ABOUT 1200 A.D., Buddhism ceased to exist in India. But the seeds of the Law had long since been sown abroad, and some of its most flourishing days were to come to pass far beyond Indian borders.

TYPES OF EXPANSION

Since the days of Ashoka, Buddhism had had a markedly missionary character. Indeed, the Buddha himself had been dedicated to spreading the Word of the dharma. Ashoka had established a Buddhist political state, so that the dissemination of the Law to which he zealously devoted himself was conterminous with the diffusion of his temporal power. Buddhism presents two modes by which this expansion was carried out. First, it penetrated neighboring countries, especially those of southeast Asia, as a form of Indian culture, the culture under whose domination such areas lay. Secondly, it spread to the further reaches of Asia, such as China and Japan, as an element of cultures that maintained their indigenous characteristics. In some areas these two types existed together.

SOUTHEAST ASIA

In the neighboring states of Nepal, Kashmir, Ceylon, Cambodia, Java, Burma, and Thailand, Buddhism was an active element in the Brāhmanism by which Indian culture was spread to those areas. In some cases (Nepal, Java), the two religions tended to fuse; in others, while Brāhmanism won the court and higher circles, Buddhism became influential among the lower classes and sometimes was in opposition to Brāhmanism.

Already in Ashoka's times, monks and nuns had penetrated into Nepal, and Buddhist colonists had begun to expand into central Asia. By around the beginning of the Christian era, Buddhism had taken hold in Funan, Champa, and Sumatra and by the fourth century in Java and Borneo. The following two centuries saw it established first in Cambodia and then in Burma. Of course, monks and nuns, while doing their part in the evangelization of the religion, do not represent the only agents by which the religion expanded. Due credit must be accorded the numerous merchant and other commercial interests which linked India with her neighbors. Colonists and traders "brought with them not only Buddhism and Brāhmanism but also the art of writing, technology, and commerce, as well as the Brāhmanic concept of the divine king. Indeed, the Dharma thus transplanted was more than the teaching of Buddha; it was a Buddhist-oriented Hindu civilization." [6]

Ceylon

The establishment of Buddhism in south and southeast Asia took place under varying circumstances. In Ceylon, where Ashoka's missionaries had carried it as early as the third century B.C., it was, from the beginning, of the Theravāda type, based on the Pāli canon. By the third century A.D., however, Mahāyāna beliefs had penetrated the island, while the eighth century saw the growth of Esoteric Buddhism (*see* p. 76) and the presence of Tantric masters and students. Hence, in Ceylon Theravāda Buddhism has incorporated numerous elements from Mahāyāna, Esotericism, and Brāhmanism. "In one sense at least, Ceylon has been faithful to the Buddhism of Ashoka's period; that is, it stands for the supremacy of Buddhism without rejecting the diverse elements of Brāhmanism and Hindu civilization."[7]

Other parts of southeast Asia present a different picture. Javanese Buddhism, Mahāyānic in nature with a certain admixture of Esoteric practices, was to coexist on an equal footing with Brāhmanism, and Hindu gods were thought of as counterparts of Buddhist divinities (*see* the Japanese parallel of *ryōbu shintō,* p. 136). The same Buddhist-Brāhman fusion is to be early noted in Cambodia, which, however, since the thirteenth century has become a stronghold of Theravāda Buddhism.

Burma and Thailand

There are other countries where Theravāda dominates, notably Burma and Thailand, where, despite the former presence of Mahāyāna, Esotericism, and Brāhmanism, Theravāda not only is considered orthodox but is the state religion as well. In Burma, despite the orthodoxy of Theravāda since the fifteenth century, there still exist important undercurrents of the Brāhmanic tradition, as well as an active animistic belief in the native *nats,* or "nature spirits." Thai Buddhism shows many similarities with the Burmese form. There the Buddhist hierarchy, unlike Burma, became assimilated into political officialdom, a situation which has given rise to tensions between high ranking Buddhists and Brāhmans.

NORTHWARD EXPANSION

Although southeast Asian Buddhism lies within the Indian cultural sphere, such is not the case of other areas where the religion spread. In its northward expansion, Buddhism was to encounter lands and peoples whose mode of life had little or nothing to do with Indian civilization, and the role of Buddhism in such surroundings was to be entirely different from what it had been in southeast Asia.

Central Asia

The importance of Central Asia in the expansion of Buddhism is impossible to exaggerate. Central Asia, peopled largely by nomadic tribes (Iranian, Scythian, Turkish, and Mongolian) with little cultures of their own, played the role of transmitter. Manichaeism, Zoroastrianism, Brāhmanism, Buddhism, and Christianity were all passed on by trader and monk alike via the Central Asian routes that extended from China in the east to the Mediterranean in the west.

Indeed, it was largely through the work of such Central Asian monks as Kumārajīva (344–413) from Kucha that Buddhism was to receive such a powerful initial impetus in China. Kumārajīva, who had studied Mahāyāna Buddhism in northern India, was taken to China toward the end of the fourth century as a prisoner. There he organized a kind of multilingual bureau of translation in which some few Central Asians cooperated with Chinese monks, the former expounding Indian Buddhist texts and the latter rendering them into classical Chinese. Thanks to the work of such translators, the Buddhist canon was made available to Chinese Buddhists, and unlike the Buddhism of southeast Asia, which continued to use Sanskrit or Pāli as the official canonical language, Chinese Buddhism was free to evolve within the framework of Chinese culture.

China

Although there are notices concerning Buddhism in China in the centuries immediately preceding the Christian era, it was only beginning in the first century A.D. that the religion witnessed a striking growth. There is a traditional story concerning the introduction of Buddhism in 65 A.D. as the consequence of an imperial dream. The account demonstrates that Buddhism had already gained imperial favor.

Buddhism never replaced the ethicopolitical system of Confucianism nor the mystic and philosophical Taoism, but in the first centuries A.D. these native systems, due to political and social disruptions, did not fill the religious needs of the Chinese. Thus it was in this native religious vacuum that Buddhism for the first few centuries was to grow almost untrammeled, continuing until the T'ang dynasty (618–906), when it reached its apex.

Chinese Buddhism, although claiming descent from Indian schools, nevertheless evolved into definitely Chinese forms, due to a number of factors. First, the basic canonical texts were no longer in Indian languages but in Chinese. Moreover, the Chinese translation of these texts did much to Sinify foreign ideas. Wright notes how the translators' reliance on native terms to render foreign ideas both changed and Sinified Buddhist concepts. "To present Buddhist ideas in Chinese language and metaphor, there was necessarily a heavy reliance on the terms and concepts of indigenous traditions. Buddhism had somehow to be 'translated' into terms that Chinese could understand. The terms of neo-Taoism were the most appropriate for attempting to render the transcendental notions of Buddhism; also useful were the Confucian classics, which continued to be studied despite the waning authority of the state orthodoxy. Thus, for example, the ancient and honored word *tao,* the key term of philosophic Taoism, was sometimes used to render the Buddhist term *dharma,* 'the teaching'; in other cases it was used to translate *bodhi,* 'enlightenment,' or again *yoga.* The Taoist term for immortals, *chen-jen,* served as a translation of the Buddhist word *Arhat,* 'the fully enlightened one' *Wu-wei,* 'non-action,' was used to render the Buddhist term for ultimate release, *nirvāna.* The Confucian expression *hsiao-hsun,* 'filial submission and obedience,' was used to translate the more general and abstract Sanskrit word *shila,* 'morality'."[8]

Persecution in China

With its steady increase of power, Buddhism in China began to incur opposition both from Confucian and Taoist factions, who naturally resented the "foreign religion." Royal favor was unpredictable, sometimes underwriting one, sometimes another of the three religions. Although Buddhism had undergone a number of persecutions, the one in 845 A.D. marked a turning point. Indeed, Buddhism, although persisting as a factor in the cultural and religious life of China for many centuries, was never again, after the massive destruction and the whole-sale secularization of 845, regarded as an essential adjunct of state power.

Despite its unstable fortunes, the contribution of Buddhism to Chinese culture is imposing. Aside from a voluminous canonical literature preserved in the Chinese scriptures—some 2,184 works in the latest Japanese edition—China produced some distinctly native developments: Ch'an (Jap. Zen), with its emphasis on a direct, intuitive approach to the Absolute (*see* p. 203); Pure Land, with its emphasis on faith as a key to salvation (*see* p. 188); and Esotericism, with its magico-mystical approach (*see* p. 136).

From the above remarks, it is clear that Buddhism in China was but one factor in the native culture; it did not pretend to the role of transmitter of Indian civilization which it had played in southeast Asia. Such was the case to a certain extent in Tibet as well.

Tibet

Officially introduced to Tibet in the seventh century A.D., Buddhism of the Tantric type (*see* p. 75), was established by the Indian Padmasambhava around 747 A.D. Tibetan Buddhism is an amalgam of a number of elements : *Bon,* the native religion, which aims at "capturing" certain mysterious and vital powers in the universe; Sarvāstivāda monasticism; and Mādhyamika and Yogachāra philosophy. The resultant mixture of magical animism, ascetic life, and abstract philosophy is typical of the Tibetan form of Buddhism called *Lamaism.*

"In Tibet we find a curious mixture of the first and the second types of expansion of Buddhism. Because of its geographical proximity to India, Tibet could be regarded in one sense as one of India's cultural satellites, but the same argument may be made in its relation to China as well. On the one hand, Tibet adopted Buddhism wholesale and translated voluminous sacred scriptures far more faithfully than Chinese Buddhists ever attempted to do; on the other hand, Tibetans appreciated and applied very little of Buddhist ethics, doctrines, and practices. Unlike China, Tibet had very little culture of its own, and yet Tibet managed to put its own mark on the Indian and Chinese elements of Buddhism and produced a unique form of Buddhism. Probably the secret of Lamaism lies in the Tibetans' 'genius for hierarchy, discipline, and ecclesiastical polity' (Eliot), which enabled them to establish a gigantic superstructure of the Buddhist Community, regardless of the quality of the faith of the priests and laity in all other aspects."[9]

PART II

Japanese Buddhism

The Introduction of Buddhism to Japan

THE TRADITIONAL DATE FOR THE INTRODUCTION of Buddhism to Japan from the Korean peninsula is 552 A.D. There is no doubt, however, that the Japanese Court, at least, must have had cognizance of the religion before then. The Annals of Japan (*Nihongi*) note under the years 284–285 (corresponding to 405 A.D.) that two men known as Ajiki and Wani (or Wang-In), probably Koreans, acted as instructors to the Japanese heir apparent in Chinese language, writing, and literature.

RELATIONS WITH KOREA

Korea in the sixth century was divided into three principal states: Koguryo (J. Kōkuri) in the north; Paikche (J. Kudara) in the southwest; and Silla (J. Shiragi) in the southeast. In between lay the little enclave of Mimana, which had a sizable Japanese population and a Japanese resident general. Koguryo had accepted Buddhism in 372 A.D., Paikche around 384, and Silla much later. By the middle of the sixth century, the balance of power among the three principal states had become unstable. It was known that the Japanese authorities at Imna had been conspiring with the government of Silla, and the Paikche king, Syŏng-Myŏng, thought it the greater part of wisdom to fend off an alliance possibly being formed against him. Thus in 545, it is known, he commanded a statue of the Buddha some sixteen feet high to be made and offered it to the Japanese emperor, Kimmei (540–571). It is not known whether this statue was ever actually sent to Japan; from the Japanese side, there is no evidence that it was received. Attested, however, is the mission that Syong-Myong dispatched to the Emperor Kimmei in 552, notifying him of the combined menace of Silla and, now, Koguryo and requesting Japanese troops. The Japanese emperor made a gracious if not entirely clear reply, with the result that later the same year, in the tenth month, the Paikche king sent another mission, this time bearing an image of the historical Buddha in gold, silver, and copper—a *different* image—as well as banners, umbrellas, and a number of manuscripts of Buddhist sūtras. In an epistle, he spoke of the merit of spreading the new religion, which, although difficult to understand—even the Duke of Chou and Confucius had not completely grasped it, he said!—leads ultimately to the highest wisdom and in which every prayer is fulfilled. The communication, having offered the information that the religion had spread across Asia from India to Korea, exhorted the Japanese monarch to continue its dissemination in fulfillment of the words of the Buddha. The political motivation behind the Korean king's piety is not to be denied, and there remains the telling postscript that in 562 he himself was ultimately killed and his country conquered by the Sillans, who in addition destroyed Imna and massacred its population.

INTRODUCTION OF BUDDHIST WORSHIP

Nevertheless, the Japanese Court gave close if perplexed attention to the Paikche king's pious epistle and especially to the religious gifts he had sent. The reception of such articles created an unprecedented situation, and the Emperor consulted with his ministers on the correct procedure to be followed. Opinions were divided; some felt that the polite thing was for the Japanese, after the example of other civilized countries, to adopt the new religion, but others expressed concern lest the native divinities be offended by the importation of new gods. Two great families who were powerful leaders in the practice of the native cult—the Nakatomi, who retained hereditary charge of the official liturgy, and the Mononobe, who headed the guard of the Imperial Family—were pitted against a no less powerful family, the Soga, who came out on the side of the new religion. The ultimate decision of this first council was to approve the worship of the courteously bestowed Buddhist image as a kind of temporary experiment. Close watch was to be maintained for any sign that the native divinities might be offended. The courtier Soga no Iname (d. 570) turned his house at Mukuhara into a temple for the worship of the image. Hardly had the temple been opened, however, than the displeasure of the native gods made itself manifest in the form of a pestilence. Accordingly the Mononobe and the Nakatomi, proclaiming that the presence of the Buddha figure was extremely inauspicious, burned the temple and threw the image into a canal.

In spite of this initial setback, Buddhist ideas, scriptures, and icons continued to filter into Japan. In 577 another mission arrived from Paikche. This time it included three priests and a nun, a temple architect, and a sculptor of images. In 579, Silla as well sent a mission accompanied by an image.

SOGA FAMILY AND EARLY WORSHIP

The latter half of the sixth century witnessed a steady strengthening of Buddhism in Japan. The reign of the Emperor Bidatsu (572–585) is noteworthy. Although not himself a believer, Bidatsu was fond of literature and the arts and tolerant of the new religion. In 574, his son, Soga no Umako (d. 626), who had embraced Buddhism, erected a temple, under the surveillance of three nuns, where he enshrined an image of the future Buddha, Miroku (Maitreya). The Soga family worshiped here until again a pestilence broke out, and again at the instigation of the Mononobe and the Nakatomi the temple was burned and the nuns ejected. This time the plague grew worse, and the belief spread that such a turn of events was not the fault of the Buddha image but rather the consequence of its rejection. The Sogas were therefore permitted to practice the religion as a family cult, and Buddhism was definitely established in Japan.

It is recorded that Bidatsu's successor, Yōmei (r. 586–587), believed both in Buddhism and in the native divinities and at his death expressed the wish to accept the Three Treasures of Buddhism : Buddha, Dharma (Law), and Sangha (monastic orders). But concerning his succession a grave dispute broke the court into two camps, the Soga and Mononobe finding themselves again at odds. In the fighting the Soga were victorious, and the breaking of Mononobe power removed organized resistance to the promulgation of Buddhism in Japan. So powerful did the Soga become that, when the Emperor Sujun (r. 587–592) expressed a dislike for the family, the Soga had him assassinated and a niece of the family enthroned as empress, under the title of Suiko.

PRINCE SHŌTOKU

Suiko's reign (592–628) marks a high point in the development of Buddhism in pre-Nara Japan. Not only was she an ardent Buddhist, but her nephew, the Imperial Prince Shōtoku (573–621), a member of the Soga clan and a son of the aforementioned Emperor Yōmei, is considered the founder of Japanese Buddhism. Also known as Umayado, "stable door," because tradition has it that he was born unexpectedly while his mother was visiting the imperial stables, Shōtoku was a scholar, acquainted with the Chinese classics (an area in which

*Prince Shōtoku by Enkai, dated 1096. Wood, height approx.
109 cm. Located in the Yumedono, Hōryūji.*

the Soga family was hardly noted), and a soldier, having gained renown fighting against certain members of the Soga family in the dispute over Yōmei's succession. Shōtoku was also called upon to play an important political role. Not long after ascending the throne, Suiko took the vows of a Buddhist nun and in large part withdrew from an active part in the government. Shōtoku was appointed regent and served in this capacity until his death. While early Buddhism in Japan had been associated with magical powers and the fear of disease, Shōtoku's faith was different in that it was truly sincere. His teachers were Korean, and their role in the formation of Buddhist ideas at this period was important. It is interesting, nevertheless, to note that, devout Buddhist though he was, in his reorganization of the government Shōtoku turned mainly to Confucian models to establish the central authority of the court. Under him, however, Buddhism flourished. Temples and images were built; in 605 a Buddha sixteen feet high was cast in bronze. Embassies were exchanged with China in 608, and Japanese lay and clerical students went to the continent, where some remained as long as fifteen years, studying continental Buddhism as well as Confucianism. By 623, according to the *Nihongi* (*Annals*), there were in Japan some forty-six Buddhist temples, 816 priests, and 569 nuns.

SEVENTEEN-ARTICLE CONSTITUTION

Shōtoku is known best, perhaps, for the famous Constitution of Seventeen Articles (*Jūshichijō no kempō*), which he promulgated in 604. At first glance this document seems to be a series of platitudes sketching in very vague, mainly Confucian terms the ideal ethical conditions for the functioning of the country. But on closer study, the Constitution reflects in an interesting way the primitive, even chaotic conditions which at that time must have obtained in Japan. The emphasis on Harmony (I) shows the factionalism which must have continually divided the court, while the condemnation of bribery (II) and forced labor (XVI) indicates that these practices must have been widespread in that day. Han Confucianism provides the ideal of government, and such passages as

> The lord is Heaven; the vassal, Earth.
> Heaven overspreads; Earth upbears.
> When this is so, the four seasons follow their due course,
> And the powers of Nature develop their efficiency. (III)

show to what extent Chinese ideas were molding Japanese thinking and institutions during the late sixth and early seventh centuries. Although mention is made of the Three Jewels and the reverence due them, there is no doubt that the Constitution was chiefly Confucian in inspiration. It actually opposed Buddhism on certain points, for while Buddhism stressed "inner light" (*prajnā*), Confucianism emphasized the heavenly bodies, an exterior light, and the maintenance of harmony between man and natural phenomena. Actually Shōtoku makes use of both Buddhism and Confucianism in his plan for government, in general assigning religious matters to Buddhism and secular matters to Confucianism.

SHŌTOKU'S BUDDHISM

Shōtoku early understood the importance of China for the cultural development of Japan, as evidenced by his sending students to the continent. A Buddhist scholar in his own right, Shōtoku is alleged to have lectured with insight on the *Shōmangyō* (T. 353) and on the *Lotus* (T. 262; *Nihongi*, II, 135). His seven volumes of Commentaries (*Jōgū no seisho*) include four on the *Lotus*, two on the *Yuima* [*kitsu*] *kyō* (T. 474), and one on the *Shōmangyō*. Buddhism flourished undeɪ him, in large part owing to his efforts, although at the same time reverence for the native gods was never discouraged. Shōtoku's commentaries show independent judgment rather than a slavish following of his Chinese predecessors. He was, moreover, responsible for propagating the moral and intellectual benefits of the new religion, as well as building temples and pagodas—the famous Shitennōji (Osaka), which he had built, was completed in 596. By 624, there were already nearly fifty temples, eight hundred priests, and well over five hundred nuns.

In the latter half of the seventh century there was a decided effort to popularize Buddhism, particularly during the reign of the Emperor Tenchi (662–671). Every household was encouraged to erect a Buddhist shrine.

Japanese Buddhism of the sixth and seventh centuries is often referred to as "national." This questionable expression means that its "origins" in Japan were connected with national interests, its aims being to protect the nation, and, as such, it was a kind of state religion. The fundamental nature of this Buddhism was subsequently molded by the law codes (*ritsuryō*) adopted from Sui and T'ang models. It was characteristic of this early state Buddhism that it took into account the native cult and its provincial traditions, which had little or nothing in common with the universality of legitimate Buddhism.

Already in the first year of Taika (645) an "edict for the propagation of Buddhism" was issued (*Nihongi, I, 202*). This edict, which conferred the privilege of worshiping the Buddha on the Soga family, stressed the role of imperial decision in the introduction of Buddhism into Japan, and the Buddhism in the early law codes tended to carry on the faith as practiced by the Soga, rather than the more legitimate type associated with Prince Shōtoku, a fact which in part explains the early Japanification of the religion. And so, while there was considerable embroidery on the part of official historians to glorify certain emperors as patrons of Buddhism, actually it was the Soga clan, rather than the emperors, who molded Buddhism prior to the Taika reform in 646.

Soga Buddhism, beginning with Umako (-626) was a worship of relics (*sharīra*). This is apparent from statements in the *Nihongi* (II, 102), and some would see further support for the idea in the stūpa-like style of the Gangōji, the temple erected by Umako. For Umako, the Buddhist relics possessed magical properties, and he supposed rewards in the form of the material good that they could confer. One may rightly ponder just how profoundly Umako's inner life was modified by such self-interested attitudes toward religion. Such Buddhism must have had, at least in these early times, but little impact on the native beliefs, while contrariwise Soga Buddhism represents a "modified" type of Buddhism, the understanding of which must to some considerable degree have been dictated by established concepts of the native cult. Buddhist precepts (*shīla*), for example, were interpreted as kinds of taboo, and so were scarcely at variance with the system of prohibitions in the native cult. Such essential Buddhist dogmas of selflessness and the monkish life had yet to make their appearance as active forces in Japanese Buddhism.

It was the Taika reform and subsequent legislation that perpetuated this "modified" Buddhism, superficially adopting a universal religion, misunderstanding it, and hence early subjecting it to the influence of the native cult.

Only with Prince Shōtoku's personal investigations into and understanding of the essence of Buddhism did a more legitimate form arise to oppose the old Soga type. Although official records (histories, temple records, etc.) show Shōtoku following in the path of Soga Buddhism, in reality he developed a Buddhism based on his personal study of such orthodox sūtras as the *Lotus* (*Hokke*), the *Shrīmālā* (*Shōman*), and the

Vimalakīrti (Yuima), to which his *Commentaries (Sangyō gisho)* are justly famous. Assuming that the *Commentaries* are in fact the work of Shōtoku—Japanese scholarly opinion differs on this question—it is interesting to note that from the standpoint of orthodox Buddhism little in them is new. The important point, however, is that striking differences become manifest when Shōtoku's Buddhism is compared to the Soga-type that had been propagated through the law codes. Whereas Soga Buddhism was largely concerned with exterior, magical powers and material advantage—in other words, a viewpoint much like that of the native religion—the Buddhism of Shōtoku directed itself toward the inner man, expounding the selflessness of all things, nature included. Such ideas stand in direct opposition to the native beliefs. The Sogas had not only overlooked some of the essential dogmas of Buddhism, but their religion had not fully comprehended the position of the monkish community as the core of the religious organization. Under them, both monks and nuns had been subject to the supremacy of the laity, and it was only gradually, during the Nara period, that the central position of religions began to be clarified. Gyōgi (670–749), among others, did much to establish Buddhism of the more othodox type, as against the Soga type that had received imperial sanction, and in large measure it was he who brought to Japanese Buddhism a universality which harkened back to Shōtoku and which began to be felt, regardless of how restricted it was to monkish circles, in the Nara period.

Nara Period
(710-784)

THE CAPITAL CITY OF NARA was laid out in 710 on the model of the Chinese capital at Ch'ang-an. It was on a grand scale, rectangular, in a balanced arrangement, with wide avenues and streets crossing at right angles. Nara was the first permanent capital, for until this time the court had regularly changed its domicile with each reign. While life went on much as it had in the past in the countryside, Nara was all Chinese, from the architecture of the temples and palaces, the costumes, the etiquette and rank of the court, to the reading of sūtras, the writing of laws and governmental communications, and even to poetry. A small aristocratic nucleus performed this revolution. Japan at this time must have had a population of about 6 million, while Nara could not have had much over 200,000. Of these, some 20,000[10] were responsible for the amazing cultural conversion that Nara was to witness.

NARA BUDDHISM

In the seventh century, Buddhism was especially valued for its magical and protective powers, particularly in the prevention and cure of sickness. Sūtras were read without understanding, their appeal being largely material. The spiritual element of the religion, however, was quickly discovered, and by the end of the seventh century the temples contained statues—of Amida (658) and Kannon (690), for example—

offered by well-to-do persons as a mark of esteem for their parents. The workings of the religion, however, were but vaguely understood, and it was characteristic of Japan that two originally unrelated elements, filial piety and compassion (*karunā*), should become associated.

Buddhism slowly began to exert its effect on Japanese life and culture. By 700, the early practice of mound burial had begun to die out, and cremation, a Buddhist import, had started to replace it. Temples and monasteries, Buddhist images, and other sacred objects were constructed to honor the dead, and all of these enriched, indeed, virtually constituted, the civilization of Nara.

Monks passed from the study of general principles to the investigation of fine points, and six different sects came to be distinguished at Nara. These were imports of six Chinese schools and depended completely on Chinese exegetical work, but already Shōtoku had shown a certain independence in his studies and not infrequently departed from the continental commentaries. It must be said, however, that no very original contributions to Buddhism were made during the Nara period, when the Japanese had of necessity to digest so many new ideas.

GOVERNMENT AND RELIGION

One of the characteristics of Japanese Buddhism from early times was the close connection between government and religion. From the early seventh century, Buddhist ritual was a part of court ceremonial. Priests performed the All Souls ceremony (J. *o-bon;* Skt. *avalambana*) for the court and regularly conducted other services. With the establishment of the provincial temples, known as *kokubunji,* Buddhism was becoming a national religion. In 684, provincial governors were ordered to erect a Buddhist shrine in their residences; in 741, doubtless in imitation of Sui and T'ang practices in

China, an imperial edict ordered the erection of a kokubunji with a seven-storeyed pagoda in each province. Each had to be served by twenty monks and ten nuns; each temple was granted sustenance land. The duties of these temples were the regular reading, in *tendoku,* or "skipping," style, of the text known as the *Saishōōgyō* (T. 665) and the saying of "masses" —public demonstrations of repentance and prayers for freedom from disease, which were observances always of interest to the government. The monks and nuns were obliged to fast six days a month.

THE DAI-BUTSU

The kokubunji were branches, so to speak, of the Tōdaiji at Nara, a sort of Buddhist headquarters, the center of numerous secular and religious functions. Here, in 749, a colossal statue of the Buddha Roshana (Skt. Lochana) was completed. Known as the Great Buddha, it was fifty-three feet high, and over a million pounds of bronze were used in its casting. Gold was providentially and auspiciously discovered in Japan in 749, and the statue was gilded all over. A huge hall was duly built to protect the statue, called the Dai-butsu-den, or "Great Buddha Hall," doubtless inspired by the Chinese temple in Lo-yang, built in 672–675. It was burned down in the twelfth century and the present hall was then erected. It is today the largest wooden building in the world, though only about two-thirds the size of the original.

Undeniably, throughout the Nara period, Buddhism was considered as an instrument for the protection of the state. This does not mean that the native cult was dead. Upon the discovery of gold in 749, the Shintō gods were thanked along with the Buddha. A rescript commemorating the occasion divided the honors between Buddhism, Shintō, and Confucianism; grants were accorded the clergy of all three.

BUDDHISM AND SHINTŌ

However, the Great Buddha at the Tōdaiji was linked to its counterparts in the provincial temples by a kind of secular order that, in a way, related Buddhism with the government. This was a detraction from Shintō prestige. To rectify what must have been considered an imbalance between the Buddha and the native gods, Gyōgi (670–749), a monk of the Hossō sect, conceived the idea of a fusion of Shintō and Buddhism, the two systems to be thought of as different forms of the same faith. In 742, he carried a Buddhist relic to the great shrine of the Sun Goddess at Ise and requested her opinion concerning the plan of erecting the Great Buddha at the Tōdaiji. Her rather vague answer, in Chinese verse liberally strewn with Buddhist phraseology, was interpreted as favorable. The priesthood henceforth was free to think of the gods as local manifestations of the Buddha, an identification that was rendered all the easier by the existence of important solar divinities in both systems.

ECONOMIC STATUS OF BUDDHISM

During the Nara period, the economic power of the Buddhist establishment steadily increased. The temples claimed great holdings of tax-free lands and received valuable gifts from wealthy patrons. Shintō could not compete with such rapidly growing affluence. Together with their religious duties, the temples were cultural centers as well, and the priests held in their hands almost all liberal learning of the times. Buddhism then became responsible in great part for the spread of institutions of a more material nature : alms houses, orphanages, infirmaries.

The rapid rise of Buddhism, unopposed in Japan by a strong native religion as it had been in China and India, brought concomitant abuses. The close connection of the clergy with the court inevitably led to a sometimes unhappy mixture of the religious and political areas. To some extent the great increase in monks must be laid to the enjoyment of tax immunity and the consequent wealth that accrued to holy office. The responsibility for supporting the temples and monks, of course, fell on the lay members and must have constituted a heavy burden as Buddhism flourished. Finally, there was a marked tendency for monks to live in unproductive indolence in the capital and for the temples to become parasitic and demoralized.

THE SIX NARA SECTS

Four sects had established themselves during the seventh century: the Jōjitsu and the Sanron (625), the Hossō (654), and the Kusha (658). Rather than independent sects, these four were philosophical schools, placing emphasis on different texts and on different interpretations of fundamental philosophical points. They were, it must be remembered, not mutually exclusive, and students of the period frequently studied under teachers of all four systems. Perhaps it is best to think of them as variations on a single theme, that of Void. In the late eighth century two more sects were founded, the Ritsu and the Kegon. Altogether they are commonly known as the Six Nara Sects.

KUSHA

The Kusha sect bases itself on a "realistic" work by Vasubandhu (J. Seshin) entitled the *Abhidharmakosha* (J. *Kusharon;* T. 1558) or *Treasury (kosha) of Analyses of the Law.* The word dharma (law), which forms a part of this title, comes from the root DHRI- "to hold," "to bear," and signifies in this instance "that which is held." Hence, the Kusha school is concerned specifically with what can be held, i.e. with things, with elements, in short, with matter. In this sense it is a "real-istic" school.

The Abhidharma School arose some time after the council of Ashoka (c. 240 B.C.), at which time the *Abhidharma* was first recognized as a part of the Tripitaka. It was particularly strong in northern India and the northwest—Kashmīr and Gandhāra.

TEXT

The author of the *Abhidharmakosha,* Vasubandhu (fifth century A.D.), was born in Gandhāra (Peshawar). He had been trained in the Sarvāstivāda School (i.e., "all exists") and in Kashmīr had studied the Abhidharma philosophy. There is a Pāli set of the *Abhidharma* in seven volumes representing the tradition of the Theravādins, while the Sanskrit, extant only in the Chinese translation, represents the Sarvāstivādin tradition. The *Abhidharma* books were composed doubtless in the first two centuries after the death of the Buddha, but the traditions were not codified much before the fifth century A.D., and since that time there has been but little development in India. The contents of the Chinese translations, in sixty *chüan,* or "volumes," deal with the elements which make up the phenomenal world, the organs which experience them, and related matters, ending with passages on knowledge, meditation, and finally the refutation of the idea of Self. Vasubandhu followed largely the work of a forerunner, Dhar-matrāta (T. 1552, 1550), although the last chapter, on the idea of Selflessness, seems to be his own.

It was the Gandhāran version of the *Abhidharma,* with the Sanskrit texts of the Sarvāstivādins, that spread to China. Chinese translations of these texts date from as early as the end of the fourh century A.D., but it was only after the trans-lations by Paramārtha, around 565, and by Hsüan-tsang, around 653, that the Kosha school (Ch. Chü-shê) came into existence and, as the numerous commentaries attest, was assiduously studied. It was introduced to Japan in 658 by Chitatsu and Chitsū, both of whom had studied under Hsüan-tsang. According to the tradition, it was introduced again in 735 by the monk Gembō. In 793, the Kusha school was registered as an appendage of the Hossō sect; in view of the limited number of adherents belonging exclusively to it, it was denied an independent position.

"ALL EXISTS"

The idea that "all exists" was not new to Buddhism. Already the Sānkhya philosophy had maintained by means of exhaustive enumeration that nothing new appears in the universe and nothing disappears, that phenomena are essentially a rearrangement of eternally existing matter. Buddhism itself had posited the idea that everything exists "instantaneously" and that there was consequently no abiding substance. Reality was split into separate elements, into constituent parts. Self then is illusory, nonexistent, for man is simply an aggregate of elements, each of which is a reality in itself. Uniting these elements does not create a distinctly new reality but a more or less temporary unity of the constituent realities, or parts. Take, for example, a house : it is a structure composed of a given number of walls, windows and doors, a roof, and a chimney. Without these elements the house does not exist. Yet the essence of the house lies in none of the composing elements. The house is not the door, it is not the windows, nor is it the roof : it is simply an assemblage of them all.

THEORY OF ATOMS

The Kusha accepts this theory and attempts to define with more or less precision the constituent elements of reality. For this purpose, it posits what some call an "atomic theory." According to this theory there are three atoms: the infinitesimal atom, the form atom, and the dust atom. The infinitesimal atom exists in theory only. It is so small that it must be conceived through meditation and hence exists only in the mind. It is, as it were, a conceptual, essential atom. Seven of these infinitesimal atoms make up a single form atom, which is the least dimension matter can assume. Seven form atoms fuse to make a dust atom, still so small that it can be perceived only by Buddhas and Bodhisattvas. Thus, the atomic theory of the Kusha sect progresses from essence (idea) through form to material, thereby explaining the composite nature of the phenomenal world. It makes no attempt to situate, in typical Buddhist fashion, anything like a "primeval atom," but procedes to enumerate all the elements (*dharma*) that constitute momentary sense data.

TIME

Time and space are correlative for the Kusha sect, the shortest time measurement being the transition of one atom to another. Early Buddhism had already posited a theory according to which a theoretical, momentary, instantaneous present existed. This was for the practical purpose of explaining the existence of the phenomenal world. Past and future did not exist, because the first by definition is no longer, and the second also by definition has not yet come into being. The Kusha school, however, maintains that both past and future are real. They explain this by the fact that the present has its root in the past—that is, exists as a result of the past—and its consequences in the future. Hence, these three states are indissolubly related in a causal relationship. However, this causal relationship does not mean a continuous one. These notions of past, present, and future actually exist separately and are limited in time. Elements thus can be real in each period, and yet these periods do not extend necessarily into each other. For example, let us suppose a vase made in 1600, existing now, and probably existing at a given date in the future. According to the Kusha idea, this vase can be thought of as existing in each of the above periods, independently. Of course, the vase is actually different in each period, it is in reality not quite the same vase, for it is continually undergoing changes of time, changes of structure, so that although the illusion of the same vase is maintained for the phenomenal world, the vase is in actuality a ceaselessly changing group of atoms. However, at any one point in time it may be posited as existing. Thus, according to this school, the three periods of past, present, and future are real, and the elements, too, are real at any given instant." So that which is abiding, unchanging, is the reality of the elements and the Void of Self.

MATTER

The Kusha school divides matter into subjective and objective groups and assumes a difference between the primary elements of pure consciousness and the secondary elements of mental function. The school establishes five categories of elements which it terms *dharmas*—seventy-five dharmas in all. They are divided into seventy-two created (i.e., made-up) and three uncreated dharmas. The created elements are: the "seed elements" (earth: hardness; water: humidity; fire: warmth; air: motion) and the elements of form (first category, eleven dharmas), that is, the sense organs and their objects plus an "unmanifested form element"; (*citta*)—meaning "mind" (second category, one dharma), that is, consciousness itself, which though one, functions in five different ways corresponding to the five sense organs; mental functions (third category, forty-six dharmas)—they include such general functions as

perception, ideal, will, good, defilement, evil; and, finally,
elements having no connection with form or mind (fourth
category, fourteen dharmas). The "unmade-up," or uncreated,
dharmas are (1) space, (2) nirvāna through mental discipline,
and (3) nirvāna through the breaking of the Chain of Cause
and Effect. All phenomena, then, are explained as being a
combination of dharmas existing by virtue of Cause and
Effect. Thus all things exist as a result of causal relations or
combinations; being itself, that is, becoming, stems from the
principle of causation. However, the school admits no enduring
soul, no substratum. The center of causation is act, that is,
one's own action : this is the universe seen subjectively. Such
action produces the causes of subsequent existences, and thus
the past forms the present and the present the future. This is
known as the theory of self-creation, that is, the forming of
self by self, for self will always be reproduced as long as the
causes of it are being produced.

"It is the great merit of the Abhidharma that it has
attempted to construct an alternative method of accounting
for our experiences, a method in which the "I" and "Mine"
are completely omitted, and in which all the agents invoked
are impersonal dharmas. . . .

"In order to make this teaching slightly more tangible, I
will return to our example of the toothache. Normally, one
simply says *"I have a toothache."* To Sariputra this would
have appeared as a very unscientific way of speaking. Neither
I, nor *have,* nor *toothache* are counted among the ultimate
facts of existence (dharmas). In the Abhidarma personal
expressions are replaced by impersonal ones. Impersonally, in
terms of ultimate events, this experience is divided up into :

1.   This here is the *form,* i.e. the tooth as matter;
2.   There is a painful *feeling.*

3. There is a sight-, touch-, and pain- *perception* of the tooth;
4. There is by way of *volitional reactions:* resentment at pain, fear of possible consequences for future well-being, greed for physical well-being, etc.
5. There is *consciousness,*—an awareness of all this.

"The 'I' of commonsense parlance has disappeared : it forms no part of this analysis. It is not one of the ultimate events. One might reply, of course : an imagined 'I' is a part of the actual experience. In that case, it would be booked either under the skandha or consciousness (corresponding to the Self as the subject), or as one of the fifty-four items included among the skandha of volitional reactions which is called a *wrong belief in self.*"[12]

Jōjitsu

The Jōjitsu ("Completion of the Truth") school maintains that neither mind nor matter exists, and it is consequently in opposition to the Kusha. It is a reflection of Hīnayāna negativism and represents a version of the ideas of the Indian Sautrāntikas, those who recognized only the *Sūtras* as authority. The Sautrāntika School stemmed from, but was a reaction against, the realism of the Sarvāstivādins (i.e., Kusha). The Sautrāntikas held their negativistic approach to the Absolute to be a reversion to the original scriptures and their own to be the orthodox school.

Text

The name of this school is taken from the *Sātyasiddhi-shāstra?* (J. *Jōjitsuron;* T. 1646), or *Treatise on the Establishment of Reality,* a work by Harivarman (250–350; J. Karibatsuma), in which he attempted to establish completely the truth as propounded by the Buddha in his original discourses. The school bases itself on three main propositions: no substance, no duration, and no bliss—only nirvāna. Relatively little is known about this system in India. Perhaps it was never an independent school there, although Harivarman's doctrine was undeniably influential. In China, it is known to have prospered until the beginning of the T'ang (seventh century), when it was absorbed by Tendai (Ch. T'ien-T'ai) teachings. The basic text was translated into Chinese by Kumārajīva (344–413) in the first years of the fifth century. It is a collection of interpretations of early Buddhist concepts. Pupils of Kumārajīva are known to have lectured on the treatise in various parts of China, and during the fifth century several lines of transmission are to be noticed. The text itself seems to have been considered differently by various Chinese, some treating it as Mahāyānistic (Fa-yun, 476–529; Chih-tsang, 458–522; Sengmin) and some as Hīnayānistic (Chih-k'ai, 531–597; Chitsang, 549–623; Ching-yin). Tao-hsüan (596–667), a pupil of Hsüan-tsang, declared it Hīnayāna (Sautrāntika) but tending toward Mahāyāna. It was introduced to Japan by Ekan, a Korean priest, who arrived at the Hōryūji in 625. The Jōjitsu was never treated as an independent school but rather as a subdivision of the Sanron sect, which will be discussed subsequently.

Jōjitsu Negativism

The Jōjitsu, being negativistic in its philosophic attitude, posits as its basic tenet the Void of Self (pudgala-shūnyatā) and the Void of All the Elements (*sarva dharma shūnyatā*). Personality consists of form perception, conception, volition, consciousness (cf. the five divisions of the Kusha), all of which are completely deprived of substratum. The universe has eighty-four elements, or dharmas, which in turn have no abiding reality. These elements are simply names of substances themselves ever changing. The aim of the Jōjitsu system, then, is to demonstrate the ultimate truth of extinction, that is, of nirvāna, by equating Void with ultimate Truth. However, the school accepts common sense phenomenality and admits the five categories under which the eighty-four dharmas are arranged. The dharmas, of course, are used in a "worldly" exposition of the truth, for actually even the dharmas do not exist, the five objects of the senses are relative, and the four elements impermanent. The Jōjitsu proceeds in a kind of eliminatory way to reduce phenomena. The objects of the senses (form, sound, smell, taste, and touch), for example, may be reduced to atoms, to molecules, to the most infinitesimal element, and hence to Void. The Jōjitsu Void is an abstracted one, that is, abstracted from entity, and hence it "exists" antithetically to existence : it is not to be confused with the transcendental Void posited by the Sanron school, but is rather a Void obtained by subtraction.

Time and Reality

Jōjitsu accepts the Chain of Causation and the idea of multiple births in order to explain "becoming." Worldly existence is, in fact, a causal combination in the present. Past and future have no entity in themselves but are together present in every moment. Reality is therefore only a moment's flash. This flash is so instantaneous that the intellectual apprehension of it is impossible, and its value is theoretical. By the fact, however, that these moments follow each other in rapid, successive groups, they give an "illusion of reality," but this reality has no actual continuity, any more than the end of a burning rope swung rapidly in a circle traces an uninterrupted circle of light. What we see in the case of the rope is the burning end in successive moments. This illusion of reality that the rapid succession of moments gives is related to Void. The dharmas are Void, just as the empty vase is Void, and just as the Void of the vase is the essential substance of the vase, so the Void of the dharmas is their reality.

For the acquisition or attainment of a state of total Voidness, the Jōjitsu establishes a discipline which aims at the suppression of the Three Attachments : to temporary name, to all elements, to Void itself. Name exists as a result of causal combinations. It is temporary because the combinations are ever changing, impermanent, temporary. Yet there is no way to show this changing existence except by name. Thus attachment to self is an attachment to a name which in turn implies a form. This name is based on elements, so that realizing its essential Voidness means realizing the Void of the elements and hence ridding oneself of dependence on them. This leads to understanding the Voidness of Self, hence to understanding Total Voidness. However, in Total Voidness there may remain a consciousness of the Void, that is, the idea of Void may persist. And it is only with the removal of this idea of Void that attainment of perfect nirvāna is assured, that there is, in other words, a Completion of the Truth (*jōjitsu*).

SANRON

MĀDHYAMIKA

The school of the Middle Path (Mādhyamika) was founded around the middle of the second century A.D. by Nāgārjuna. It approached salvation through the contemplation of Void (*shūnya*), by which it meant "suchness," or "nonduality," terms it proposed as synonyms for void or emptiness. Wisdom (*prajnā*) was gained through a middle path which eschewed all polarity. "Emptiness is the non-difference between yes and no, and the truth escapes us when we say 'it is,' and when we say 'it is not'; but it lies somewhere between these two. The man who *dwells in emptiness* has neither a positive nor a negative attitude to anything. Nāgārjuna's doctrine is not a metaphysical one at all, but it describes a practical attitude of non-assertion which alone can assure lasting peace. Nothing is more alien to the mentality of the sage than to fight or contend for or against anything. This peacefulness of the true sage is the germ of Mādhyamika dialectics."[13] Nāgārjuna was of south Indian origin and the wisdom literature of the Mādhya-mikas shows a subtle dialecticism rather different from the earlier literature of the north. Since Nāgārjuna's doctrine, by avoiding the extremes, tries to attain the resulting Void, his teaching is also termed *shūnya-vāda*, "School of the Void." The school flourished in India until around 1100 A.D. after which it disappeared together with Buddhism.

TEXTS

The Sanron ("Three Treatises") school was introduced to Japan in 625 when Ekan (Hyegwan), a Korean monk, taught the doctrine at the Gangōji in Nara. There were two other orthodox introductions during the seventh century: one by Chizō, a pupil of Ekan, and another by Dōji. Never an independent sect in Japan, Sanron teachings nevertheless profoundly influenced Japanese Buddhist thought. Sanron led in developing the philosophical side of Buddhism in Japan; indeed, Sanron very likely represents the first concentrated attempt of the Japanese to understand the Buddhist philo-sophic systems.

Of the three treatises on which its name is based, the most important is a work by Nāgārjuna (second century A.D.) entitled the *Mādhyamikashāstra (Treatise on the Middle Path;* T. 1564; J. *Chūron*), which was first translated into Chinese around 409 by Kumārajīva. It teaches that all phenomena are unreal and stresses the relativity of the phenomenal world. By rejecting all pluralistic ideas, it endeavors to rectify the "wrong views" of the Hīnayāna. The second treatise is the *Dvādashadvārashāstra (Treatise on the Twelve Gates;* T. 1568; J. *Jūnimonron),* which also was translated into Chinese by Kumārajīva. This one attempts to correct the errors of the Mahāyānists. The third treatise is the *Shatashāstra (One Hundred Verse Treatise;* T. 1569; J., *Hyakuron),* written by Āryadeva, a pupil of Nāgārjuna. It is a refutation of the heretical views of Brāhmanism. Curiously enough, the name Four Treatises *(shiron)* may also be applied to this sect, because sometimes a fourth text is added : the *Prajñāpāramitāshāstra? (Great Treatise on Knowledge;* T. 1509; J. *Daichidoron),* composed by Nāgārjuna and translated into Chinese by Kumārajīva. It is a firm exposition of the monistic view.

The Sanron school in China (where it is called San-lun) owes much to Kumārajīva. This amazing scholar is responsible not only for the translation of the texts on which the school bases itself but also for the training of numerous students. Men such as Fa-lang (507–581) and Chi-tsang (549–623) were influential in this flourishing school under the Sui (581–618) and early T'ang (618–906).

SANRON AND MIDDLE PATH

The Sanron school aims at a refutation of all positive views of other schools. Through dialectic negation it opposes heretical views—what it considers the one-sided ones of the Hīnayāna—and the positive, dogmatic views of the Mahāyāna. The basic philosophy of this school has as its goal the suppression of all polarity, all extremes, so that opposites exist no longer (e.g., neither left nor right, up nor down). The argument is based on the four possible answers to any question : (1) yes; (2) no; (3) either yes or no, depending on circumstances; and (4) neither yes nor no, depending on circumstances. Such argumentation logically reaches a point at which there is no polarity of thought either positive or negative, a point not unlike the Void. The aim of such a teaching is to combat erroneous views by the elucidation of right views which are nondogmatic, neither negative nor positive, that is, which are the Middle Path. For this purpose the school establishes a distinction between the worldly truth and the higher Truth. The Middle Path it posits is of eightfold negation : it is Buddhahood, the state in which all traces of the phenomenal world are rejected. The Middle Path is Void; at that point, it implies, nothing is acquirable. Simple refutation of error means, of course, the selection of a right view : this very selection is in a sense acquisition. The only way to avoid even this "acquisition" is to make refutation into elucidation. Hence refutation means the rejection of any views conceivably based on acquisition, such as Kusha realism and Jōjitsu negativism (*see* above pp. 105 and 111). For the Sanron school, the "right teaching" is the Middle Path, because the Middle Path is devoid of both name and character and implies that truth is attainable only by negation or refutation of wrong views. Retaining wrong views, of course, is blindness to reason. At the end of verbal teaching, the Middle Path begins; and, although it has no name, for convenience it is called "the right as elucidated."

TWOFOLD TRUTH

The Sanron teaching divides its concept of right into substance and function : that is, right in substance corresponds to transcendental Truth, while right in function corresponds to the twofold (higher and worldly) truth. The worldly truth (*samvriti-satya*) is the teaching of the Buddha concerning causation and the existence of the dharmas. The higher Truth (*paramārtha-satya*) expounds the relative existence (*sarva-*

shūnyatā) of all the elements : that is, all the dharmas are in reality Void. The Sanron accepts this concept of a twofold truth as a means of instructon and calls it "word teaching." Other sects tend to conceive of this twofold truth as the very principle that the Buddha taught. That this concept is taken to be a means to instruction rather than a principle is peculiar of the Sanron school.

In the view of the Middle Path, then, existence is transient and evanescent, just as nonexistence is temporary and impermanent. Neither is real. Everything is the result of causality. When the extremes of being and nonbeing are removed—when, in other words, one arrives at the Middle Path—nonexistence is existence and existence is nonexistence, just as Void is form and matter and vice versa.

EIGHTFOLD NEGATION

The Eightfold Negation consists of four pairs of opposites—birth/death, one/many, determinate/undeterminate, going/coming—which express the wholesale polarity of the universe and its negation. Everything is matched by its opposite, so that the refutation of wrong is at the same time the elucidation of the right. It is only when refutation and elucidation are both suppressed that absolute right, that is, Truth, is attained. This is the Middle Path. A fourfold Middle Path is used for practical purposes and corresponds in large measure to the general negation of the eightfold path.

The Sanron school divides its teaching into two groups, the shrāvaka, or "hearers," (Hīnayāna) and the Bodhisattvas (Mahāyāna), and further into the so-called Three Wheels of the Law (*dharmachakra*). These Three Wheels correspond to different elements of the canon : the root Wheel to the *Avatamsaka,* which contains the fruit of the Buddha's Enlightenment. But the message of the *Avatamsaka* is too difficult for human understanding, and the Buddha therefore brought into being the numerous texts of the Hīnayāna and Mahāyāna canon. They are thought of as the branch Wheel. The third Wheel is the *Lotus* sūtra, which contains the essence of all teachings from the *Avatamsaka* on down.

Hossō

YOGACHĀRINS

In India, the Yogāchārin School, which had begun to rise around the first century A.D., by 500 had come to dominate much of Mahāyāna thought. The Sarvāstivādins had long emphasized Wisdom (*prajñā*) which they understood as coming from meditation on the dharmas. The Yogāchārins carried on this trend, but emphasized such Yogic practices as the trance. Actually, the Yogāchārins were reacting against the dialectics of the Mādhyamikas (Sanron), who, with their Middle Path, tried to negate thought; that is, they reacted against those who sought to arrive at the truth by emphasizing the thought process as a means.

TEXT

The Yogāchārin School, founded by Asanga in the fifth century, is based on a text written by him entitled the *Yogāchāryābhūmishāstra*, or *Treatise on Yoga* (J. *Yugaron*; T. 1579). The ideas of the school were systematized by Vasu-bandhu (fifth century), who set forth the idea of "only ideation" (*vijñānamatra*; J. *yuishiki*). According to this concept, nothing outside the mind exists; the phenomenal world prevails only through the ideas we have of it. However, ideation does exist. The Yogāchārins held the Absolute to be only thought (*chitta-mātra*). This theory was not actually new, for it had been set forth in numerous scriptures. "What seemed important to them was the statement that the absolute is 'thought' in the sense that it is to be sought not in any object at all, but in the pure subject which is free from all objects."[14]

Vasubandhu further elaborated theories concerning the storehouse consciousness, beings, and the three bodies of the Buddha.

The Golden Hall of the Hōryūji.

TRANSMISSION

The Yogāchārin school disappeared from India around 1100 A.D. along with Buddhism. It was brought to China under the name of *fa-hsiang*, a translation of the Sanskrit *dharma lakshana*, "characteristics of the dharmas" (J. Hossō), where under the T'ang dynasty it largely replaced the San-lun (J. Sanron). Among its important teachers were Hsüan-tsang (c. 602–664; J. Genjō), his pupil K'uei-chi (632–682; J. Kiki), and Paramārtha (500–564; J. Shindai), who in 546 A.D. had come to China from his homeland in east India.

Hsüan-tsang had studied the Yogāchāra doctrine in India at the famous Buddhist intellectual center of Nālandā (c. 632), and thence carried it to China. He relied chiefly on Dharmapala (sixth century; J. Gohō), the abbot of Nālandā, in his interpretations. Hsüan-tsang's school is known as the Wei-shih (J. Yuishiki), or "Only-Thought" sect. In Japan, the school is also called *shōzō-gaku*, "the study of nature and characteristics," and is particularly concerned with describing the dharmas. It is considered to be largely Mahāyānistic.

The Hossō school was introduced to Japan in 654 by Hsüan-tsang's pupil, Dōshō (628–700), who was also interested in Zen practices and who was connected with the Gangōji in Nara. Dōshō's first pupil was Gyōgi (667–748), who thereafter taught the Hossō system at the Gangōji. The line via Gyōgi is called the "transmission of the Southern Monastery." There were other lines of transmission too: via Chitzū and Chitatsu (c. 660); via a Korean named Chihō; and finally via Gembō (d. 746), a pupil of K'uei-chi, who, having studied in China since 717, returned to Japan in 735 and taught at the Kōfukuji. Gembō's line, called the "transmission of the Northern Monastery," is considered the orthodox one.

IDEATION

In the Hossō teaching, things exist for us through the projection or reflection of their image on our minds, that is, through our consciousness of them. This consciousness coordinates our reactions to things, to the phenomenal world about us, and is hence a kind of storehouse of our ideas concerning the world of phenomena in which we live—a so-called "ideation store," which itself exists through causal combinations; that is, being subject to the action of the Chain of Cause and Effect, the "ideation store" creates the phenomenal world by imagination. This, of course, is not pure ideation, since "pure" ideation can proceed only from Buddha Enlight-

enment. Pure ideation means that no distinction exists between
subject and object, and hence it implies the existence of
absolute unity. This is nirvāna. The phenomenal world exists
through the mixture of pure and tainted ideation.

CHARACTER OF THINGS

According to the Hossō, a sharp distinction is observed
between the specific character of the dharma (*lakshana*) and
the nature (i.e., thusness) of the dharmas. This distinction may
be compared to our concept of the distinction between the
worldly truth and the transcendental or absolute Truth. The
Hossō aims particularly to describe these dharmas (it will be
remembered that the school's name means "Characteristics of
the Dharma"). It aims, that is, to distill and isolate the idea
that gives rise to the dharmas, for, according to its teaching, no
element (*dharma*) is independent of the ideation which is its
cause : "all dharmas are mere ideation." In fact, every thing
exists through ideation. The external, phenomenal world exists
for us in the appearance which internal ideation projects of it.
Hence, there is no real, phenomenal world but simply ideation
of it. Likewise there is no self : self is ideation. Of course, this
school does not deny the illusion by which we are surrounded,
but it does stress the importance of realising that it is illusion.
Self and the phenomenal world, the Hossō maintains, are very
like a river. Now, a river presents a certain appearance, with
its meanderings and yet its continuity. Yet where exactly
is the river? At what point can we say, this is the river,
separating it from the myriad drops of water that go to make
it up? We say the river is an entity, yet its waters are never
the same and its very appearance is constantly in flux. *River,*
then, is the name we give to an illusion that defies definition,
that can never be grasped, because it does not in actuality
exist except as a combination of elements forever changing
and reforming. The Hossō applies the same kind of definition

to the self, to the phenomenal world. By studying the elements which compose self, which make up phenomena, it aims to gain a clear idea of the nature of the illusion they present. For this purpose, the school proposes a hundredfold division of the dharmas in five general categories, comprising all forms of consciousness. This consciousness has four functions: objective, subjective, self-witness, and rewitness. Again, if we take the example of a house, these functions correspond to: (1) the house as seen (or its image projected by creative imagination on the mind); (2) our seeing of the house with the eyes as a measuring instrument; (3) recognizing the dimensions of the house according to the measurements the eye provides; (4) the recognition of the accuracy of the measurement.

Objects of the outer world are divided into three groups: those immediately perceptible, that is, objects of the five senses noted as they are; illusion, that is, the image of phenomena which one projects on one's imagination; and the original, or essential, substance, which is not actually perceptible as it is.

The Hossō school recognizes a difference in the nature and the specific character of the dharma. Principle is different from fact: "The thing in itself is different from the thing for us." The chief concern of the Hossō, as a result, is to discover the exact manner in which the elements are manifested in order to learn the exact manner in which illusion is projected. Thus, while other schools deal with the principle behind the elements, the Hossō school is most particularly concerned with their specific character. Of course, the Hossō school does not recognize that every being has within it the Buddha nature. The Hossō also posits a Middle Path, which is Thusness, ultimate Reality. The ideation we make of things, their projection on the screen of our consciousness (our imagination), has no real existence and hence is Void. Causation occurs through ideation, so that it may be said that the action which stems from this causation is "the result of ideation." As a result, causal combinations, if we accept that they stem from nonreal ideation, do not exist—compare the example of the river above—and yet they form a kind of illusory, or temporary, reality, which the Hossō recognizes in order to give practical explanations of phenomena. The Middle Path, then, is neither this temporary reality that results from causal combination nor the Void of the nonexistent. For the Hossō school, it is transcendental and mystical; and, as such, it stands in opposition to the eliminatory Void which characterized the Middle Path of the Sanron school.

RITSU

CHINESE ORIGINS

With the evolution of Buddhism in China, interest in dialectics, the exegesis of difficult texts, encouraged a growing academic intellectualism in Buddhist circles. Certainly the basic Hīnayāna ideal of a community of monks was becoming less and less a fact of Chinese Buddhist life. In order to counter this tendency, Tao-hsüan (596–667; J. Dōsen) founded a sect which he called the Lü, or "Rules," a translation of the Sanskrit *vinaya* (J. Ritsu), rules governing the life of the Community. For Tao-hsüan, the doctrine per se was of less importance than the leading of a disciplined religious life. Discipline and morality, he claimed, were the cornerstones of a monk's life. He accordingly placed great emphasis on the Vinaya. He followed Indian precedents by making the *Dharmaguptavinaya* (T. 1428?; J. *Shibunritsu, The Rules in Four Parts*) the authoritative text of the sect. Nevertheless, "the idea of thus emphasizing the Vinaya seems to have originated in China and not to have been imitated from any Indian movement." [15]

During the first half of the eighth century, the emperor Shōmu (724--748) sent two priests to China to invite an able teacher to instruct Japanese priests and nuns in the Discipline (*Ritsu*). In 733, the invitation was extended to Ganjin (687–763; Ch. Chien-chen, J. var. Kanshin), but for political reasons, as well as the fact that the Chinese emperor Hsüan-tsung favored Taoism, he was not given permission to leave the continent. Ganjin, after five abortive attempts and a sixth perilous crossing—he was blinded in a shipwreck during the fifth attempt—finally arrived in Nara in 753, at the age of sixty-six. He stayed at the Tōdaiji, before which was built a platform (*kaidan;* Skt. *sīma*), and both the emperor and empress, along with some four hundred others, received ordination according to the prescribed rule. Previous to Ganjin's officially correct performance of the ordination ceremony, the ordination rules had doubtless been lax.

ORDINATION

The idea of ordination was closely connected with the idea of correct transmission, so that correct ordination by a qualified master was felt to be necessary in establishing the orthodoxy of a given teacher or temple. These ordinations took place on such a special platform, or kaidan, as the one built at Tōdaiji. During the Nara period, there were three places of ordination: the Tōdaiji in Nara, the Kanzeonji in Tsukushi, and the Yakushiji in Shimotsuke. The Tōshōdaiji was ultimately made the authorized headquarters of Ritsu training.

PRECEPTS

Ritsu is a kind of nondenominational school common to both Hīnayāna and Mahāyāna. (Hīnayāna Buddhism inclines toward observing the letter of the law, while the Mahāyāna stresses more the spirit of the rules.) The Ritsu texts (Skt. *Vinaya*) pertain specifically to the operation of the Community and consist of some two hundred fifty articles for priests and

A kaidan — Mt. Kōya.

three hundred forty-eight for nuns. The Discipline calls for weekly convocations to see if any of the Community has committed an infringement of the rules. These convocations are concerned with confession, repentance, and, if an infraction warrants it, expulsion from the order. The rules of conduct, or precepts (*shīla*), are both positive and negative. The positive rules pertain to the cult : they deal with sūtra reading, rites, medicines, and so forth. The negative precepts are chiefly prohibitions against "sins"—intemperance, lying, etc.—or against acts leading to sin.

The precepts involved four aspects of discipline: (1) elements of discipline; (2) essence of discipline; (3) action of discipline; and (4) form of discipline. Of these four, essence of discipline is considered to be the most important. It is conceived of as being active in nature. It is a kind of consciousness of the acceptance of the Discipline. Vows taken at the time of ordination are felt to constitute an active, moral force henceforth affecting the mind and, through it, all subsequent actions. This essence of discipline is subject to varying interpretations by different sects. For the Kusha, for example, it is one of the forms of matter; for the Jōjitsu, it is a special element, neither matter nor mind. For the Hossō, it is a perceptive form conceived at ordination and proceeding from the "store seed" of thought.

KEGON

According to tradition, the sect known in Japan as Kegon, or "Flower Ornament" (Skt. Avatamsaka), was founded in China as an independent school, the Hua-yen Tsung, by Fashun (or Tu-shun [557–640]). The final systematization of the philosophy was effected by Fa-tsang (643–712) through whose translations and lectures the *Avatamsaka* doctrines were widely disseminated. In India the *Avatamsaka* was one of the texts used by the Yogachārins (cf. p. 119). "The Avatamsaka takes up the teaching of the *sameness* of everything, and interprets it as the interpenetration of every element in the world with everything else. The one eternal principle of the universe, which is the *serenity of Mind,* is reflected in the cosmos, its presence charges everything with spiritual significance, its mysteries can be beheld everywhere, and by means of any object one may generate all virtues and fathom the secrets of the entire universe."[16] Actually, however, the Kegon school stems from the system founded in China on Vasubandhu's commentary on the *Dashabhūmika-sūtra* (T. 285–7). That system split into two branches: a northern branch, taught by Tao-ch'ung, which propounded the concept of a "storehouse consciousness" that was considered to be unreal and separate from Thusness; and a southern branch, taught by Hui-kuang (468–537), which set forth the idea of a "storehouse consciousness" (*ālaya*) that was considered to be real and the equivalent of Thusness. It is the latter branch which produced the Kegon school.

Tradition has it that the sect was introduced to Japan around 736 by Bodhisena, an Indian monk who is supposed to have arrived in Nara some ten years earlier and to have taught the *Avatamsaka* doctrine there. Bodhisena (704–760) had been born a Brāhman, in South India, and is consequently also referred to as the "Brāhman bishop" (*baramon sōjō*). Another tradition, perhaps the more reliable, attributes the introduction of the sect to Dōsen (596–667). The Kegon probably did not exist as an independent school in India.

CAUSE AND INDRA'S NET

The goal of the sect coincides with that of its basic text, the *Avatamsaka-sūtra,* which tells of the visit of Sudhana to some fifty-three Buddhist worthies, both religious and secular, to realize the principle of the *dharmadhātu,* "World of Dharmas or Principle." This World of Principle is twofold in nature, depending on the aspect from which it is viewed. For the Kegon, it refers both to Absolute Truth and to phenomena, made up of dharmas, hence the name dharmadhātu. This dharmadhātu is posited as an active state, and the school supports a theory known as "causation by dharmadhātu." This causation is fourfold: (1) by action and the result of that action; (2) by ideation (-store); (3) by Thusness; and (4) by dharmadhātu, that is, by essence. This fourfold theory of causation represents a completely relative world in which all beings exist mutually dependent on each other, for they are the cause for the existence of every thing in the universe and at the same time they undergo the effect of this existence. Hence, beings are their own cause and their own effect, that is, they represent what is known as "causation by common action influence." In the Kegon school, this state of affairs is regularly represented by a figure known as "Indra's Net"—a huge net which bears at the point of intersection of each of its cords a reflecting jewel, which by imaging the stones immediately adjacent to it images the infinity of jewels in the outer spaces of the whole net, for each jewel is the bearer of its neighbor's image. Thus the universe is represented by the net and causation by the imaging. The universe is represented as being correlative, interdependent, and mutually originating This universal interdependence of all things, which is a characteristic teaching of Kegon, was to be influential in the formation of Zen thinking in the thirteenth century and later.

Of course, like other schools, Kegon holds the theory of causation by mere ideation. Here it is called "universal causation by the dharmadhātu"—by Ultimate Truth. This concept is the climax of a theory of causal origin based on the above fourfold theory, which Kegon develops in two directions. For example, causation was explained by action-influence; but since action originates in ideation, action is actually ideation-store. Yet ideation-store is the repository of seed-energy, and so ideation must be considered Thusness. Finally, and as a consequence of the preceding three statements, causation exists by dharmadhātu, or through (the world of) essence. Further, the Kegon continues, since beings are universally interdependent, since they create themselves and the universe in which they exist, they exist by what may be termed "causation by the common action influence of all beings." Seen from this angle, then, the universe *is* the manifestation of Thusness, although the reason for the existence of the universe is only in the unverse itself. Kegon consequently accepts no single being as existing independently, and the only independent state is that of nirvāna.

CLASSIFICATION OF BUDDHIST DOCTRINES

The Kegon attempts to classify and summarize the whole of Buddhist teaching by dividing it into what are known as the Five Aspects : (1) The Hīnayāna, which is essentially "realistic" and which admits the existence of all elements, for which nirvāna is total extinction, and in which causation is attributed to action-influence. The Kusha school is held to be representative of this aspect. (2) Mahāyāna of an elementary type which is based on the specific character of all the elements and represented by the Hossō school, but which is also based on the negation of all elements, an idea, it will be remembered, already set forth by the Sanron school. It may be noted here that the foregoing views are held to be elementary in view of the fact that neither of these two schools admits the existence of the Buddha-nature. Further, Hossō is representative of causation by ideation-store based on phenomenal characteristics of the component dharmas; while Sanron, although admitting the unity of being and nonbeing—in other words, positing the ultimate absence of polarity—bases itself on a one-sided view of Void according to one's own nature. (3) The Final Doctrine of the Mahāyāna, which teaches the Thusness of all elements (*dharmatathatā*), the existence of the Buddha-nature in all beings, and hence the ability of all beings to attain Buddhahood This, called the Doctrine of Maturity, corresponds to the theory of causation by Thusness, that ultimate, nameless state of being. (4) The Abrupt Doctrine of the Mahāyāna, which implies training by word and which is a direct appeal to insight and sudden enlightenment. This aspect corresponds to the Zen teachings. (5) The Round Doctrine of the Mahāyāna, or the "perfected Mahāyāna teaching," that is, the doctrine which is composed of the preceding four aspects and which, being the essence of them, is superior to any one of them. This means that the "three vehicles" (i.e., Hīnayāna, Mahāyāna, and Abrupt) become the "one vehicle" (*ekayāna*). According to the Kegon, the best and fullest account of the Buddha's enlightenment is found in the *Avatamsaka-sūtra,* and hence the Kegon considers its own teaching the most nearly fundamental and perfect. As a result the highest state is reached, known as the One Vehicle of Distinct Doctrine, in which Kegon alone is considered the *summum,* the perfect exposition thereof, since it analyzes the totality of the Buddha's teachings.

The Kegon further posits a fourfold universe, the views of which are again represented by various schools. There is, first, the world of reality, which, as explained above, corresponds to the Hīnayāna; and, second, the world of principle, represented by Sanron and Hossō, which view phenomena as being different from essence and accept principle as different from fact. Third is the world of principle and reality united, encompassing an identity of fact and principle. This world is represented by later Tendai teachings (*see* p. 138). Finally, there is the world of all realities existing in perfect harmony, which is symbolized by Kegon itself. The existence of this perfect harmony is closely connected with the correlation of all things, that is, their coexistence and interdependence, as Indra's Net represents. In such a universe, things arise simultaneously without distinction of past, present, or future. All things at all times compose one entity.

NATURE OF THE DHARMA

The Kegon school, although not concerned with the nature of the dharma in the way the Hossō is, nevertheless propounds a sixfold specific nature of all elements (*dharma*) by which it explains the functioning of things. This sixfold nature is actually composed of three pairs of opposites: universality/

specialization; similarity/diversity; and integreation/differentiation. Universality designates the totality of the parts—a machine, for example, is the totality of the gears, bolts, etc., while specialization designates the parts as they form the totality—the gears, bolts, etc., are the essential, vital elements of the machine. Of course, universality and specialization exist together and are simply different views of a given object, be it the machine or the universe. Similarity implies the harmonious existence of all the parts within the whole; with the machine, all the different parts work together for a similar end, i.e., the functioning of the machine. Diversity then means that all the individual parts are different, they all have individual features, but they work together harmoniously. Integration signifies the fusion of the parts into a whole, as the interworking of the gears to make the machine function. Differentiation means that, although the specific parts make up a whole, at the same time they do not lose their special, individual features.

SUMMARY OF THE NARA SCHOOLS

As we have observed, the various Nara sects constituted not so much schools, in the sense of independent systems, as different approaches to, or variations on, the theme of Void. The KUSHA school maintains that all exists, that every thing is made up of constituent realities called elements, or dharmas. The notion of the existence of the dharmas is associated with that of time; and for this school both past and future are real because they are related to present by cause and effect. But past, present, and future exist separately; that is, the school does not posit an enduring existence extending from a point in the past through to a point in hte future. Existence therefore is momentary.

In opposition to the Kusha, the JŌJITSU, reflecting Hīnayāna negativism, claims that nothing exists, there is no abiding reality, such as were the dharmas for the Kusha school.

Ultimate truth is Void. For the Jōjitsu, past and future have no reality, for the one is gone and the other not yet come. The school posits a present which is instantaneous. The SANRON school teaches the Middle Path, that is, it aims at a metaphysical point at which all polarity has ceased to exist. It comes to this point by means of four basic arguments, which compose in reality all possible answers to all possible questions : yes, no, either yes or no, neither yes nor no. The middle path between all these poles is Void, which is equated with the Middle Path. The aim of the school is the refutation of all the positive views of other Buddhist schools. The HOSSŌ school attempts to describe the dharmas, but it tries to go further than the Kusha, for example, saying that only idea exists (*yui-shiki*). The world is explained as being composed of dharmas. Yet phenomena are simply the projection of ideation, that is, imagination, and are themselves Void. Thus all is Void, and Void is the Middle Path.

The RITSU school, mainly nondenominational, deals with the rules of the order, common to all schools. It stresses the correct transmission and observance of these precepts, or Discipline (*ritsu*), and through its ordinations it establishes the orthodox lines of all schools. It stresses an "essence of discipline," a kind of moral force which the adept is made aware of at the time of ordination and which subsequently exerts a dominance over him. The KEGON school aims at the realization of the "world of Principle" (*dharmadhātu*). It stresses universal causation and the comprehensive interdependence of all things. Further, it attempts to fit the various facets of Buddhist teaching stressed by other sects into its own system. Rather than denying these other attitudes, it labels them as partial views of the Truth, which is fully expounded only by the Kegon. All beings possess in themselves Void and are hence possessors of the Buddha-nature, which like nirvāna can be "realized." This is realizing dharmadhātu.

Heian Period
(794-1185)

IN 784, THE IMPERIAL CAPITAL was transferred from Nara to Nagaoka and from there in 794 to Heian, the present-day Kyoto, where it was to remain, in name at least, until 1868. It is not entirely clear why the capital was removed to Heian. Possibly the growing influence of the Nara sects and their hold on the court had something to do with it. There is no doubt that as the power of Buddhism grew, its interest in secular matters increased, and it is probably true that the Emperor Kammu (782–805) decided to remove from Nara at least partly in order to escape ecclesiastical influence.

THE CAPITAL OF HEIAN

The new capital was given the title of Heian-kyō, "capital of peace and tranquility." Heian-kyō was modeled on the T'ang capital at Ch'ang-an (Sian). Like Nara, it was laid out in a balanced rectangle, measuring three and one-half miles north and south by three miles east and west. Located on a gentle slope, it was provided with flowing water. Fourteen gates permitted access. The principal palace, in the Chinese fashion, was located in the north center, although numerous other palaces graced the city.

HEIAN BUDDHISM

Perhaps hoping to make a fresh start by exerting control over the church, Kammu officially limited the number of

134

temples and of priests, but in practice this little affected the proliferation of both over the entire country. Kammu also attempted to suppress the sale of tax-free land to religious organizations, but to no great avail; temples and shrines grew apace.

Nara Buddhism, though externally Mahāyāna, had been concerned basically with Hīnayāna doctrines and tended to be limited to rather narrow, monkish circles. What popular appeal it had was largely through ritual and magic. In Heian, therefore, the time was ripe for a more encompassing type of teaching. The doctrines of the Chinese school of T'ien-t'ai seemed to be just that. T'ien-t'ai, or Tendai (discussed more fully below), was formally introduced to Japan in 807, when the monk Saichō, with official permission and a grant of official funds, ordained some one hundred followers on Mount Hiei, near Heian. The new sect provoked immediate and vigorous jealousy on the part of the older Nara schools. There were doctrinal differences, of course, but, more pointedly, the Nara sects were jealous of the patronage and success of the new and rival institution. They centered their attacks on Saichō's request for permission to erect an ordination platform (kaidan) and to perform further ordination ceremonies. So insistent was their opposition that permission was actually delayed until after Saichō's death.

The court favored the new sect, not only for the reasons mentioned above, but also because its site, Mount Hiei, lying conveniently beyond the city precincts, seemed, after the troubles with the Nara monasteries that had lain within the capital, to be auspiciously distant. Moreover, according to Chinese ideas of geomancy, the northeast, the compass point towards which Mount Hiei lay, was a dangerous direction, a "demon entrance," and it was hence thought that the new sect would serve to protect the capital.

The more comprehensive schools of the Heian period rapidly

gained in strength at the expense of the more rigid Nara sects. Their eclecticism contained the seeds of most of the subsequent evolution of Buddhism in Japan.

ESOTERICISM

A contemporary of Saichō, Kūkai, brought back from the continent, where he too had spent a period of study, still another school, the Esoteric worship of the solar divinity Vairochana. The school had the Chinese name of Chen-yen, in Japanese, Shingon. A form of Tantrism, it is commonly referred to as Esotericism (discussed in detail below). Shingon and Tendai were to be the characteristic forms of Buddhism practiced in the new capital, for, although the Nara sects were by no means abandoned, their geographical remoteness from the new cultural center led inevitably to a lesser role than they had played.

With Tendai, Shingon fostered the idea of what was to be known as Dual Shintō, an amalgamation of Shintō and Buddhism, which was especially favored by the existence of solar divinities in both systems. This syncretism was referred to by Shingon as *ryōbu Shintō*, "Shintō of the Two Parts" (of the universe) and by Tendai as *ishijitsu Shintō*, "Shinto of the One Truth." Under Shingon inspiration, images of the gods were placed in Shintō shrines, although Shintō had from the beginning been a religion without images. Both Saichō and Kūkai had accepted as normal the common practice of worshiping Shintō and Buddhist divinities in the same building or on the same grounds, a practice which naturally tended to bring the two faiths into relation. There was not a complete fusion of the two systems, however, and Dual Shintō did not evolve fully until the end of the period, around 1100. The spread of Buddhism, it must be added, did not do away with other beliefs of the Japanese, who continued to venerate not only the Buddhas and the Shintō gods but also the Chinese cult of Heaven and the always important *yin* and *yang* concepts.

LATE HEIAN BUDDHISM

The tone of the later Heian period is quite different from that of the beginning. The vigorous enthusiasm of the earlier times gave way to a certain disillusionment. By the eleventh century, the idea of *mappō,* or "end of the Law," had captured the popular imagination. Mappō, used technically in the *Sūtras* to express the third and last period in a cosmic cycle, was reckoned to begin around the middle of the eleventh century and to mark the end of civilized order. That such an end seemed to be approaching was evidenced by the growing strife and disorder, the weak rulers, the greedy clergy, and, in general, the flagrant disintegration of morals that characterized the late Heian. The aristocratic Tendai and Shingon sects seemed preoccupied with materialistic matters, while the old Nara schools were at most obsolescent. The need of the times was a revival of faith by popular methods. Such a revival was led by men like Kūya, who taught in a simple, revivalistic way the invocation of the Buddha's name and its saving power. The movement was crystalized by Genshin (942–1017), a Tendai priest, who in his *Essentials of Salvation* urged the worship of Amida, a Buddha of long life (Skt. Amitābha). His teachings, easily understood by the common man, promised help from an outside source (*tariki*), that is, from Amida himself, and contrasted sharply with the Nara teachings, which, following Hīnayāna precepts, had stressed one's own power (*jiriki*). Salvation meant rebirth in the Western paradise, open to any and all who called on the name of Amida. It was obviously a religion which attracted people weary of troubled times and in need of a simple, more intuitive belief.

TENDAI

The founder of the Tendai sect is traditionally recognized to be the third patriarch, Chih-k'ai or Chih-i (J. Chigi, 531–597), who lived and taught in the monasteries on Mount T'ien-t'ai in southern China (Tendai is the Sino-Japanese reading of the Chinese T'ien-t'ai). The school is variously called the Hokke-shū, or Lotus sect, in view of the fact that it bases itself primarily on the *Lotus* sūtra (Skt. *Saddharmapundarīka-sūtra*). The *Lotus* text had been studied as early as the beginning of the sixth century A.D., and intensified research on it was begun in China after Kumārajīva's translation in 406. During the fifth century, eight Chinese commentaries were written on it. The Kumārajīva translation was in twenty-seven chapters, filling seven volumes, but Fa-hsien discovered another chapter (on Devadatta), and the present *Lotus* contains twenty-eight. Although the *Lotus* is by far the most important text of this school, the *Nirvāna-sūtra* and the *Parinirvāna-sūtra* (T. 374 *et al.*), which were widely studied in the south, were ultimately absorbed by the Tendai. The latter text sets forth the idea that nirvāna is a state which shows that the Buddha remains as dharmakāya (essence, scripture) even after his death. Dharmakāya was conceived of as a "spiritual body" that survives forever. All beings have the Buddha-nature and hence partake of this dharmakāya, variously identified with permanence, bliss, self—all being essentially contradictory to traditional Buddhism. Nevertheless, the idea of dharmakāya was to influence all Chinese Mahāyāna schools. Although the principal texts are the ones mentioned above, place is found in Tendai teaching for all scriptures, which are considered as forming a kind of progressive revelation of the Truth. Emphasis is on eclecticism, much as in the Kegon of the Nara period, for Tendai endeavors to fit into its teaching the doctrines of all Buddhist schools which had preceded it, thus incorporating the various views on Truth which had been evolved during the course of time. This eclectic emphasis makes it difficult to isolate ideas which are purely Tendai in nature. But this very eclecticism has made Tendai the source from which the chief Buddhist sects in Japan subsequently arose: Amidism, Zen, and Nichirenism.

Origins of Tendai doctrines

The systematizer of Tendai in China is considered to be Hui-wen (550–577), who based himself on a verse found in Nāgārjuna's *Chūron* (Skt. *Mādhymamikashāstra,* IV, ch. 24, v. 18):

> The various causes and effects produce the dharmas.
> Yet I (Nāgārjuna) explain them as being nonexistent.
> Further, this nonexistence is given a temporary name.
> Indeed, this is the meaning of the Middle Path.

That is to say, while causes and effects produce the elements, these elements are essentially Void, no matter by what name they are called. And this Void is in reality the Middle Path. From this passage, hence, comes the Triple Truth of Tendai: Void, Temporary, and Middle Path. The example of the mirror is often used to illustrate their relationship. The brightness of the mirror is Void, because it is in reality nonexistent. The objects reflected in the mirror are Temporary, since their appearance there lasts only as long as does the cause for the imaging. The mirror itself is the Middle Path and stands for the true state of all things. This triple truth, of course, must be understood as a unity, as three inseparable aspects of one truth. This concept is expressed in Tendai by the phrase *isshin sankan,* "one heart, three meditations," signifying a threefold meditation on the one essence, a perfect fusion of the three truths through meditation.

SAICHŌ

The T'ien-t'ai monasteries of China were well known in Japan. In the eighth century, Ganjin, when he brought the Ritsu teachings to Japan, had also brought T'ien-t'ai writings, but it was not until 806 that Tendai was formally introduced by the monk Saichō (posth. Dengyō daishi, 767–822). Saichō had been ordained in 785 in the city of Nara, but he left in 788 to establish himself on Mount Hiei, to the northeast of the new capital of Heian. There he built a small monastery (Enryakuji), which, being situated near the capital, was to become identified with it. Saichō had studied Tendai teachings at Nara under the followers of Ganjin, and in 804 he was sent to China by the Emperor Kammu in order to inquire as to the best form of Buddhism for adoption at the new Japanese capital. In China, Saichō became the pupil of Chan-jan (717–782). He studied Tendai (under Tao-sui), Shingon (under Shun-hsiao), and Zen teachings, none of which had existed as independent sects at Nara. It is probable that Saichō did not at first plan to found a new sect on his return from China, for in his first temple he enshrined Yakushi, the healing Buddha, as in the Nara sects. He taught Tendai, Shingon Esotericism (which gradually came to dominate it), and both Zen and Ritsu, although he was to stress Tendai teachings above all.

Intellectually, Saichō seems to have been a notably honest man, and he carried on his search for the right teaching throughout his life. On his return from China, although convinced of the wisdom of Tendai teachings, he was quick to study other systems and to recognize their virtues. Thus his relations with the great Shingon master Kūkai, at first amicable, exercised considerable influence on his thinking and consequently on Tendai teachings, which gradually became more and more impregnated with Esoteric ideas. Ultimately

these relations with the unbending Kūkai were to end un-
happily, owing largely to the adamant stand of the Shingon
master, who imperiously suggested that Saichō would go far
toward discovering the truth if he were to come to the Shingon
center at Kōya as a disciple. Kūkai's attitude, tinged with more
than a little arrogance, was responsible for the final estrange-
ment of the two leaders. Nevertheless, the esotericizing of
Tendai, begun by Saichō himself, was to continue until, like
most of subsequent Buddhist thought in Japan, it was to be
completely dominated by Esoteric ideas.

Saichō had returned to Japan in 805 and resumed the
position of abbot at the Enryakuji, which he had founded in
788. He was strongly opposed by the Nara sects, however, and
was not allowed to perform ordination ceremonies. Saichō
himself had been correctly ordained at Mount T'ien-t'ai in
China, and hence he considered himself qualified to perform
the ceremony in Japan. This he finally did in the last month
of 807, as described above, but owing to the pressure by the
Nara sects, there were no more ordinations until after his
death in 827.

Besides a commentary on the *Lotus* sūtra, Saichō wrote the
interesting work *Shugo kokkai-shō, Defense of the Country,*
in which he saw Tendai teachings as a kind of protection for
Japan. Indeed, Saichō's monastery was called the "Center for
the Protection of the Nation." Along with a certain nationalistic feeling in his writings, as well as the great reverence he
paid the sovereign, Saichō presages the rise of the strongly
nationalistic Nichiren sect, whose founder indeed had received
training in the Tendai doctrine.

Saichō's Tendai

Tendai, as Saichō conceived it, stressed enlightenment for
all and assumed a basic unity between the Buddha and all
other beings. Indeed, the Buddha-nature exists and is to be

ed in every being, that is, to be attained through a life
l purity and meditative discipline. Saichō criticised
ivara Buddhism (with the exception of the Kegon sect),
claiming that these schools were all based on secondary sources
(commentaries) rather than on primary ones (*Sūtras*). In this
sense, then, Tendai was superior to the Nara sects, for it was
founded on the primary sūtra itself, the *Lotus*. Moreover,
Saichō subjected his Tendai monks to a twelve-year term of
rigid discipline in the seclusion of the Mount Hiei monastery,
where they were trained in the *Sūtras* and in the method
known as *shikan,* "concentration and insight." Such a life
contrasted with the comparatively lax discipline of the Nara
sects, whose monks lived in the old capital city with all its
distractions.

THE FIVE PERIODS

Tendai views the entirety of Buddhist teachings from the
standpoint of the so-called Five Periods and Eight Doctrines.
As in the Kegon system, these form a kind of classification of
all Buddhist doctrine, reaching a climax with the Tendai
exposition of the Truth. Typical of Buddhism, this classification is nonexclusive, accepting the views of the different sects
as aspects of the composite and complete Truth expounded by
Tendai. The First Period, the Time of the Wreath, refers to
the *Avatamsaka-sūtra,* the central text of the Kegon school.
As an elucidation of the Buddha's enlightenment, this text is
essentially true, but it is so concentrated as to be unintelligible
to the common man. The Second Period is that of the Deer
Park, in which the Buddha preached the early *āgamas,* or
long, medium, short, and "number" sūtras. These texts,
directed to people of inferior capacity, were meant to attract
commoners to the higher doctrine. This period is hence also
called the Time of Inducement. The Third Period is that of

Development, that is, the time when Hīnayāna evolved into Mahāyāna, when the restricted teachings based largely on self-advancement through discipline evolved into the Savior doctrine that was characteristic of the Mahāyāna. This Period is also called the Time of Rebuke, for the Buddha often berated the arhants, saints of the highest kind, for their shortsighted views. The Fourth Period, that of Wisdom (*prajnā*), corresponds to the preaching of the *Prajnāpāramitā-sūtras*, which reject all ideas of acquisition and distinction and teach the ultimate doctrine of Void. The Fifth Period, as one may expect, is the time of the *Saddharmapundarīka-* and *Nirvāna-sūtras*, a time of the fusing of the doctrines. Although these five time periods are presented in chronological order, it is to be remembered that the arrangement is arbitrary, for the Buddha was able to utilize all five at the same time, depending on the occasion.

THE EIGHT DOCTRINES

Of the Eight Doctrines, the first is the Abrupt, in which the Buddha teaches without any expediency (i.e., the Kegon) and which is essentially incomprehensible to the lower orders of beings. The second is the Gradual, corresponding to the predications in the Deer Park, in which the Buddha modified his teaching so that it would be more easily understandable. In the third, the Mystic Doctrine, each hearer thinks he alone hears and understands the doctrine. At this stage, the hearers receive the doctrine separately and variously. To the fourth, the Indeterminate Doctrine, all listen together; it is exoteric, nonmystical. These first four doctrines apply to Buddhism prior to the preaching of the *Lotus*. The fifth doctrine, that of the Canon (*pitakas*), designates all of Hīnayāna teaching. The sixth is the elementary doctrine of the Mahāyāna, common to all. The seventh is the Distinct Doctrine, the developed Mahā-

yāna, in which the doctrine of the Middle Path is taught. The
eighth is the Round or Perfect Doctrine, which expounds the
independent and separate Middle Path, a teaching which of
course is typified by the Tendai teaching of the *Lotus* sūtra.

THE THREEFOLD BODY

Another important Tendai teaching is that of the Threefold
Body, composed of the *hosshin (dharmakāya)*, the *hōshin
(sambhogakāya)*, and the *ōjin (nirmānakāya)*. The hosshin, or
Principle Body, is the Buddha existent as an ideal or principle,
that is, without personal, historical existence. This existence
is identical with the Middle Path. The hōshin, or Enjoyment
Body, is the body attained as a result of long causal action and
in consequence represents a person endowed with profound
insight. It is conceived of in two ways : a body for Self-
enjoyment, that is, in which a person may enjoy his own
enlightenment; and a body manifested for the enjoyment of
others, corresponding to the body of a Bodhisattva. The
Transformation Body, or ōjin, is capable of assuming various
forms for the purpose of saving sentient beings. It also has two
aspects : one exclusively for Bodhisattvas, another for those
beings prior to becoming Bodhisattvas. It is to be remembered
that every Buddha has these three aspects, or bodies,
simultaneously.

MEDITATION PRACTICES

Since the central text of the Tendai is the *Lotus,* the chief
personage of which is the historical Buddha, Shākyamuni, it
is not surprising to find that special reverence is paid to him.
In fact, all Buddhas are considered to be aspects of him. They
are all nonetheless given full recognition. Tendai recognizes
Vairochana, the solar pan-Buddha, as an expression of the

dharmakāya and Shākyamuni as a manifestation of the nirmānakāya. Since the dharmakāya is considered as a higher aspect, the existence of Shākyamuni is explained as a condescension to the weakness of human intellect. Amida, the Buddha of life and light who ruled over a Western Paradise, or Pure Land, too, was recognized, but his role was simply that of one of many Buddhas. *Nembutsu,* or calling on his name for succor, was practiced, but in the Tendai system nembutsu was merely an adjunct to worship. It was used as a means of clearing the mind for a disciplined concentration on Amida. Concentrated meditation, which was later to be organized under the school of Zen, was never a popular or important part of the Hiei curriculum and hence was never a subject for discussion. It cannot be denied, however, that Zen practices were to be of great influence on Tendai doctrine. Meditation was employed under a system known as *shikan,* "concentration and insight," which led after long discipline and training to the realization of the Truth. This truth, however, was not quite the sudden, intuitive variety that Zen was later to teach; under the Tendai system, emphasis was on a long preparation in concentration practices.

ENNIN AND TENDAI ESOTERICISM

After Saichō, Tendai was to come under the leadership of Ennin (Jikaku daishi, 794–864). Ennin had gone to China in 838 with the embassy of Fujiwara no Tsunetsugu (d. 840) and spent his time studying at various Buddhist centers. Returning to Japan in 847, he introduced into Tendai such Esoteric practices as the study of the two mandala (*see* below under Shingon), Esoteric anointment ceremonies (*kanjō*), and the nembutsu (i.e., of the type described above and known as the Esoteric nembutsu). The Esotericism of Tendai was to differ essentially from the traditional Shingon type. While Shingon, originating in China chiefly from Kegon teachings, had as its central tenet the incompatibility of the exoteric and esoteric doctrines, Tendai esotericism originated in China from the esoteric discipline of T'ien-t'ai itself and was based on the belief that the exoteric and esoteric teachings are simply two aspects of one teaching. Esotericization was continued by Annen (c. 890).

ENCHIN

Another important figure in eleventh-century Tendai was Enchin (posth. Chishō daishi, 814–891). A nephew of the Shingon master Kūkai, Enchin studied in China from 852 to 858 and on his return founded a center of study at the Miidera (or Onjōji), a temple originally founded in 674. Later the Miidera was made a dependency of the Enryakuji, and Enchin was appointed abbot in 868. The position of abbot was subsequently held by monks belonging to the lines of both Enchin and Ennin. In 933, however, as a result of a succession dispute involving one of the abbots in the Ennin line, the Enchin faction broke away, left Mount Hiei, and formed a virtually independent school at the Miidera. There were frequent disputes between Miidera and Hiei, sometimes so violent that on several occasions the former was reduced to ashes (e.g., in 1081). In these disputes, as well as others concerning misunderstandings with the secular authorities in Kyoto, a type of warrior monk (J. *sōhei*) became powerful.

MILITANT CLERGY

These militant clergy arose particularly with the spread of Esotericism. As was mentioned above, Ennin was succeeded by Enchin, who in 873 was appointed head of the Miidera. The opinions of Enchin's disciples, differing from those of

Ennin's, resulted in the sect's splitting into two factions: the *sammon*, or "Mountain Order," at the Enryakuji (Hiei), and the *jimon*, or "Church Order," at the Miidera (Ōtsu). This was in fact no fundamental division in the sect but rather a bitter rivalry, which broke into open dispute at Enchin's death in 891. From this time dates the use of monks known as *akusō*, "Bad Monks," developing into the large monk armies of later times. About 970 mercenaries were first recruited as a general protective agency for religious bodies. This was done under the Tendai head Ryogen (Jie daishi), who decided to retain such a permanent force in a dispute with the Gion Shintō shrine. After him the practice grew, and by 1100 all the great Tendai monasteries had standing armies, and some of the Shintō shrines (such as Gion and Kumano) had them as well. In 1081, for example, the Kōfukuji (Nara) united with another monastery and attacked both Mount Hiei and the Miidera, burning the latter and making off with much loot. Troops of sōhei, while originally used in disputes between monasteries, later descended on the capital against the government. Mount Hiei was the most troublesome. Between 981 and 1185, troops numbering several thousands again and again entered the capital to support one or another of the monastery's claims. The court was helpless. The cause of these incursions was originally doctrinal difference, but this in time gave way to greed for power and for possessions of a purely secular kind. Shingon, being centered on Mount Kōya rather far away from the capital, remained largely out of the strife, except for Negoro, about which more later. In their forays into the capital, the monks took to bringing with them their sacred car (*mikoshi*) in which the divinity was transported, against which an attack by government troops was sacrilege. Sometimes the monks would return to their monastery leaving the holy carriage unguarded. This was a form of blackmail, for the angry deity would supposedly remain in the streets until the monks could be induced to come back for the mikoshi. Such a thing was first done in 1082, by the monks of the Shintō shrine of Kumano.

SHINGON

Like the Tendai, the Shingon school established its independence from the Nara sects by setting itself apart from the old capital. It established its center on the summit of Mount Kōya, far removed from large urban centers. So, unlike the Tendai, situated relatively close to Kyoto and consequently never quite free from political tensions, the Shingon was completely withdrawn from the political activities of the time. This isolation, although it was to mean less power for the Shingon in secular circles, was in the course of the centuries to spare the sect from the numerous repressions that the Tendai ultimately suffered.

Shingon is a branch of so-called Right-handed Tantrism, which was discussed above (p. 76). It placed great emphasis on ritual, imagery, and magnificent ceremony, and it is not surprsing that its spectacular rites had great appeal for the Heian population. Of equal importance was the use of magic and the occult, in particular formulas (*mantra*) composed of magical sounds, for accomplishing very human ends. There is no doubt but that Shingon incorporated a great fund of superstition, both continental and Japanese in origin. It would be wrong, indeed, to assume that the Buddhism of this sect—and this is true of other sects, although to a lesser degree—owed its success in Japan to its purely metaphysical appeal. It is a fact that, before the establishment of Shingon at the beginning of the ninth century, mystical practices existed, in such systems as the Ritsu, whose use of the *kanjō*, or ceremony of anointment, contained several magical features (e.g., the transference of Knowledge to the neophyte).

LINES OF TRANSMISSION

From the standpoint of doctrine, Shingon was not an Indian import to Japan via China, but a system formulated by Kūkai, in which he incorporated secret rites of Indian origin that he had learned in China. There are, therefore, two traditional lines of patriarchal transmission : those teachers who propagated the doctrine, and those who handed down the secret rites. The doctrinal line is composed of Nāgārjuna, Nāgabodhi, Vajrabodhi (J. Kongōchi), Shubhakarasimha, (J. Zemmui), Amoghavajra (J. Fukū), I-hsing (J. Ichigyō), Hui-kuo (J. Eka), and Kūkai. The line of secret or ritual transmission traditionally includes Vairochana (J. Dainichi), Vajrasattva (J. Kongōsatta), and the others as above, without Shubhakarsimha and I-hsing.

KŪKAI

The man who was to fuse the fund of magical practices long existent in the Buddhism of past centuries was the monk Kūkai (posth. Kōbō daishi, 774–835).

Birth

The fifteenth day of the fifth lunar month in the era known as Hōki, or "Treasure Tortoise," corresponds to July 27, 774 A.D. On this date a son, the second of four children, was born to Saeki Yoshimichi, a local noble. He was named Mao. The Saeki family was then located in the province of Sanuki in modern Shikoku, the smallest of the four main Japanese islands, lying across the expanse of Inland Sea from Osaka. The event took place in the small town of Byōbu-ga-ura, the present-day Zentsūji, not far from the town of Kotohiro. On his mother's side—she was Ato no Tamayori (-hime)—the young boy was related to the Ato family, active in Chinese learning and destined to influence the course of his life. It was in fact Ato no Ōtari, a maternal uncle and Confucian scholar, who assumed responsiblity for Mao's education. Thus in 789, at the age of fifteen, the youth accompanied his uncle to the capital (Nara), where he settled down in earnest under Ōtari's tutelage to the arduous task of studying the Chinese classics. Along with composition of literary Chinese, he concentrated particularly on the Confucian *Analects,* passages collected by the pupils of the Master and illustrating, although not systematically, his ethical ideas. By studying the Taoist classics, he gained insight into this highly mystical religiophilosophic system according to which the universe, all that is in the world, is subject of a kind of cosmic law, the Tao, or "Way," that underlies the function of all things. He completed his knowledge of the heroes of the past by a detailed study of the historical biographies of the *Shu ching,* or *Classic of History.* These studies were to influence him, notably in his early intellectual development, and it is impossible to judge in what subtle ways they are to be found reflected in his later, more characteristically Buddhist activities.

The Indications

At seventeen, in 791, young Mao entered the Confucian college at the capital, where he continued his Chinese studies, concentrating, it is recorded, on the famous *Spring and Autumn Annals (Ch'un-ch'iu).* These annals were a chronological report of the events that took place during the years 722– 479 b.c. in the state of Lu, homeland of Confucious, to whom, indeed, the work is traditionally attributed, although the attribution is not given much credence by modern scholarship. During this period of study, Mao had become increasingly interested in Buddhism. The fruit of his interests in Chinese learning and his new attraction for Buddhism is a work entitled *Indications to the Teachings of the Three Religions (Sangyō shiki),* which was an attempt to evaluate

Procession of Shingon priests — Mt. Kōya.

the respective contributions of Confucianism, Taoism, and
Buddhism. It is attributed by some to the year 791, but if that
is true, it must be recognized as a truly remarkable achieve-
ment for one so young. The version of 797, which would
make the author twenty-three at the time, is perhaps closer
to a plausible date; it is Mao's first important work.

In the *Indications,* we see that the young man has been
completely won over to Buddhism, for, while he does not at
all reject the teachings of both Confucianism and Taoism, he
proposes to show how both fall short of the goals of Buddhism
in concern for man's future existence and in the systematization of the religious experience. Buddhism not only went
beyond these two religions in its concept of man's existence
but, according to the author, "actually contained all that was
worthwhile in the other two beliefs. We can thus find even in

this early work signs of the syncretism which marked his [Mao's] mature philosophy. Although [Mao] clearly reveals himself as Buddhist in the *Indications,* we know that he was not satisfied with the forms of the religion known to him in Japan. In later years he recalled that period of his life : 'Three vehicles, five vehicles, a dozen sūtras—there were so many ways for me to seek the essence of Buddhism, but still my mind had doubts which could not be resolved. I beseeched all the Buddhas of the three worlds and the ten directions to show me not the disparity but the unity of the teachings.' " "

Entry into Buddhism

At nineteen, Mao left the capital to become the disciple of the priest Gonsō, in the Makinoosanji (Izumi), and it was under this teacher that the young man shaved his head and took the religious name of Kyōkai. Under Gonsō he studied both Mahāyāna and Hīnayāna doctrines, especially those set forth by the Three Treatises school (Sanron), emphasizing the Mahāyāna doctrine of the Middle Path. Later, leaving the Makinoosanji, he returned to the capital, and at the Great Eastern Temple, the Tōdaiji, one of the three centers for orthodox ordination ceremonies of all sects, he received ordination in the 250 rules regulating the life of monks (*gusoku-kai*). This was in April, 795, and at this time he changed his religious name to Kūkai, "Sea of Void," by which he has been known throughout the centuries.

Departure for China

In his *Indications,* Kūkai had already expressed discontent with Confucianism and Taoism, finding them incapable of providing the final answers for man's life. If he assumed that Buddhism was better qualified to give this answer, Kūkai was nonetheless unable to find it among the types he had studied, that is, among the various schools that were flourishing during the Nara period. The Middle Path of the Three Treatises school, if going well along the way, did not furnish a definitive solution, and although Kūkai had become acquainted with the famous *Dainichikyō,* or *Sūtra on the* [solar divinity] *Vairochana,* it presented to him numerous problems in comprehension that he was not able to resolve alone. It was hence in search of a type of Buddhism which would unify the various teachings he had culled from his studies that he set out to China at the age of thirty. This was the twenty-third year of the Enryaku era, April, 804.

Taking advantage of the fact that the imperial ambassador Fujiwara no Kadonomaro (754–818) was just at that time setting out for T'ang China, Kūkai joined his retinue. Another great ecclesiastic was also a member of the same ambassadorial party, Saichō, although the two monks were on different ships. It is not unreasonable to suppose that the two men met, although there is no account of the fact. Kūkai arrived in the T'ang capital of Ch'ang-an in December, 804. In February, 805, he obtained imperial permission to reside in the Hsi-ming-ssu, and he soon met the great master Hui-kuo (746–805). Hui-kuo was the seventh successor, or patriarch, in a line which traced itself to quasi-mythical origins in India. According to traditional reports, Kūkai was warmly received by the Chinese master and in a surprisingly short time initiated into the secrets of the Esoteric teachings.

Studies in China

He had begun his studies in June, 805, and already by August had received ordination (*abhisheka*) to the degree of "master transmitter of the law," at which time he was accorded the epithet of "universally illuminating thunderbolt" (*henjō kongō*), a reference to his anticipated role of disseminator of the Thunderbolt, or Esoteric, Vehicle. From this point on, Kūkai participated in all the ceremonies of the temple, becoming familiar with cult procedures and the use of cult implements. He had been warned by the master that these latter were essential for the conducting of Esoteric ceremonies, and Kūkai took pains to begin his collection. He employed ten men to make copies of the kongōkai mandala, which will be discussed below; twenty, to copy the *Kongōchōgyō,* which after the Great Vairochana Sūtra (*Dainichikyō*), was the most important Esoteric text. He also obtained fifteen cult instruments, one priest's robe, and some eighty relic containers. By December of this year he had gathered together over 300 scrolls of holy texts.

Prajña

Kūkai is said to have studied with the Kashmirian monk Prajña (J. Hannya), although there seems to be some doubt about this. Prajña is known to have worked in Ch'ang-an from 785 to 810, and it is not at all impossible that the two met. It is traditional belief that Kūkai studied Sanskrit under this teacher from whom he is said to have learned the *shittan,* a transcription of the Sanskrit *siddham,* a type of Sanskrit writing—the word itself means something like "realized through magic powers"—transmitted across Central Asia to China around the seventh to eighth centuries by Buddhist Tantric scholars. And, indeed, it is interesting to speculate to what degree such writing may have influenced the modern Japanese syllabary, which is attributed to Kūkai himself. From Prajña, Kūkai is said to have received sūtras and a rosary with which he is frequently portrayed in Japanese representations of him.

In an amazingly short time, considering the complexities of the doctrines, he was considered sufficiently instructed to be chosen by the master as the eighth patriarch of the sect and entrusted with the transmission of the secret doctrine to Japan.

Hui-kuo died in December, 805, and it is indicative of the position Kūkai must have enjoyed among his Chinese colleagues that he was chosen to write the master's funeral inscription, an even greater honor for a foreigner.

Return to Japan

Although he had been urged by the master to import the newly learned doctrine to Japan, it is nevertheless surprising to find Kūkai leaving for his homeland in 806, but a few months after the death of his teacher. From his arrival on Chinese shores in August, 804, to his departure in August, 806, his whole trip scarcely spans two years. In view of the fact that it was not uncommon for monks to study in China for much longer periods, sometimes as much as thirty years, one may rightly ponder the causes for Kūkai's relatively short stay. If we consider the extremely complex doctrine he intended to take with him to his homeland, we must assume that some extraordinary circumstance obliged his return. Just what this circumstance, or circumstances, may have been cannot be clarified with any degree of certainty. Perhaps after Hui-kuo's death Kūkai may have provoked the animosity of his Chinese colleagues before whom he had been signally honored by the master. Perhaps, too, he had spent a good part of the money allotted to him for the trip in purchasing the many cult instruments, statues, and paintings necessary in Esoteric ceremonies, which were, of course,unavailable in Japan. Then too it may have been convenient for him to return with the Japanese Tachibana no Hayanari, a nobleman who had also studied in China and who was just then setting sail for home. In any event, his biographers do not explain the details of his return, and his reentry into Japan in 806 had best be accepted as a simple fact without further conjecture.

On his arrival in Japan, Kūkai took up residence at the Kanzeonji in Kyūshū, where he seems to have been obliged to await the pleasure of the court before proceeding to the capital. The emperor, in fact, was uncertain as to whether the Tendai teachings brought back from China two years previously by Saichō or Kūkai's Esotericism should be thought of as orthodox. In October (806), Kūkai sent up to the court a list of the sūtras and commentaries which he had brought back from China, and in April, 807, he was permitted to return to the capital. In October of the same year, he delivered his first lecture and in June, 808, he was appointed abbott of the Makinoosanji. According to some scholars this latter date marks the founding of the Shingon sect.

Early Activities at the Capital

The years from 808 until 815 mark a steadily increasing number of Shingon ceremonies performed in connection with the welfare of the country and hence with the functions of the government and the court. In October, 810, for example, Kūkai memorialized the throne for permission to perform the Esoteric ceremony for the protection of the state according to the sūtra known as the *Ninnō gokokugyō,* the sūtra which explains how "benevolent kings may protect their countries." It must indeed be remembered that Buddhism since its introduction to Japan in the sixth century had been intimately connected with protection of all sorts, particularly against enemies of the country and disease, and the Benevolent Kings sūtra had been much used in the Nara period. Now Shingon with its magical powers was being called on to protect the new capital of Heian. In the same year Kūkai was appointed superintendent (*bettō*) of the great Tōdaiji. So important a place had Shingon teachings assumed that in December, 812, Kūkai performed an ordination ceremony (*abhisheka*) for some 145 persons, among whom was present the famous Saichō himself.

Founding of Kōya

But Kūkai had doubtless begun to feel the pressures of life in the capital. They were distracting to the serious performance of religious duties. Also increasing involvement with the government meant political commitments and plays for power that Kūkai correctly feared would be the source of future ills for his sect. Saichō had established Tendai on the mountain called Hiei, which lay to the northeast of Kyōto, a convenient location, and propitiously distant from the center of the inevitable political intrigues of the capital. And so it was that on July 14, 816, Kūkai requested a grant of land on which he could construct a monastery whose activities would be untrammeled by the political factions of the court. His request was granted on August 3 of the same year, and, accordingly, 816 is most commonly accepted as the date of the founding of the Shingon sect.

The place he chose was a wooded mountaintop, Kōya, in the remote province of Kii, not far from present-day Ōsaka. Actually, Kūkai's purpose in requesting the grant of Kōya was in order to establish a *shuzen dōjō,* or "place for practicing *zen* (meditation)," and he referred to the *Zengyō,* or *Meditation Sūtras* (Skt. *Dhyānasūtra*), in support of his demand. There it is stated that all things belong to the Master of the State and that all monks are accordingly beholden to him, a not unskillful reference under the circumstances to the omnipotence of the emperor and the esteem in which he was held by the Shingon sect. In 823, Kūkai was also given the still uncompleted Eastern Temple (Tōji) in Kyōto, which he proceeded to finish. Kūkai intended Kōya essentially for the practice of meditation, and hence he established the Tōji as the official center for Esoteric practices and as a place of learning where the principal treasures of the sect (statues, sūtras, etc.) were to be stored. Echoing the perennial protective role of Buddhism in Japan, he gave it the name of Kyōō-gokoku-ji, or "Temple of Doctrine Kings, Protectors of the State." Kūkai wished the Tōji to remain the center of "pure" Shingon practice and stated this in his will. Today, while Kōya is the center of monastic practice, the Tōji remains officially the chief temple of the sect, and it still houses many Esoteric treasures within it.

Other Activities

Kūkai's career from 816 on was a series of successes. The monastery on Mt. Kōya grew apace and the master not only devoted himself to the abundant religious matters in connection with the court but to the building of temples, roads, irrigation canals, and to the invention of a simplified Japanese script. He was in short a kind of universal genius lending to the glory of his sect an outstanding personality. "In all the annals and legends of Japanese Buddhism there is no more celebrated name than this [Kūkai], and whether as saint, miracle-worker, writer, painter, or sculptor he is familiar alike to the most learned and the most ignorant of his countrymen. The equivalent of our phrase 'Homer sometimes nods' is in Japanese 'Kōbō mo fude no ayamari; Even Kōbō sometimes makes a slip of the pen.' "[18]

Death

Kūkai died on April 20, 835, at the age of 61. Already in 831 he had been stricken and must have known that the end was not far, although tradition holds that he was miraculously restored to health. The faithful in fact believe that he never really died but rather simply entered into a deep meditative trance known as the "Diamond Meditation" (*vajradhyāna*). In this state, he exists in the so-called Tushita heaven, Heaven of the Satisfied, and is to return to the earth once again with the arrival of the future Buddha, Maitreya. His earthly form is believed to remain uncorrupted in his tomb on Mt. Kōya, where he is regularly worshiped as a kind of deified saint. In 921, he was accorded the posthumous title of Daishi, or "great teacher," and he is widely referred to by the name Kōbō Daishi, although it cannot correctly apply to him before this date.

SHINGON-TENDAI *vs.* THE SECULAR

Like Tendai, the Shingon school established its independence from the Nara sects by separating from the former capital. As we have said, it founded its center on the summit of Mt. Kōya, which was removed from the close proximity of large, urban centers. So, unlike Tendai, which was situated relatively close to Kyōto and consequently never completely free from political tensions, Shingon found itself completely withdrawn from the political activities of the time. This location, although it was to mean less secular power for Shingon, was to spare the sect in the course of the centuries from the numerous repressions that Tendai ultimately underwent.

TANTRIC MAGIC

Shingon is a branch of what is called Right-handed Tantrism. Such Tantrism specialized in the worship of masculine gods and was largely free from the sexual aspects which characterized the Left-handed type and its emphasis on the feminine facet of divinity. Shingon placed great emphasis on ritual, on imagery, and on ostentatious ceremony, and it is not surprising that its pleasing spectacles from the tenth century on exercised widespread appeal on upper and lower classes alike. Of equal importance was the use of magic and of occult methods, in which special formulas composed of magical sounds were used to accomplish very human ends. There is no doubt but that Shingon incorporated a great fund of superstition of continental, as well as of Japanese, origin. It would be wrong indeed to assume that Buddhism of this sect—and this is true of other sects too, although to a lesser degree—was successful in Japan simply through the appeal of its metaphysical speculations.

Kukai's Successors

Kūkai had a number of successors who were to play important roles in the evolution of Esoteric ideas in Japan: Yakushin (827–906), who founded the Hirosawa school, which prescribed special methods of study but presented no new doctrine on any important point; Shōbō (832–909), who founded the Ōno school; and later Kakuban (1095–1143), who founded a new branch of Shingon, called the Shingi-shingon. Shingi-shingon stressed meditation on the Buddha Amida as an important part of its teaching. Amida, in this branch, becomes almost identified with Vairochana (Dainichi), the supreme Buddha of the *Dainichikyō*. The position of this Buddha gives proof in the twelfth century of the growth of Amidist ideas and particularly of the spread of the idea of the Pure Land, Amida's paradise, which according to Shingi-shingon can be attained by Esoteric practices.

Definition of Shingon

Kūkai's borrowings are mainly from the type of Buddhism known as the Mantrayāna ("Vehicle of Formulas" [mantra]), mentioned above. And indeed, the word Shingon, which means "true (*shin*) word (*gon*)," is a rendition of the Sanskrit *mantra,* for the ultimate efficacy of the Esoteric rite is dependent on the correct formula, that is, on the *shingon (mantra)*. The Mantrayāna had been introduced to China by Vajrabodhi (Kongōchi) in 719, but it had been popularized most particularly by Amoghavajra (Fukū) and disseminated by his disciple Hui-kuo, under whom, we have seen, Kūkai studied during his stay in China.

TEXTS

The Shingon sect bases itself mainly on the *Dainichikyō* (*Mahāvairochana-sūtra*), the *Kongōchōgyō* (*Vajrashekhara-yoga-sūtra*) and the *Soshicchijikarakyō* (*Susiddhikara-mahāt-antrasādhanopāyikapatala*). There are others, but the preceding may be considered the most important. These are all late Tantric works, not translated into Chinese until soon after the beginning of the eighth century A.D. They involved a pantheon heavily influenced by Hinduism, containing numerous divinities not purely Buddhist.

PANTHEISM

Shingon posits a kind of pantheism in which the whole universe is a manifestation, an emanation, of the central solar divinity, Vairochana (J. Dainichi). The concept of a cosmic Vairochana was doubtless anticipated by such notions as the Tendai eternal Buddha. While in the Tendai sect this concept of Buddhahood was revealed to the historical Buddha, Kūkai's Vairochana was the limitless cosmos itself. The appeal of Esoteric Buddhism lay in its aesthetic concepts, for it believed that only art can convey the profound meaning of the sūtras. By art was meant a fourfold group: (1) painting and sculpture; (2) music and literature; (3) gestures and acts; and (4) implements of civilization and religion. Ability in these fields is gained by mastery of the Mysteries. For Kūkai what is beautiful partakes of the Buddha.

MANDALA

The concept of the cosmic Vairochana is portrayed by means of two graphic representations of the cosmos called *mandala* (J. *mandara*). Separately they represent the dual aspect of the cosmos, together they demonstrate the essential unity of the universe despite its appearance of duality. Actually duality is present in unity as an aspect of it, and consequently these two cosmographs can never be dissociated in a discussion of the universe or of its parts. They exhibit the essential duality-unity that obtains in everything. One of the mandalas is termed the *kongōkai* (Skt. *vajradhātu*), or "World of the Diamond." The diamond symbol is chosen for its hardness, its stability, and this mandala represents essence, the unchangeable, principial idea, the mind. On a psychological level, the World of the Diamond represents the cosmic conscience, the great prototypes that are the essence of all things. Movement in this mandala tends to converge inwards and represents thereby a resorption of the personality, a reintegration of multiplicity to unity. The other mandala is called the *taizōkai* (Skt. *garbhadhātu*), "World of the Womb." Here *womb* is chosen, as opposed to *diamond*, for its softness, its movement, and this mandala represents phenomenon, change, act. Psychologically the World of the Womb represents the multiplicity of phenomena, which are ever evolving from our central conscience; it represents the multiplicity of aspects into which our central conscience is continually breaking. Movement hence is outward from the center, from the unitary to the many.

Mandala Forms

Originally mandala referred to a circle that formed a kind of sacred precinct in which a divinity was worshiped. Hence, especially in India, mandalas could assume many different forms and be composed of many different objects. Sometimes they were simply sketched on the ground, with ritual objects placed at designated points. In Japan, however, Shingon mandalas have become stylized so that the Diamond World is regularly represented by a square divided into nine square sections and the Womb World by a circle containing various secondary divisions known as courts. Shingon mandalas, moreover, are regularly composed of images, symbolic attributes, or Sanskrit letters (*bīja*; J. *shuji*), this latter being a very common form in Japan. The practice of the mandala involves a progressive projection into it by means of successive meditations on the divinities in their ritual order. Meditation on the divinities implies an assumption of their powers, for one of the underlying ideas of Tantrism is the transference of qualities from the object meditated on to the meditator. Gradually, as the meditation progresses toward the central divinity, that is, Vairochana, the adept finds himself increasingly endowed with insight and understanding, until, arriving at the supreme meditation of the central, solar Vairochana, he becomes mystically fused with the essential godhead. Psychologically this corresponds to the complete reintegration of the personality. Just as each divinity possesses certain aspects of the central One, so the various parts of the human personality are simply manifestations of a singular, central consciousness. By "realizing" the parts, one attains reintegration into the whole.

ART AND SHINGON

Since, as was mentioned above, Shingon believed that art was a means of revealing most perfectly the essence of the divine, it is not surprising that the Esoteric sects (Tendai and Shingon) most of all fostered the representation of their divinities both in painting and in sculpture. Their sacred

The homa *fire on the inner altar of the Great Stūpa, Mt. Kōya.*

representations, however, are meant to be more than merely aesthetically pleasing, for they embody the profound, mysterious forces that compose the divinity. This means that any representation of the divine in painting or sculpture, since it contains the essence of the godhead, must be treated as the bearer of essential forces, which, in the belief of Esotericists, are transferable through meditation from the divinity in his representational form to the believer. This transfer of powers characteristic of Esotericism has served to endow Esoteric art with an importance not usually attached to the sacred images of other sects.

First Buddhist Images

Early (Hīnayāna) Buddhism had already held within it the seeds of a plurality of Buddhas and Bodhisattvas, but it was only with the development of Mahāyāna, and especially Tantrism, that any visual multiplicity was to be observed. Early Buddhism had been aniconic, and there were numerous passages in the *Sūtras* prohibiting the representing of the historic Buddha in human form. This prohibition was circumvented by the use of a number of symbols which were conventionally understood to stand for the Buddha presence : the wheel, with or without flanking deer; the throne; and others. The representation of the Buddha in human form occurred around the beginning of the Christian era in India and the first images doubtless owed much to Greco-Roman influences, particularly in the northwest (Gandhāra), for the early Buddha images surprisingly recall the Apollo type common to Greco-Roman art.

Symbols

Gandhāran images were for the most part representations of the historical Buddha. The images themselves were largely indistinguishable one from the other, their specific functions being clarified by the use of symbols and other methods. With the rise of the Tantric school and the plethora of divinities that accompanied it, it was of course necessary to evolve a system of symbols that would make quite clear the "aspect" of godhead that a given divinity was supposed to represent, since it was not possible to vary infinitely and successfully the appearance of the statues themselves. There arose, therefore, the use of a number of attributes that could be held in the hand, as well as certain hand and body postures that specified the religious import of a given statue.

Symbols, body postures, and hand signs are commonly

known under the generic title of *mudrā,* the Sanskrit for "sign" or "seal," although the term is most regularly used to refer to hand gestures. Early Indian (Gandhāran) mudrā were somewhat vague in their usage, and it was only with the codification of the Tantric schools around the seventh century that they were to be subjected to a more specific employment. In the Tantric schools, hence in Shingon, the mudrā tended to assume a mystic value. It was used as a kind of "seal," one of the primary meanings of the word in Sanskrit, in order to guarantee the efficacy of the spoken word, in this case the magic formulas (*mantra* and *dhāranī*), which they were meant to accompany. They were associated with Act of the Three Mysteries, and were hence intimately connected with the secret workings in the order of things as exposed by the Tantric schools. It is not within the scope of this work to expose in full the mudrā system, but it will be necessary to bear in mind that, since the Buddha image itself is largely invariable, Esoteric iconography is meaningless without some knowledge of the often abstruse symbolism.

Tantrism, in order to represent the multiple aspects of divinity, admitted an enormous pantheon, encompassing not only Buddhist divinities alone, but those of Hinduism and other religions as well. This means that the number of divinities is particularly great, ranging from the many secondary gods, personifications of natural phenomena borrowed from Hinduism to the metaphysical abstractions represented by the Buddhas. It will suffice here to mention a few of the most important.

The Five Buddhas

The mandalas are largely formed around a group of five Buddhas known as the five Jina, or "victors." These Buddhas are personalizations of aspects of the central godhead. They are "realizable" by knowledge of these aspects gained through

Dainichi (Vairochana) in the Great Stūpa, Mt. Kōya.

meditation, hence their Japanese name *gochi nyorai*, or "five knowledge Buddhas." The most important of these Buddhas are the following.

Vairochana, or Dainichi

Vairochana (J. Dainichi) is the central, solar divinity of whom all other Buddhas are an aspect. As the sun is the center of the universe, so Vairochana is the center of the cosmos and hence of the mandalas, the point toward which all integration moves and from which the multiplicity of the phenomenal world comes into form. Represented regularly in a seated posture, his role as center of a centrifugal or centripetal universe is made manifest by the mudrā he forms: that of concentration for the former (Womb World mandala) and that of knowledge for the latter (Diamond World mandala). His marked solar character made it particularly easy to establish a relationship with the native sun goddess Amaterasu, in the Dual Shintō system which we will discuss below. Sometimes almost indistinguishable from Vairochana is the Buddha Locana, a personification of the Buddhist doctrine (*dharma*). In the *Bommōkyō, Sutra of Brahmā's Net,* he is described as seated on a great lotus throne, the thousand petals of which constitute each an individual universe, each having its own historical Buddha. Secular, political parallels to such a system were not lost on the Nara Court, which constructed a great statue of this Buddha at the Tōdaiji, where it stands today.

Amida

More popular even than Vairochana is the Buddha Amida. His place is properly in the west, the location also of his Pure Land, or paradise. Amida is the saving Buddha, highly revered by Amidist sects but present also in the Esoteric pantheon,

Amida with two attendant bodhisattvas. By Genshin Sōzu.
Painting on silk, decorated with cut gold leaf. Height approx.
33 cm. Konkaikōmyōji, Kyoto.

where he is the object, like other Buddhas, of meditation. He is twofold in nature, the two aspects being apparent in his Sanskrit names: Amitāyus, "long life"; and Amitābha, "limitless light." The Japanese *Amida* combines these two aspects, although if necessary a distinction may be observed. The origin of Amida is perhaps to be sought in the frontier regions of northwest India. While Iran with Ahura Mazda offers a number of striking similarities, both Greek and Christian influences are not to be ruled out. The fact that Amida is essentially a saving divinity and regularly represented as part of a trinity would seem to place him in relationship with Mediterranian concepts. The outstanding quality of this divinity is his generosity toward the worshiper, whose every sin he forgives and whom he goes out to meet and welcome into his paradise. Perhaps of all the Buddhas, Amida is most popular in Japan. In Esoteric mandalas, he is regularly represented in the gesture of concentration or in that of preaching. There is a group of nine Amidas known as the *kuhon Amida,* or "Amidas of the nine classes." The various classes of meditation on this Buddha are manifested through graduated mudrā. The system in Japan seems to date from around the tenth century.

The Historical Buddha

Concerning the historical Buddha, Shākyamuni, suffice it to say that the earliest Indian Buddhist images, in Gandhāra, were mostly of him, and subsequent Buddhas were all portrayed in his likeness. He is regularly represented with curled hair and a cranial protuberance (*ushnīsha*), sign of his Buddha knowledge. It is said that the form of his body was borrowed from the wide breast and narrow waist of the lion and the head from the bull, while the eyes recall the lotus bud, the eyebrows the Indian bow, and the three folds of the neck the undulations of the conch shell. Although he figures in the

Shaka, with the bodhisattvas of medicine, Yakuō and Yakujō,
dated A.D. *623 (Asuka period). Bronze, height approx.* 6½ *feet.*
Golden Hall, Hōryūji.

Esoteric pantheon, he is not a principal divinity. His importance in the *Lotus* sūtra, of course, makes him the chief divinity of the Tendai sect.

Miroku and Yakushi

Two Buddhas of lesser importance are the future Buddha, Miroku (Skt. Maitreya), and the healing Buddha, Yakushi (Skt. Bhaishajyaguru). Maitreya is universally recognized by all sects of Buddhism, and he is represented in the oldest statues of Gandhāra. Despite his importance in Buddhist theory and his not infrequent representation in art, he was never the object of a popular cult in Japan. Perhaps this was due to his other-worldly nature. Yakushi, on the other hand, was already worshiped at Nara. Indeed, the earliest statue surviving from this period (607) is of this healing divinity, now located in the Kondō of the Hōryūji. The early appreciation of this Buddha is not surprising in view of the relationship of early Japanese Buddhism with disease and its cure. His origins are uncertain and his entry onto the iconographic stage in the Far East was relatively late, the basic text first being translated into Chinese only in 615 A.D. Besides his duties as a healing Buddha, Yakushi was also Master of the East, in which direction he had his own paradise. Although this Eastern Paradise was not unknown since early times, it was never to rival with the Western Paradise of Amida, and Yakushi's main function was always healing. He is often represented in a seated posture, his hands folded in his lap, while on them rests a small medicine jar, his special attribute.

Kannon

Of the Bodhisattvas, most important is doubtless Kannon (Skt. Avalokiteshvara). Originally a masculine divinity in India, it is uncertain just when the concept of this god's

Kannon (Avalokiteshvara) with the Wishing Jewel. Asuka period (552–646). Gilt bronze, height approx. 13 inches. Smithsonian Institution.

feminine character evolved. In India the divinity is regularly masculine, and early statues of him around the seventh century in China show him thus. It is not until the Sung dynasty (960–1279) that he becomes definitely feminine. Perhaps there was confusion with Tantric female divinities, such as Tārā and Hāritī, which effected this transfer of sex. In any case, in China and Japan at least, the accent is never on the sex of the god. Kannon is the personification of divine mercy (*mahā-karunā*) and in this is intimately associated with the Buddha Amida, an image of whom appears regularly in the Bodhisattva's headdress. Like Amida, Kannon is the great savior of the world, for which role he is able to assume any form he desires—a concept which of course would explain his change of sex. The forms of the divinity are varied from the two-armed to the "thousand-armed" variety in which the god holds an attribute in each of his hands. There is even a horse-headed Kannon, supposedly to commemorate a former incident in the life of the historical Buddha in the form of a horse (Varāha).

Monju and Jizō

Of less popular appeal is the Bodhisattva Monju (Skt. Manjushrī), the personification of wisdom and intellect. He is regularly portrayed holding the sword of knowledge and a book which represents the sacred writ. Although Monju was an important personage in some of the sūtras, he has never been the object of a popular cult, like that, for example, of the Bodhisattva Jizō (Skt. Kshitigarbha). Jizō as a popular divinity developed later than the other Bodhisattvas. He was never important in India, although in both China and Japan he has appealed strongly and constantly to the popular imagination. His name means "earth store," and he has a double much less popular than himself, Kokūzō (Skt. Ākāshagarbha), "void store." Jizō has a number of feminine traits, and in previous existences is said to have been a woman. This would

*Jizō (Kitshigharba). Kamakura period, fourteenth (1365)
century.*

account for the fact that he is especially devoted to the help of women and to their children. In Japan, there is the still-active belief that he leads dead children safely through the nether world. He is regularly portrayed holding an alarm staff—he is also thought to be the guardian of roads—and carrying in his other hand the wishing jewel (*cintāmani*).

Fudō and Aizen

Among a secondary group of divinities called Wisdom Kings (*myō-ō*) are to be mentioned Fudō (Skt. Achala), the Immovable, a form of Shiva. The object of a popular cult in Japan, Fudō is a defender of the Law. He is regularly portrayed holding in his hands a sword and rope; with the former he cuts down the evils of the world, and with his rope he binds them. He is often shown on a rock throne, with a terrible face from which two fangs protrude, while behind him arises a background of flames. Similar to him is Aizen, god of Love (*kāma*), despite his terrible appearance. Among other attributes, the latter brandishes a bow and arrow with which he shoots down the passions that bind beings to the phenomenal world.

EXOTERIC AND ESOTERIC

The core of the Esoteric doctrine is centered around three mysteries: thought, word, and act. These three elements all derive from Vairochana and serve to explain the existence of the phenomenal world in its multiplicity. They may be studied in literature, as indeed they are in traditional Buddhism. This is called the Exoteric teaching (*kengyō*). But Shingon maintains that their essence can only be seized by the comprehension of the mysteries (Skt. *guhya;* J. *mitsu*), transmitted orally from teacher to initiate. This is called Esotericism (*mikkyō*), the teaching represented by Shingon.

The basic idea of Esotericism lies in the Three Mysteries.

They represent three ways of approaching the ONE and are
three inseparable aspects of the Great Unity. Equivalent each
to the other, they are united in every phenomenon of the
ordinary world. "The doctrine of the Three Mysteries maintains that thought, word, and activity are only different expressions for one and the same reality, for in the great Oneness
reigns equality and identity 'in the same way that the ocean
has everywhere the same salty taste.' The doctrine of the fundamental unity (*samatā*) of the three actions is a dogma essential
to Esotericism, for it alone permits one to consider as equiv
alent, or even as identical, meditative imagination, mystical
formulas, and exterior material things; such is the condition
required for all practical activity of a magical nature."[19]

MEDITATION AND FORMULAS

Thought in the Three Mysteries is represented by meditation, by Yogic concentration. Tantrism maintains that by
such disciplines it is possible for the adept to gain possession
of the "forces" inherent in the cosmic symbols about him.
These symbols are arranged in ritual order in the mandala, so
that his meditation has a given form. Each object of meditation, be it a statue or attribute or graphic symbol, bears its
own forceful aspect of the central divinity, an aspect which
meditation permits the adept to acquire. Meditate he does
until his powers are equal to those of the divinity itself, until
in effect he becomes the central divinity. Thought is also
placed in connection with the Five Wisdoms, methods of
apprehending the Truth.

As aids to meditation, magic formulas (*dhāraṇī*) are used.
They correspond to the "word" of the Three Mysteries and
constitute a kind of support for meditation. These formulas
are often successions of syllables of a purely magical nature.
Sometimes contained in these magic formulas are clusters of
phonemes regularly ending with a nasal, the meaning of which

is to be sought on a profound, mystical level. Their repetition tends to set up vibrations in the human body, most particularly in the head, while the resonance of the mantric groups creates a state of consciousness independent of the phenomenal world and propitious to religious experience. "The mantras constitute objects ('supports') of meditation for the Conscience. Consciousness of them comes during meditation on them by the development of the 'seeds' (*bīja*) which they contain."[20] Three examples may suffice: *om Akshobhya hūm* ("Oh! Akshobhya. Oh!"); *a-ban-ran-kan-ken* (Skt. *a-vam-ram-kam-kham*), being one of the three formulas of Vairochana; and *om mani padme hūm* ("Oh! Jewel in the Lotus. Oh!").

Act of the Three Mysteries is represented by mudrā, or symbolic gestures, and includes postures of meditation and handling of ritual instruments. Mudrā are meant to accompany the mystic formulas and serve as kinds of "seals." In other words, the meditation of the adept is "supported" by formulas, whose efficacy in turn is guaranteed by symbolic gestures. In this way all three elements of the Three Mysteries are brought simultaneously into play in the Esoteric religious act. The ability to remember the vast number of formulas and their associated mudrā, as well as the long training required to master the techniques of meditation—the whole symbolic paraphernalia is passed from master to adept largely by spoken word, implies not only a patient heart but a devotion to the cause that is not given to all. This means, of course, that Shingon, understood in its profoundest sense, was to be largely restricted to monkish circles. The common people saw in this system the ritualization of magic practices, the efficacy of such and such a formula against disease, for causing rain, as protection against evil, etc. As such, Shingon was widely, if superficially, known. Of course, the splendid ceremonies and the mysterious beauty of Esoteric iconography was an aesthetic pleasure independent of a knowledge of the deeper meanings, and this could not be denied to the simple man in the streets any more than to the more sophisticated courtier.

TEN STAGES OF THE HEART

Like other sects which endeavored to classify Buddhist teachings, Kūkai set forth a system of his own. This was a theory of the development of spiritual life, which he exposed in his *Jūjūshinron, Treatise on the Ten Stages of the Heart.* The work was the result of an imperial decree issued in 830, commanding the Buddhist sects to submit the articles of their faith. It is written in Chinese—an accomplishment of no little merit in itself. Kūkai divided religious consciousness into ten ① stages beginning with (1) animal existence, the state of uncontrolled passions in which there is only desire to satisfy appetite. The list proceeds as follows : (2) The second stage is known as ② "the heart of a foolish boy who fasts" and indicates the practice of secular virtue. It is the state of the ordinary man who disciplines himself just enough to avoid disorder. In the realm of religion, it corresponds to Confucianism with its stress on moral order, but from the Buddhist standpoint, it lacks spiritual motive power. The next stage (3) is for those who ③ have religious aspirations but who do not understand the true essence of their faith. It is called the "heart of the young boy without fear." As for religions, it corresponds to Taoism (sometimes Brāhmanism), which teaches long life and magical practices, maintains hope for heaven, but remains ignorant of the nature of this latter. The fourth and fifth stages represent two aspects of Hīnayāna beliefs, that is, of partial understanding : (4) that of no-self, that is, self being made up of ④ separate parts (*skandha*) and hence subject to disuniting, a belief which falls into the error of nihilism; and (5) that of ⑤ Enlightment for oneself as typified by Hīnayāna *pratyeka*-Buddhas, for whom Enlightenment is only for themselves, not for others. The sixth stage is that of Mahāyāna beliefs, ⑥ most specifically those corresponding to the Hossō sect, which stresses thought as the basis of reality and investigates the character of all existence. Typical of the Mahāyāna beliefs of this stage is compassion (*karunā*) and the desire to save others. The next three stages are representative of various Mahāyāna views : (7) the eight denials of the Sanron sect; (8) the Oneness of ultimate reality and the phenomenal world of Tendai; and (9) the universal interdependance of the Kegon school. The tenth stage is represented, of course, by Shingon Esotericism itself, in which man is united with cosmos and the cosmos with Vairochana through the mystic rites. This "order of merit" was of course open to discussion, and Hōnen (1133–1212), the great Amidist, was later to criticize Kūkai's arrangement, maintaining that it was a violation of the truth to represent Buddhist sects in a graduated scale, as if truth itself could be more or less complete.

It has been often observed that Esotericism (as it was practiced in the Miidera [Tendai] also) gradually began to infiltrate all of Japanese Buddhism. It is certainly true that no sect organized after the Heian period is free of Esoteric influences. This is doubtless due to the proclivity of the Japanese to magical beliefs to which Shingon catered, as well as to the extremely developed aesthetic side of the religion in the graphic arts, sculpture, and architecture. Along with Zen, it may truthfully be said that Esoteric Buddhism has exercised the most profound influence on Japanese religious and secular life.

TACHIKAWA SECT

Early in the twelfth century, a branch of the Shingon sect arose called the Tachikawa school. It was organized by a Shingon believer and a teacher of the Chinese system of *yin* and *yang*. This curious hybrid maintained that the Way of Yin and Yang, which they equated to woman and man, led ultimately to the state of Buddhahood. Practices were founded on some of the principles found in the shakti cults of Left-handed Tantrism. Hence, the two mandalas stand for the male and the female principles, and their unity for the union of the two sexes. There were other parallels, and sexual intercourse was an important practice of this school, as it was in the shakti sects. There exists very little literature pertinent to this branch of Shingon. What is known is largely revealed through the opposition which it engendered, for the Kōya monks in 1335 presented a memorial protesting it, and as a result the leaders were exiled and the books burned. Traces of its beliefs still remain.

SHINTŌ AND BUDDHISM

Since Esotericism exerted influence on a large portion of Japanese religious beliefs, it is pertinent to note briefly its relation with Shintō, and this latter with Buddhism.

The native cult, before contact with Buddhism, consisted of a relatively simple, animistic belief. Natural objects were considered imbued with a kind of vitality which was superior in one way or another to other objects of the same category. This quality was termed *kami*, the fundamental meaning of which is "upper," "topmost," "superior." A high mountain, a curiously bent tree, an odd-shaped rock could all be styled *kami* and hence worshiped as something superior.

NATIVE MYTHS

In general lines, the native myths trace the activities of the sun goddess Amaterasu and her brother Susano-o, the Impetuous Male, and his exploits, boisterous and headstrong, contrast continually with the more gentle nature of his sister. These myths show striking points of similarity with those of the South

Seas as well as with those of the northern Asiatic continent, a
fact which would seem to point to the areas of origin of the
Japanese people.

NATIVE CULT

The main interest of this cult is in the conditions of fertility
and pollution or defilement, the first, because in a system of
belief which animates nature in its various aspects, the agricultural cycles of growth and decay were of the utmost importance. Just as growth is a desirable state, so decay is an
undesirable one, to be avoided. The end point of decay is
death, of course. Death is the essence of defilement, the
counterpart of life, and anything that leads to death is by
definition polluted (sickness, the indisposition of childbirth,
etc.). As a result, a good part of Shintō ritual is directed toward
ceremonies the aim of which is to insure purity by exorcising
pollution, to assure (agricultural) fertility by exorcising decay.
Cleanliness of body, of course, went hand in hand with ritual
purity.

SHINTŌ

Just how early Shintō was organized as a "religion" is hard
to ascertain, but records indicate that by the middle of the
eighth century (737 A.D.) there were over 3,000 shrines. The
name itself, that is, Shintō, or "Way of the Gods," was not
used until after the introduction of Buddhism, when it became
necessary to distinguish the two forms of belief. The first
reference occurs in the *Nihongi, Chronicles of Japan*, a history
of the country from earliest times to 697 A.D., under the year
585. There is little doubt but that Shintō in the pre-Buddhist
period remained a rather vague cult, with no sacred books, no
established dogma or moral code. But with the introduction

of Buddhism into the country, that is, from the sixth century on, and subsequent contacts between the two beliefs, Shintō assumed a more definitive form.

DUAL SHINTŌ

Anthropomorphic concepts of divinities doubtless began to develop early, yet they remained vague and unsystematized. By around 900, however, images of Shintō divinities on the analogy of the great number of Esoteric Buddhist figures were being produced. This trend in the originally aniconic native religion was in later times explained by the concept of *honji suijaku*, "traces of descent from the original land." This meant that Shintō divinities were regarded as local manifestations, as it were, of Buddhist divinities. For example, the native sun goddess Amaterasu became the counterpart of the Buddhist solar deity Vairochana (Dainichi), while Hachiman, later the Shintō god of war, was identified with the role of the gentle Buddhist Bodhisattva (or even the Buddha Amida!), the first instance being recorded in 783 in connection with the Usa Hachiman, who had made such startling proposals to Dōkyō. This tendency to relate the two systems had begun in the Nara period. Gyōgi (670–749) is said to have set forth the idea, and it was propagated by Ryōben (689–773). However, an imperial edict of 765 seems to indicate that the process of amalgamation was not yet complete, for it reflects the view that Shintō gods were the guardians of the Buddhas. Actually, the chief period of growth for this concept of syncretism took place during the ascendency of Esoteric Buddhism, from the beginning of the ninth century. Since, according to the Shingon concept, the universe was divided into "two parts" (*ryōbu*), upon which the two mandalas were based, it seemed but a step to see in the divinities of Shintō the members of a pantheon which formed one part of the beliefs of Japan, while Buddhism formed the other. The former, indeed, was a manifestation of the latter. This curious alliance was termed *ryōbu Shintō,* or Dual Shintō, and this is a peculiarly Japanese development in the evolution of these two religions.

The fusion of Buddhism and Shintō was at no point complete, and the native divinities continued to reign over their own shadowy domains, even though restricted to a greater or lesser degree according to the fortunes of Buddhism. Only after the end of the Heian period, say 1100, did a fully syncretic form come about. In 1272, for example, the Gion shrine, a Shintō establishment, was made into a Buddhist temple under the name of Gion-ji. It was not uncommon indeed for Shintō shrines to be governed by Buddhist priests. Both Kūkai and Saichō are accredited with the founding of Dual Shintō, but it is hard to find the basis of such assertions in the writings of these men. Perhaps the most that may be said is that they favored the syncretic development of the two religions by the very catholicity of their views, a quality markedly characteristic of the general Japanese attitude toward religious practice. As Sansom says : "They saw nothing irregular in the common practice of combining both forms of worship in the same building or the same precincts, but the more specific theory (expressed in the formula *honji suijaku,* "traces of descent from true home") which regards the gods as manifestations of the Buddhas, was elaborated in later times."[21]

Kamakura Period
(1185-1333)

FUJIWARA POWER BROKE DOWN IN the middle of the twelfth century, and by 1185 the Minamoto clan had defeated its opponents, the Taira, and its leaders had become the *de facto* rulers of Japan. They preserved the imperial institution, but, to escape the heady and enervating influence of the court, they located themselves in the small village of Kamakura far to the east. From this place they ruled as representatives of the throne in Kyoto. Their leader demanded, and was granted, the title of generalissimo (*shōgun*). The time of their rule is known as the Kamakura period and their government, as the *shōgunate*. It is a period of developing feudalism.

CHARACTERISTICS OF KAMAKURA LIFE

Life and attitudes toward it were different in Kamakura and Kyoto. Kyoto was dominated by the elegant, refined courtier; Kamakura by the simple, direct warrior. With the disturbances that accompanied the fall of the Fujiwaras in the mid-twelfth century, the essentially refined but optimistic attitude toward life that typified the courtier gave way to a pessimism characteristic of the troubled times and of the temperament of the warrior, constantly concerned with death. Emphasis was placed on the evanescence, the impermanence of things, on the gradual disintegration of the world. This concept was formalized by the Buddhist expression *mappō*, "end

of the Law," mentioned above, a period which was thought to
mark the end of the world. As a result of political and social
change, Buddhism evolved too. Distinct from the intellectual
Nara cults or the ostentatious Esoteric cults of Heian, Kamakura saw the rise of a Buddhism that stressed salvation, a
concept stemming from the vicissitudes of the warrior's life.

POPULARIZATION OF BUDDHISM

For the first time, Buddhism became a truly popular
religion. The first and perhaps most important reason was the
decline of the aristocracy. Concomitantly a new society arose
headed by a new class, the warriors (*bushi*). Although some of
these men were of noble lineage or of the provincial gentry,
the class as a whole, almost by definition, included great
numbers of common retainers, whose new importance did
much to set the tone of the period. The decline of Heian
society had been accompanied by the increasing corruption of
a patronized clergy, more and more out of touch with the
lower classes. All this, set against the background of disorder
and confusion, contributed to emphasizing the idea of salvation for the warrior. He was not attracted by the Esoteric
ceremonies of the Tendai and Shingon schools, with their
beautiful but impersonal rites, nor by the coldly intellectual
concepts of the older sects. The warrior insisted on the imme-
diacy of salvation, and he favored the sect that could offer him
this. Salvation was no longer confined to the monasteries; it
was now to be sought on the battlefield as well.

By this time, learning had gradually come into the common
ken. Chinese, which had been used as the intellectual language
since the Nara period, was still important, but in the twelfth
and thirteenth centuries, treatises were more and more being
written in the more easily understood Japanese syllabary
(*kana*).

The popularization of Buddhism kept pace with its "nationalization"; that is, as Buddhism filtered down to the people, it became for the first time truly Japanese in nature, and the sects that developed in the Kamakura period were more sincerely Japanese in feeling and expression than any that had come before. This popularization was partly a reaction against the Buddhism of the late Heian period. Although during the Kamakura period the Nara sects, especially the Kegon and Ritsu, experienced a revival, the new sects (Jōdo, Shin, and Nichiren) best demonstrate the nature of this reaction. A third aspect of the popularization was the rise of Zen and, in the following period, the growth of its influence.

AMIDISM

ORIGINS

The origins of the cult of Amida (Skt. Amitābha/Amitāyus) are difficult to trace. Somewhat before the first century A.D., texts appeared that dealt with a Western paradise presided over by the benevolent Amitābha, god of longevity and infinite light (Amitāyus), one of the several Buddhas of the Mahāyāna pantheon. Certainly, remarkable parallels may be drawn with the Iranian *Avesta* and its Ahura Mazda, also a divinity of light, enthroned in a Western Paradise, access to which is obtained through calling on his name, a practice with which one must compare the Japanese nembutsu, calling on the name of Amida. And, despite the entirely Indian tone of the early Amida texts (*Sukhāvatī-vyūha;* T. 360–364), there are other signs of a foreign origin. For example, in the oldest Buddhist texts of India, Amitābha is unknown, and when he does appear he is by no means an important Buddha. As far as we know, his cult was never organized into a separate school on Indian soil. Moreover, the essential idea of the Amida cult

—that is, of a transfer of merit from the Buddha to the worshiper; in other words, of salvation through the good works of others—stands in opposition to early Buddhist ideas, which instead stressed self-responsibility and a system of self-advancement toward Enlightenment.

AMIDISM IN CHINA

Knowledge of Amitābha was introduced to China at an early date; and, doubtless under the influence of Taoist humanism, this Buddha evolved a definite personality. By the time knowledge of him reached China, he had developed a number of distinctive traits that must have been attractive to the Chinese. He dwelt in a Western Paradise; the Chinese had a Western Paradise of their own, presided over by the Queen Mother of the West. His identification with longevity was at one with the Taoist aim of attaining immortality, and the Taoist notion of "original nothing" (*pen-wu*) paralleled the Mahāyāna concept of Void as it is expounded in the *Prajñā-pāramitā-sūtras*. The Chinese teacher Tao-an (312–385) had taken up Mahāyāna Buddhism, particularly the study of the *Prajñāpāramitā-sūtras* and the practice of meditation. His disciple Hui-yüan (334–417) is credited with introducing into cultivated Chinese Buddhist circles the ideas he had learned from his master. This was made possible chiefly by the fact that he remained a nobleman while living a monk's life. It is Hui-yüan who is credited with the real founding of the Pure Land sect, as it was called. Like his master, he stressed the Mahāyāna practice of meditation, claiming that it was the ecstasy of meditation that permitted a vision of Amitābha's Pure Land. Meditation permits a fusion with the Absolute. Although by the fourth century a definite school is said to have been organized by Hui-yüan, the general popularity of the cult prevented its monopoly by any one sect. Hence, one notes

the presence of Amitābha, among other Buddhas, in Tenda
and Shingon as well as in other sects, and it was recorde
that the *Sukhāvatī-vyūha* was publicly recited in Japan in 640.

Amida's presence in the Tendai and Shingon sects testifies
to his existence as an Esoteric divinity. Thus, like the other
Esoteric gods, Amida was an object of meditation, the goal, as
with other Esoteric divinities, being to possess the virtues of the
god, which were transferable through meditation. Merely calling on Amida's name (*nembutsu*), was not sufficient; the
Esoteric use of the divinity's name was rather as an aid or
"support" for the meditative process. This is called the *Esoteric
nembutsu*. Moreover, although Amida was thought particularly suitable, concentration on any Esoteric Buddha was
believed to be a way of attaining paradise. The Amida form
was undoubtedly popular, for by the end of the eleventh
century in Japan, an Esoteric Amida had been established as
a meditative object, together with a ninefold (*kuhon*) graduated system of meditation on the divinity. This system, elaborated in China, is said to have been transmitted to Japan in
847 by Eun (798–869).

TENDAI AND SHINGON AMIDISM

Long before the Pure Land theory was molded into a
Japanese sect, it was part of the teaching and practice of other
schools. In the seventh to the ninth centuries, the practices of
praying for the dead (*tsuizen*) and invoking Amida (*nembutsu*)
were known in the Nara sects and most particularly in the
Tendai and Shingon sects of the Heian period. Amidism in the
Nara and early Heian periods, however, was completely confined to monasteries and to scholarly religious circles, whose
main goal was an emulation of T'ang learning. Amidism

(Jōdo) was still theoretical at this stage and exerted little influence on the aristocratic society.

INVOCATION OF AMIDA'S NAME

The nembutsu is said to have been introduced to Mount Hiei in 851, and it is known that a concentration hall existed there. The nembutsu, however, was considered as only one among various methods of concentration, as Amida simply was one among various gods. Amida invocation (known also as the *hanju zammai*) took the specific form of the so-called *jōgyō zammai*, in which for ninety days the devotee circumambulated an image of Amida, meditating on, and calling all the while upon the name of the divinity. Although the jōgyō zammai evolved into the nembutsu as Hōnen later conceived it, at this time it was really an Esoteric type of nembutsu (*tendai nembutsu*), which, rather than a simple invocation, was more a magical formula pertinent to Amida, in fact, an utterance of the dhāraṇī type. Accordingly, the importance of the nembutsu in the Tendai sect should not be overlooked.

FUJIWARA AMIDISM

Amidist ideas gradually began to flourish in early Fujiwara times, and their popularization was accentuated in the tenth to eleventh centuries. Yōkan (1032–1111), in his *Ōjōjūin, Ten Conditions for Rebirth in Paradise,* emphasized the protection of Amida along with the efficacy of meditation; Chingai (1091–1152), in his *Ketsujō ōjōshū, Collection of Passages on the Certainty of Rebirth into Paradise,* founded a new branch of Shingon (Shingi-shingon), aspiring to rebirth into the Pure Land of Amida by invocation and meditation on the divinity. For the last, Amida was simply an aspect of Vairochana, and the Pure Land was Vairochana's palace. Identification with the godhead by the Shingon process of meditation assured the realization of the paradise in this very world. Yōkan, however, felt the doctrines of such sects as the Tendai and Shingon as too subtle for immediate understanding. He therefore expounded the simple repetition of the nembutsu, largely dissociating it from the meditative aspects it possessed under Kakuban. Chingai's views were similar to those of Kakuban, though adding that rebirth in the Western Paradise was attainable only if there was sincere aspiration along with the desire of salvation for all sentient beings.

GENSHIN

There were other precursors of Amidism outside of the purely Esoteric schools. Perhaps the most important is Genshin (Eshin sōzu, 942–1017), who indeed is often called the first Japanese patriarch of the Amidist sect. Genshin held that the mere repetition of the nembutsu, or calling on the name of Amida, was sufficient for salvation in the form of rebirth in the Western Paradise. In 985, he published a treatise concerning his views on salvation, which he entitled *Ōjōyōshū, A Collection of Essentials Concerning Rebirth in the Western Paradise* (i.e., Amida's Western Paradise). Indeed, it was through the reading of the vivid descriptions of paradise in Genshin's work that Hōnen was later to be inspired.

RYŌNIN

Another precursor was Ryōnin (1071–1132), a Tendai monk, who is responsible for forming the first sect for the exclusive worship of Amida (1124) and so paving the way for Hōnen's teachings. Ryōnin's sect is called the Yūzū-nembutsu. Interestingly, the Yūzū-nembutsu doctrine is based not on Amida sūtras, as might be expected, but on the *Lotus* and the

Kegon, and through these texts it maintains a close connection
with the Tendai and Kegon schools. The main idea of the
doctrine is that the nembutsu should be performed on behalf
of others as well as of oneself. This idea was based, so the
adherents claimed, on the personal inspiration of Amida and
Bishamon.[22] In fact, the school maintained that calling on the
name of Amida was even more meritorious if done for others
than if done for oneself, an idea that curiously was never taken
up and developed.

HŌNEN

The real founder of Japanese Amidism was Hōnen (Genkū,
1133–1212). Although Hōnen's Amidism was not recognized
as an independent sect until the time of Ieyasu (1542–1616),
it was Hōnen who organized and taught the Amidist doctrine
as an independent teaching, thereby establishing the Jōdo, or
Pure Land, sect.

Hōnen's father was an official in Mimasaka province who
died exhorting his son to become a priest. His mother permitted him to study at Mount Hiei, where he showed great
promise. Ordained a priest, he retired to Kurodani on the out-
skirts of Kyoto, renounced the world, and devoted himself to
prayer. He is said to have read the Buddhist Tripitaka five
times, but he was not satisfied with the religion as he had
learned it. Most important for him was the peace of religious
life, in contrast to the period of civil wars through which he
had lived. He is said to have achieved Enlightenment upon
reading Genshin's *Ōjōyōshū*. The *Ōjōyōshū* was based on a
commentary to the *Amitāyurdhyāna-sūtra* (T. 360) by the
monk Shan-tao (J. Zendō, 613–681), the third patriarch of
Chinese Amidism. This work set forth that the practice of the
nembutsu would bring about salvation in accordance with the
Buddha's vow. This was the religious peace Hōnen was seek-

ing, for it depended not on one's own strength (*jiriki*) but the strength of another (*tariki*), that is, on the intervention of the saving Amida. At the age of forty-three (1175), Hōnen began to teach what he had learned, and this date is accepted as traditional for the founding of the Jōdo sect.

Hōnen believed he had a message for his age. In 1198, he wrote the *Senchaku* [*hongan nembutsu*] *shū, Collection of Passages* [*on the Original Vow and the Nembutsu*], in sixteen chapters. The "collected passages" were from Amida sūtras and included not only commentaries by Zendō, whose interpretation of these sūtras he generally followed, but Hōnen's opinions as well. Hōnen was opposed by the clergy of the great Tendai monasteries, and in 1204 the priests of Mount Hiei attempted to condemn his thesis. In an open letter of a conciliatory nature, Hōnen forbade the slandering of other Buddhas besides Amida.

The emperor Toba II (r. 1184–1198) was friendly to Hōnen, but in 1206 a serious misunderstanding arose. Two maids of honor from the court had become Amidist nuns, and it was suggested that their reasons for so doing were improper feelings toward certain Amidist priests. The priests, hearing of this, quoted Zendō to the effect that unbelievers are jealous of those who act according to religious principles. They were promptly beheaded for their unwise admonition, and Hōnen himself was exiled to Tosa (1207) and later to Sanuki, on the northeast of Shikoku. His exile lasted only ten months, but he was not allowed to return to the capital until 1211. The following March he fell ill and died, in his eightieth year of age.

It is not too harsh to say that Hōnen was neither a remarkable preacher nor a moving writer. Though he believed earnestly in his own ideas of salvation and his system of Amida worship, he was unassertive in preaching them against the opposition of the older, established sects. Yet the gentleness that caused his excessive diplomacy, to avoid giving offence, was the very quality that drew him to the common people and them to him.

JIRIKI AND TARIKI

Nevertheless, Hōnen was considerably more of a teacher than Genshin. In his *Senchakushū,* he divided religious practices into two paths: *shōdō,* or Holy path, and *jōdo,* or Pure Land path. These paths respectively parallel the subjective and objective attitudes toward salvation already mentioned: jiriki, reliance on one's own strength; and tariki, reliance on another's (i.e., Amida's) strength (help). Hōnen maintained that hope for mankind lay ultimately in the Pure Land path. The basis for these ideas was a series of vows made by Amida to save sentient beings: Amida accepted Buddhahood on certain conditions, stated in the form of vows, forty-eight in all. Of these, the eighteenth vow is the most important. It states that anyone calling on the name of Amida at least ten times will by virtue of this act be 'reborn into the Western Paradise' (*ōjō*). Of course, faith in the Buddha Amida does not mean renouncing all other Buddhas, for they represent the Holy way, even if only Amida's is the Pure Land way. Shākyamuni, for example, is important, for he came into the world in order to explain the eighteenth vow of Amida.

PURE LAND

In the Pure Land, Amida's Western Paradise, all enjoy wonderful powers of body and mind. Sometimes it is considered as a dwelling place for all eternity, although this is a later, popular concept. In the *Sūtras,* it is a place of peaceful and blissful sojourn on the way toward the attainment of nirvāna or even Buddhahood. Hōnen, in fact, believed that one who had arrived at the Western Paradise could return to the world and labor for the salvation of others. But it should not be assumed that such a returning meant a re-entry into the cycle of birth and rebirth. Rather it was the power of the Buddha state, as Amidists conceived it, to influence the samsāric world but to remain free of its chain of causality.

Amidism recognizes also a kind of purgatory, called the *keman-kai,* where the spirits of doubters are obliged to spend a certain time. Hōnen does not speak of the keman-kai, but the Amida sūtras tell how the faithful are born on lotus flowers while the doubters remain some five hundred years inside the flower until their doubts are dispersed.

RECITATION OF NEMBUTSU

Hōnen emphasized the repetition of the nembutsu with faith, holding that meditation on Amida, the principle of the Esoteric practice, was superfluous. In this teaching, his system is directed to the ordinary man for whom the divinity is always and immediately available. The believer is thus relieved of the long training necessary for the practice of Esoteric rites. Basing himself on the Chinese monk Zendō, Hōnen associated the recitation of the nembutsu with Three States of Mind, by which he defined "recitation with faith." The nembutsu was to be recited (1) with a sincere heart, that is, with genuine devotion, (2) with a deeply believing heart, and (3) with a longing heart, that is, with a desire, implemented by the merits of preceding existences, to attain birth in Amida's Pure Land.

Amida is all merciful, and even sinners are pardoned if they call on him with the triple sincerity just described. Opponents of the Pure Land sect accused it of giving free reign to sin and then excusing sin by the simple recitation of the nembutsu.

But Hōnen stressed also the idea of good conduct, which he related to correct faith, for if faith is not right, Amida cannot save.

DISCIPLES OF HŌNEN

Hōnen was a simple and, as we have observed, gentle man. He set forth his ideas in direct, untechnical language, trying always to avoid contradicting the beliefs of the other sects. Six prominent disciples carried on his work: Shōkōbō, Zennebō, Ryūkan (1148–1227), Chōsai (1184–1228), Kōsai, and Shinran. Shōkōbō (Benchō, 1162–1238) founded the Chinzei school, and this branch represents ordinary Jōdo (Pure Land) Amidism as it exists today. He elaborated Hōnen's views only slightly, stressing the need for the nembutsu. He also emphasized Amida's twentieth vow, that practices other than the nembutsu will ultimately permit entrance into the Pure Land. Zennebō (Shōkū, 1777–1247) founded the Seizan branch of Jōdo, which today is recognized as the orthodox branch and has its headquarters at the Zenrinji (Kyoto). He emphasized an intimate union between the faithful and Amida, a kind of mystic concord between the divinity and the believer—a concept not unlike Esoteric mysticism. For Zennebō, rebirth into the Western Paradise means the entry of Amida into one's own heart. Everyone, therefore, contains the seeds of his own rebirth, and his salvation is achieved by "realizing" his oneness with Amida. For Zennebō, furthermore, the nembutsu is essential to salvation. Buddha means Enlightenment or profound Wisdom, and since all Buddhas share in this Enlightenment, all are as one in the Amidist Wisdom.

OPINIONS OF NEMBUTSU

Various points of view concerning the nembutsu gave rise to a division among the disciples of Hōnen. It was a question of "one or many callings," that is, of the efficacy of a simple nebutsu as against calling on Amida many successive times. Hōnen himself favored the continuous use of the nembutsu until death. Repetition was a kind of insurance that the nem- butsu said with the threefold sincere heart would be realized. His disciple Kōsai (1163–1249), however, claimed that, although there is no harm in the repetitive use of Amida's name, one calling, a sincere and true one, was enough. Furthermore, Kōsai, who had undergone Tendai training and hence was open to Esoteric influences, maintained that Amida possessed two personalities: the original nature (*hommon*), which is identical with the Buddha-nature in us all and has a parallel in the Three Body Theory (i.e., the essence body: dharmakāya), and the incarnate nature (*shakumon*), that is, an historical manifestation, corresponding to the transforma- tion body (ōjin). Hōnen took issue with Kōsai's theory of one calling, claiming that it was against Zendō. Not only did he expel Kōsai from the sect, but he also issued a writ denouncing the "one calling," with the result that Kōsai's "heresy" came to nothing.

TRUE PURE LAND SECT

By far the most important disciple of Hōnen was Shinran (1173–1262), founder of a type of Amidism known as Jōdo Shinshū, the "True Pure Land Sect." Shinran selected the name Shinshū (True Sect), by which this school is regularly known, from a passage in Zendō in which it is stated that "the shinshū (true sect) is hard to find." However, Shinran indis- criminately used the name to refer to Hōnen's teachings as well as to his own, and it is unclear just when his sect became distinct from Hōnen's. For a long time, both Jōdo and Jōdo Shin were considered the same.

The monk Shinran (1173–1262). Ashikaga period (1392–1568). Wood, 12½ inches. Musée Guimet, Paris.

Shinran

Shinran (also known as Zenshin and Shakku) was the son of a court noble, and in his veins flowed both Fujiwara and Minamoto blood. Orphaned early, he entered Mount Hiei at the age of nine. But Tendai teachings did not satisfy him. He visited Nara and then returned to Mount Hiei. We are told that he dreamed Kannon instructed him to study with Hōnen, which he began to do in 1201, becoming the Amidist master's

favorite pupil. Shinran married the regent Kaneza
daughter, known as Eshin the Nun. He was what was kno
as a *shami* (Skt. *shrāmanera*), a person who while leading ...
religious life does not follow the strict monastic rule. Shinran
and Hōnen were essentially in harmony; both were friends of
the regent, both were exiled in 1207, and both returned to
Kyoto in 1211. In 1211, Shinran set out on a missionary trip
to the northeast. Only after Hōnen's death does a schism seem
to have arisen in the Amidist sect. Shinran lived in the
province of Hitachi, and there he preached, although he spent
a part of his time at Inada, where he founded the Jōdo
Shinshū. In 1224, he published his teachings in a work
regarded as the basic Shinshū text, the *Kyōgyōshinshō, Doctrine, Practice, Faith, and Realization,* consisting of 143
selected passages from twenty-three sūtras, Amidist and other.
About 1230, Shinran returned to Kyoto, where he spent the
last, uneventful years of his life.

It may be said that, in discipline and ritual, Jōdo is much
the same as the older sects. It is a monastic order; it honors
other Buddhas and Bodhisattvas besides Amida, although it
clearly holds that salvation is most readily attained through
the recitation of Amida's name. Shinran, on the other hand,
abolished monasticism. He permitted the marriage of the
priesthood, an innovation approved by Kōsai but scotched by
Hōnen's strong opposition. Further, Shinshū approved only
the worship of Amida, although Shaka (Shākyamuni) and
other Buddhas are invoked in the funeral ceremony and salvation is attained through faith, Amida's gift to sentient beings.
There are no relics or images of divinities other than those of
Amida and, less frequently, Shaka. The headquarters are
located in the two Honganji ("Temples of the Original Vow")
in Kyoto.

Twofold Truth

Shinshū presents a twofold truth: faith and morality, *shintai zokutai.* Shintai, real truth, or faith, applies chiefly to the next world; it concerns the salvation offered by Amida and how to attain it. Zokutai, common truth, or morality, refers to man's duty as a member of the social order. In the religious sense, Shinshū sees this duty as the spirit of right conduct arising from faith.

Married Priesthood

One of Shinran's distinctive innovations was that of a married priesthood. Thus he sought to break down the division between clergy and laity which other sects maintained through monasticism. Shinran's zeal to simplify his religion extended not only to the pantheon, which he reduced essentially to one Buddha, Amida, but also to the practice of the nembutsu in his advocacy of the "one calling," although, out of gratitude, he admitted a multiplicity of callings.

Further evolution of Amidist beliefs was brought about by successors of Shinran, notably the seventeenth patriarch, Ryōyo Shōgei (1341–1420), who applied the concept of "abrupt Enlightenment" (*tongyō*) to Amidism. Tongyō is the "abrupt presentation of the Buddha of his ultimate Doctrine, without preparation and without temporizing devices." He taught that both the Western Paradise and Amida, who welcomes beings into it, are metaphorical: Amida is omnipresent, and his Paradise is absolute Reality, concepts that are not without parallel in Zen.

Ippen

Another successor of Hōnen, Ippen (Yūgyō shōnin, 1239–1289), originally a Tendai priest, identified the native deity of Kumano, Ietsunomiko or Shōjō *gongen,* with Amida, whose teaching he claimed was revealed by this god. He established rules for reciting the hymns of Zendō at fixed intervals, times a day, and hence founded a sect called the Ji, mean. "Time." Like Kūya (903–972), who disseminated Amidist ideas among the common people by chanting Amidist ditties and dancing in the streets, Ippen based his time theory on the *Lotus* sūtra. Insisting that his teaching was the religion for the age (*ji*), Ippen publicly distributed cards bearing the inscription "namu Amida butsu" ("Honor to the Buddha Amida"), and thus spread the Amidist gospel. He agreed with Hōnen's doctrine of calling on Amida with faith, and interestingly enough he appealed to the divinity through the god at the Kumano shrine. He not only considered this deity to be a manifestation of Amida; to Ippen, all Shintō gods were manifestations of Buddhas. In consequence, the nembutsu was directed to Shintō divinities as well as to Buddhist. Faith for Ippen was an "act of the mind" and, as such, subject to corruption and ultimately useless. Consequently Ippen insisted on a complete abandonment to Amida, the mysticism of which is, again, paralleled in Zen.

RENNYO

Rennyo (1415–1499), the eighth patriarch of the True Pure Land sect, sometimes referred to as the second founder of Shin, stressed particularly the observance of moral precepts. Shinran had taught that, though faith was essential to salvation, the mere calling on Amida is sufficient. Rennyo, on the other hand, held that the nembutsu is powerless without faith. Pure faith, he claimed, means an abandoning of selfish desires. More precisely it means an observance of the Confucian virtues and civil law. The faith of Rennyo and his followers in the efficacy of the nembutsu and the mercy of Amida bordered on the fanatic. Their militancy gained them the name of *ikkō*, "single-minded," and Rennyo's Shin was called the Ikkō sect.

In the fifteenth century, Shinzei (1443–1495) attempted to combine the recitation of the nembutsu with ordinary Buddhist ceremonies and ritual. This, of course, was diametrically opposed to Hōnen's and Shinran's beliefs. Thus his sect, called Ritsu, is accepted as a branch of Tendai rather than Amidist thought.

SUMMARY OF NEMBUTSU

The chief characteristic of the Amidist sects is the nembutsu, the development of which parallels the evolution of Amidism. For Genshin (942–1017), the nembutsu was fundamentally meditative, although he maintained that a simple repetition of Amida's name was sufficient for rebirth into his paradise, and a method practicable for all. The nembutsu purifies man of sin and assures his rebirth into the Pure Land. Of course, this is true when one calls on any Buddha, but Amida is by far the most important. For Genshin, it is imperative that the believer keep a picture of Amida in his mind.

Ryōnin (1072–1132) established a kind of universal identity in which one man was identical to all men and vice versa. This was true also of religious practices, hence the calling of the Buddha's name a single time was the same as calling it a million times. This universalism had its roots in Tendai and Kegon. Also under Tendai influence, Kakuban (1095–1143) established an equivalence between Amida and the central Esoteric divinity Vairochana. For him the pronunciation of the nembutsu was a kind of mystical formula. He also claimed that the Buddha land was within one's self, that salvation was essentially an interior process.

Yōkan (1032–1111) rejected the single repetition of the nembutsu and claimed that it must be repeated constantly in order to be efficacious. Hōnen, basing himself largely on the Chinese monk Shan-tao (Zendō), carried this tendency even further, rejecting both meditation and intellectual comprehension as means of worshiping Amida. He stressed faith as the only necessary element for rebirth into the Pure Land, and he extended the idea to mean absolute faith in the nembutsu. Among Hōnen's followers, Shōkōbō, who founded the Chinzei branch of Jōdo, held that the nembutsu was meant to assure the constant companionship of Amida and urged its constant repetition, although he accepted other methods of worship as being efficacious. Zennebō, founder of the Seizan branch, distinguished between the teachings of Shaka and those of Amida. Through only the latter was ultimate salvation possible, and the nembutsu was the chief means. The division of the sect between advocates of the "one calling" and those of the "many callings" was represented respectively by Kōsai and Ryūkan. Shinran conceived of salvation much as Hōnen did, but he agreed with Kōsai's concept of "one calling." He admitted "many callings" but insisted on the "one calling with faith" as the most important.

ZEN

It is difficult to know to what degree Zen represents either a dressing up of Taoist ideas in Buddhist garb or a response to a Chinese ideal. There is, however, no doubt that this largely meditative sect bases itself on latent Indian ideas, such as that of *dhyāna,* which were transferred to China along with the earliest Buddhism.

ZEN AND EARLY BUDDHISM

Meditative practices had been an essential feature of Buddhism from earliest times. For Hīnayāna, contemplation had been of considerable importance; it had, in fact, formed the end point of the so-called Eightfold Path that was the kernel

of Hīnayāna practice. The Buddhist legend had recounted as
well the tutoring of Shākyamuni by various Indian ascetics,
the discipline including Yoga breathing techniques, whose
climax was often confounded with nirvāna itself. And, as a
kind of supreme recognition of the role of meditation in the
Buddhist system, the historical Buddha himself set the example
through his own ecstatic concentration under the pīpal tree,
which was to lead ultimately to his Enlightenment.

Although the legend shows the undeniable place that meditation as a practice was accorded in early Buddhism, that
theory was no less established in the sūtras, especially those of
the Mahāyāna. Among these writings, for the history of Zen
at least, perhaps the most important was the group known
as the *Prajnāpāramitā-sūtras* (J. *Hannyaharamittakyō*),
Sūtras of Transcendental Wisdom, the oldest of which go back
to the first century B.C. These typical Mahāyānist writings are
not philosophic treatises but religious messages, whose kernel
is the exposition of the idea of Void (*shūnya*) and selflessness.
Things do not have a self of their own, they are nonexistent,
they are Void. True Void is apprehended through the eyes of
Wisdom (*prajnā*), which is one with Enlightenment and
Knowledge. Somewhat later, probably toward the second
century A.D., Nāgārjuna built his idea of the Middle Way on
these sūtras. The *Prajnāpāramitā-sūtras* are studied today in
Zen cloisters, and their concept of the ultimate Void of all
things continues to influence Zen thinking.

The *Avatamsaka-sūtras* (J. *Kegonkyō*), which are the basis
of the Kegon school, are also intimately connected with Zen.
They teach a kind of cosmotheism in which the various aspects
of the universe are completely interdependent. The metaphor
of Indra's Net (*see* above, p. 128) is used to exemplify this
relationship : the slightest change in the universe immediately
affects every multiple aspect of its parts. Moreover, the

Buddha-nature is in everything, as much in a grain of dust as in man. It is interesting to note that the fifth patriarch of this school in China, Kuei-feng Tsung-mi (J. Keichō Shūmitsu, 770–841), was also the head of a flourishing Zen school of his time. Certainly both doctrines observed the total universe as interdependent.

The *Vimalakīrtinirdesha* (T. 474–479) are particularly interesting in their relationship with Zen. They are concerned with such problems as "right meditation," that is, the correct method of concentration. While accepting, as the afore-mentioned sūtras do, the Void of all things, the *Vimalakīrtinirdesha* stress the Zen practices of "right begging and non-possession." In fact, the climax of these scriptures is a pure Zen experience. Two hundred and thirty Bodhisattvas set forth their ideas concerning the nonduality of things, with the final word from the great Bodhisattva of Wisdom, Manjushrī (J. Monju), who claims that in the last analysis one can never really speak of things or explain them, for Truth lies outside discussion. Thereupon Manjusrī challenges Vimalakīrti (Yuima) to take up the argument, but Vimalakīrti remains silent. This is consummate Wisdom, and he receives the praise of the Bodhisattva for his silence on a subject concerning which nothing can be said.

The *Lankāvatāra-sūtra* (T. 670–672) also shows remarkable touches of Zen feeling in another sense. This sūtra was highly esteemed in early Zen circles, and the four-volume Chinese translation was given to Hui-k'o (J. Kei-ka, 487–593?) by his teacher, the famous Bodhidharma (c. 520 A.D.), with special recommendations concerning its value as a basic text. The *Lankāvatāra-sūtra* consists of 108 questions and answers which take place between the Buddha and the Bodhisattva Mahā-mati. The questions as well as the answers are often cryptic and terse, and in this sense the whole text may be likened to

the *kōan,* the famous paradoxes used particularly by the
Rinzai sect. The underlying idea here, as in all Mahāyāna
sūtras as well as in Zen, is that the ultimate cannot be comprehended without inner Enlightenment. The sūtra emphasizes
the Void of all things, the ultimate understanding of phenomena being the result of a kind of imaginative insight, for
essence cannot be expressed in words. Buddhist teachings concerning the fundamental value of illumination as the only way
of apprehending the universe in its totality, the ultimate futility
of words to express the truths of the cosmos and the nature of
things, the attitude toward meditation as a practical means of
approaching Enlightenment : such concepts run through all of
Mahāyāna writings and are in fact the basis of Zen.

ZEN IN CHINA

Although the essential meditative practices and the metaphysical bases for Zen had, to a degree, been present in Buddhism since early Indian times, it was in China that an independent school was first formed. This school, which called
itself Ch'an (J. Zen), a rendition of the Sanskrit *dhyāna,*
"meditation," was in large part a Chinese adaptation of the
mystical element in Buddhism. At an early date, in order to
clarify the metaphysical abstractions that abounded in Indian
Buddhism, the teachers drew parallels with ideas known to the
Chinese through Taoism. Thus the Mahāyāna concepts of
Void and nirvāna were explained in terms of the Original
Nothing (*pen-wu*) of Taoism; the famous Middle Way was
equated with the Chinese concept of the Mean (*wu-wei,* "non-
action"); and the Absolute, as understood in Enlightenment
(*sambodhi*), was compared with the Great One (*T'ai-yi*). If it
was easy thus to simplify the abstractions of Indian thought in
Chinese terms, the very practice of meditation was even more
easily transferable. Taoists had long honored the institution of

the solitary hermit, pictured in Chinese painting meditating in his mountain fastness on the underlying Truth of nature. Hence the Buddhist dhyāna was immediately comprehensible as a practice. Basic forms of Buddhist meditation, such as concentration on Amida and the contemplation of the transcendental Wisdom (*prajñāpāramitā*), were early practiced in China. Tao-an (J. Dōan, 312–385), who also studied the *Prajñāpāramitā* texts, placed particular stress on meditation.

His disciple Hui-yüan (J. Eon, 334–417) was the real founder of the Amida sect in China. Hui yüan emphasized meditation in order to experience a vision of Amida and thereby unite with the divinity. Such meditation contains Buddhist and Taoist elements. A disciple of Kumārajīva, Tao-sheng (c. 360–434), sometimes called the actual founder of Zen, went far in assimilating Buddhism to Chinese thought. He stressed the importance of a "sudden Enlightenment," and recalled the example of the historical Buddha under the pīpal tree. For him, the Buddha was equated with the Tao and the cosmic law with *Li*. We know that Tao-sheng visited Hui-yüan on Mount Lu, but he does not seem to have been influenced by Amidist beliefs. In fact, he shows special mistrust for scriptural writings and icons, such as were a part of Amidist practices. Quoting the *Chuang-tzu,* he said : "Throw away the fishnet when the fish is caught,"[23] a phrase he applied to Buddhist meditation. For Tao-sheng, "gradual Enlightenment" was impossible, metaphysically speaking, and he compared the instant of Enlightenment to a fruit that falls suddenly when ripe.

BODHIDHARMA

Tao-sheng and others were precursors, or perhaps pioneers, of the Zen school and were important in the evolution of early

Zen ideas. But Zen traditionally recognizes a line of patriarchs who transmitted the so-called "seal of Enlightenment." The first Chinese patriarch (twenty-eighth in the full Buddhist line) is Bodhidharma (c. 470–534). Bodhidharma was the bringer of a new tradition :

> A special tradition outside the sutras,
> Independent of word and writ,
> Pointing directly to man's heart,
> Seeing (one's own true) nature and becoming Buddha.

His teaching goes back traditionally to that of the Buddha himself, who once while preaching held up a flower and smiled. Only Kāshyapa understood that the Buddha meant to symbolize the inadequacy of words to express the essence of his Doctrine. This is the "wordless tradition" Bodhidharma brought to China, the transmission of which henceforth depended on intuitive apprehension of the Absolute.

We know little concerning Bodhidharma. He appears to be of south Indian origin, from a Brāhman milieu, and to have traveled considerably, often wandering as a mendicant monk. One of his journeys took him to southern China, where he spent a relatively short time, proceeding thence to the north, where he remained more than forty years. He was in Lo-yang, at the Yung-ning monastery, from 515–526, and he died before 534. Even if the known facts concerning his life are few, the manifold legends that have sprung up attest to a truly remarkable man. The story of his interview with the Liang emperor Wu (502–550), when he informed the monarch of the futility of his good works in temple building, is famous. He is reputed to have crossed the Yangtse River on a reed, and he is often so portrayed in Zen paintings. Moreover, according to the story, he spent nine years in meditation—so long, in fact, that his legs are said to have fallen off from disuse. From this legend derive the modern Japanese dolls called *daruma*—Japanese for Bodhidharma—which when tipped over always roll back to an erect sitting position.

Hui-k'o

What we know of the life of the second patriarch Hui-k'o (484–590 or 487–593) is equally uncertain. The legend tells of his attempt to convince his master Bodhidharma of his serious desire to follow Zen discipline at the Shao-lin monastery, at whose door he waited in the snow to be accepted. In spite of this exhibition of patience, acceptance was not forthcoming; Hui-K'o accordingly cut off his arm and presented it to the master, whom this act convinced. (Another version relates that the monk's arm was cut off by robbers.) During his youth Hui-k'o had studied not only Buddhist philosophy, but Taoism and the Chinese classics in general. After Bodhidharma's death, Hui-k'o became a wandering monk. His master had passed on to him his four-volume Chinese translation of the *Lankāvatāra-sūtra,* which emphasizes the Oneness of all things. Hui-k'o himself stressed direct experience, that is, self-illumination, which he conceived as a direct apprehension of the Absolute.

Tao-hsin

The fourth patriarch, Tao-hsin (J. Dōshin, 580–651), was a man of great refinement and strong personality. Unlike his predecessors, he did not lead a life of wandering and alms seeking but rather established a more or less permanent base. While the lone itinerant monk could depend for his livelihood on the alms he received during his wandering, such an uncertain source of income was insufficient for a stable community. Thus, under Tao-hsin a new step was made in the evolution of the Zen clergy: the monks began working for themselves in garden and field. From this point, daily work became a part of Zen discipline. Under Tao-hsin there was a division of chores in the monastery, a system of shifts, so that a part of each day could be set aside for religious practice. Tao-hsin's slogan, "work, live, meditate, sleep," stresses the importance of ordinary daily living as a part of Zen discipline in the community under him. This important evolution of Zen practice opened the doors for lay participation in the religious exercises in a way that had not previously been possible. This lay participation is today a characteristic trait of the Zen community in Japan.

The early masters emphasized the realization of the Buddha through meditation. The reading and interpretation of sūtras was considered of great value, in contrast to the sect's later antiliterary tendencies. One hears but rarely of kōan, the paradoxical stories that were subsequently to become typical of Zen teaching. After Bodhidharma, two types of monk evolved, the alms beggar, generally a solitary, wandering monk, who depended for his livelihood on chance donations, and the teacher, a type which, particularly after Tao-hsin, tended to develop with the founding of communities and with the economic independence the sect gained through self-support.

NORTHERN AND SOUTHERN SCHOOLS

After Hung-jen (J. Gunin or Kōnin, 601–674), the fifth patriarch, a division occurred in the Zen community; two camps, the northern and the southern, arose. They were represented by the master's two disciples, Shen-hsiu (J. Jinne, 606–706) and Hui-neng (J. Enō, 638–713). The northern sect, with its center at Lo-yang, where Shen-hsiu had established himself, we know largely through the writings of its opponents in the southern sect. Generally speaking, the reproaches against the northern school fall into two groups: (1) straying from the correct line of transmission, that is, the usurpation of the patriarchy; and (2) a mistaken concept of Illumination and practice. As to the latter criticism, one of the differences between north and south was "sudden" versus "gradual" Enlightenment. The southern sect believed that an individual's original character is realized through Illumination, which is a sudden realization of his own Buddha-nature. Generally, the south opted for "sudden" Enlightenment, stressing, however, the "moment of Awakening." Shen-hsiu was a man of great strength around whom many disciples rallied, but the northern school did not long survive him. Its failure, due perhaps largely to the incessant attacks of the southern sects, was a fact with the death of Shen-hsiu's two disciples, P'u-chi (651–739) and I-fu (658–736).

HUI-NÊNG

Hui-nêng, the sixth patriarch, is often called the second founder of Zen. As the leader of the southern sect, he represents a kind of protest against the prevailing scholasticism of the north. Hui-nêng spoke of the mirror nature of the spirit and the spirit nature of reality. "All reality is spirit, the spirit is one and like a mirror is motionless, quiet and yet active, for its light clearness gives a complete reflection." Hui-nêng rejected "gradual" enlightenment and daily practice. To see the pure mirror of the spirit, concentration is not necessary but rather a suppression of duality; that is, Illumination is a "realization" of the entirety of one's Self. For him, ecstatic meditation and wisdom go together like the lamp and its light. As the *Prajñāpāramitā-sūtras* had set forth, spirit means Void; that is, ecstatic meditation implies an absence of thought, a state where the spirit has no object but is like a pure mirror. Hui-nêng spoke of Substance and Function in order to represent the relation of Meditation (*samādhi*) and Wisdom (*prajnā*), and in so doing he expressed Buddhist ideas in Chinese form. Most of all, Hui-nêng insisted on "experience" as the most important way to Enlightenment. By this he meant an intuitive, direct, personal apprehension of Self. For this experience, words, just as texts and icons, are superfluous; they are merely "steps" to the ultimate realization, and so Hui-nêng rejects them. Hui-nêng's emphasis on "sudden" Enlightenment is remarkable, because it would be more typically Chinese to follow, on the analogy of the civil service, the gradual step-by-step approach. In this sense, then, Hui-nêng's attitude is new for China.

KōAN

The period between 713, the date of Hui-nêng's death, and 845, that of the persecutions of Wu-tsung (r. 841–846), may be thought of as the golden age of Chinese Zen. Numerous personalities carry it to an apogee. One of these, Ma-tsu (707–786), was responsible for the extended use of the paradoxical kōan and the introduction of the shocking yell "katsu!" (Ch. *ho*), which Demiéville calls "a kind of eructation." Kōan are, so to speak, undeveloped themes, which often illogically confound the intellect and appeal to the intuition for understanding. Like the yell "katsu!" they are meant to establish a direct intuitive understanding, bypassing inhibitive intellectual processes. A famous kōan of Nan-ch'üan (J. Nansen, 748–834) may serve as an example. Monks of the northern and southern halls of Nan-ch'üan's monastery engaged in a rowdy dispute over the possession of a kitten. Catching the cat, Nan-ch'üan held it up before the disputing monks and said, "If any among you can tell me why I should not kill this cat, I will spare its life." Since none of the monks spoke, Nan-ch'üan dashed the kitten to the ground and killed it. The monk Chao-chou (J.

Jōshū, 778–891), returning to the monastery after a day's absence, was greeted by Nan-ch'üan and asked what he would have answered had he been present. Chao-chou removed his straw sandals, placed them on his head, and left the presence of Nan-ch'üan. Whereupon Nan-ch'üan said: "If you had been there, the cat would have been saved." Chao-chou's action implied neither affirmation nor negation. In other words, it expressed the Void that is the only answer to any problem, and his pointing out the nonexistence of the problem constituted the saving word which was never spoken.

To the use of the yell and the kōan was added that of the stick. This was introduced by Te-shan (Tokusan, 780–865), perhaps the most important of Hui-nêng's disciples. It is said that whenever he ascended the meditation platform he took with him the stick which, like the yell, was used—corporally— to startle the mind to sudden enlightenment. The use of such measures was to be characteristic of the Rinzai sect.

Po-chang

During the T'ang period (618–906) Zen life was conducted according to rules established by Po-chang (J. Hyakujō, 749– 814), and these same rules apply in large part to modern Japanese Zen monasteries. Begging could support the lone monk in India but not in the colder climate of north China, where continual wandering was more difficult. Hence under Tao-hsin (J. Dōshin) group living became the custom, in which work and daily life were accepted as an integral part of the Zen discipline. According to Po-chang, "One day without work means one day without food." Such self-sustenance made Zen independent of other sects. Po-chang feared lest the desire for daily existence should change into a desire for existence per se, which Buddhism as a whole tries ceaselessly to annihilate. Hence he constantly admonished the monks "to be attached to nothing, to desire naught," "to think neither on Good nor on Not-Good."

THE FIVE HOUSES

Hui-nêng and his successors up to the third and fourth generation represent the high point of Chinese Zen. Under these masters Indian Buddhist teaching was assimilated to Chinese traditions and thoroughly mixed with Taoist ideas. After the persecutions of 845, from which Buddhism in China never fully recovered, Zen was perhaps the most flourishing of all sects. Toward the end of the T'ang and through the Five Dynasties (907–960) arose the Five Houses, which represent the traditional lineage in southern China. In general, these sects represent the same line, the two most important being the Ts'ao-tung (J. Sōtō) and the Lin-chi (J. Rinzai).

TS'AO-TUNG (SŌTŌ)

The Ts'ao-tung (J. Sōtō) sect takes its name from the two founders Ts'ao-shan (840–901) and Tung-shan (807–869), who in turn had taken their names from the mountains on which their cloisters stood. The first use of the name Ts'ao-tung is of uncertain date, possibly the beginning of the tenth century. Ts'ao-tung emphasized the "Zen of silent Enlightenment" (J. *mokushō-zen*) and stressed the importance of sitting in meditation (*zazen*), a discipline which, carried on over a period of time, leads to Enlightenment through a modification of the whole life and personality of the meditator. This sect reacted against the "sudden Illumination" arrived at as a result of meditating on the kōan. In short, the Ts'ao-tung sect, quietistic in nature, strove through meditation for a "gradual enlightenment." It emphasized the importance of daily living and of the full participation of the whole personality in the

Buddhist nuns meditating (Koide-machi, Niigata Prefecture).
The guardian nun holds a stick with which she strikes those
who are remiss in some aspect of meditation practice.

experience of Illumination. For it, the most important practice
is seated meditation, zazen. The goal of meditation is the realization of the real nature of things and the discovery of the
Buddha-nature in one's Self. In a dialectic typical of the
Ts'ao-tung variety of Zen, the meditation concerns the fundamental unity of Absolute and Relative, divided into five steps
and represented by five symbols: (1) The Absolute in the

Relative, that is, the subject observing the object, represented by ◑; (2) the Relative in the Absolute, that is, an opposite movement from the above, the object seen in the subject, represented by ◐; (3) the Absolute alone, that is, the subject treated as an entity, represented by ⊙; (4) the Relative alone, represented by ○; and (5) the Absolute and Relative together, unity of subject and object, represented by ●. In 1 and 2, Absolute and Relative are interdependent, in 3 and 4 they are independent, and 5 establishes their unity.

Lin-chi (Rinzai)

Of equal importance is the Lin-chi (J. Rinzai) sect, whose founder, after whom it was named, was a remarkable man. His real name was I-hsüan (J. Gigen, d. 867) of Lin-chi. There are numerous stories concerning his Zen career and his life in the cloister of Huang-po. Lin-chi's method of approach to Enlightenment is characterized by the abundant use of blows and yells ("ho!"). The following conversation with a disciple will serve as an example: "The Master questioned Lo-p'u saying: 'One strikes with a stick, another calls out "ho!" Which is nearer Reality?' Lo-p'u answered, 'Neither is near.' The master said, 'How can one then come near Reality?' Lo-p'u called out 'ho!' and the Master struck him."

The most important method of Enlightenment of the Lin-chi sect, however, was that of the kōan. The kōan placed complete stress on provoking an instantaneous Enlightenment for which no preparation was possible. In this sense, Lin-chi was opposed to the gradual disciplinary methods adopted by the Ts'ao-tung sect. The use of kōan was transmitted to Japan by Eisai. The Lin-chi sect rose to its highest point under Yang-chi (922–1049), in whose time, indeed, the kōan became a characteristic feature of the Lin-chi method. Their extended use began with the end of the T'ang. There was a tendency

*Lin-chi (Rinzai), by Soga Jasoku. From the Daruma Trip-
tych, late fifteenth century. Height 87 cm. Yōtoku-in Temple,
Kyoto.*

to look back on the acts of past masters and to use them as models. The number of kōan mounted to over fifteen hundred. Two principal collections have preserved them : the *Pi-yen-lu* (1125), containing a hundred kōan plus short explanatory strophes; and the *Wu-men-kuan* (1228) containing forty-eight kōan, collected by Hui-k'ai (1184–1260), concerning the Enlightenment of the Master Wu-men (J. Mumon). It should be pointed out that even in the Lin-chi sect, the kōan are not to be considered as an end but as "helpful means" to Enlightenment. As the Lin-chi teachings reproach the passivity of the Ts'ao-tung, so those of the Ts'ao-tung point to the danger of accepting the various means of the Lin-chi as ends in themselves. Further reproaching the Lin-chi for accentuating the sudden, momentary Enlightenment that such expedients as the kōan are meant to inspire, the Ts'ao-tung training endeavors to induce a partaking of the experience rather by the "whole personality."

EARLY ZEN IDEAS IN JAPAN

The introduction of Zen to Japan is generally attributed to Eisai, who in the twelfth century imported the Rinzai (Lin-chi) sect. However, Zen ideas were present in Japan much earlier. Dōshō (628–700), who had introduced the Hossō sect to Nara in the seventh century, had become aware of Zen ideas during his training with the Chinese master Hsüan-tsang. He was aware of the Bodhidharma tradition, and on his return to Japan he built a Zen hall in the Hossō temple at Nara. This was the first Zen temple, although under Hossō authority, to be constructed in Japan. In the eighth century (710), Tao-hsüan (J. Dōsen, 596–667), who incidentally belonged to the northern line of Shen-hsiu (*see* above, p. 210), was the first Chinese Zen monk to visit the Japanese islands. He maintained a close relationship with the Kegon and Ritsu sects. Tao-hsüan is said to have passed the rules of Zen meditation to Gyōhyō,

Takuan, the Zen master. Artist unknown; late sixteenth century.

who in turn instructed the famous Tendai master Saichō (767–822), thus explaining in part the Zen element in Tendai. In the middle of the ninth century, the wife of the emperor Saga (810–823), Tachibana Kachiko (787–851), received instruction from the Chinese master I-k'ung (c. 840), of the Rinzai sect. She later erected a temple for him, the Danrinji (Kyoto), where Zen was taught. I-k'ung, however, seems to have had little success, and he returned to China. Subsequently, for some three hundred years, although Zen practices found their way into other sects, especially the Tendai and Shingon, Zen evolved no further as an independent school.

EISAI

Only with Eisai (Zenkō kokushi, 1141–1215) did Zen become an independent sect. Coming from a family of Shintō priests in the district of Okayama, Eisai had spent his youth in Tendai Buddhism. In 1168, he undertook his first trip to China, where he visited the Zen centers on T'ien-t'ai. He was much impressed by what he saw and felt that in Zen discipline lay the salvation of Japanese Buddhism. On a second trip in 1187, he hoped to visit the sources of Buddhism in India, but his travel beyond the Chinese borders was opposed by continental officialdom, and he had to content himself with a sojourn in China. He studied at the Zen center of T'ien-t'ung-shan until 1191. Eisai's visit to China was at the time when Sung culture flourished at Hangchou, yet of all Buddhism he found only Zen teachings really prospering in eleventh-century China. Both Zen and the syncretic Confucianism of Chu Hsi were actually in vogue. Eisai received the "seal of Enlightenment" in the Huang-lung lineage (Rinzai) and returned to Japan, where he built the first Rinzai temple in 1191 at Hakata (Kyūshū), the Shōfukuji.

Eisai's concern with Zen teachings was opposed by Tendai circles who, claiming that he placed Zen above Tendai, sought to have the new sect outlawed. But Eisai enjoyed the protection of the shōgun, Minamoto Yoriie (1182–1204), who in 1202 awarded him the direction of the Kenninji (Kyoto). Eisai, like Nichiren, attached Zen to the national welfare, and in his tract, *The Spread of Zen for the Protection of the Land,* he went far in establishing Zen as a recognized sect. Eisai was forced, however, into continual compromise with Tendai and Shingon. The Kenninji was not a purely Zen institution; Eisai was obliged to maintain places also for Tendai and Shingon worship. Until his death, Eisai recited Shingon sūtras, and even today the Kenninji celebrates Tendai ceremonies. At the order of the shōgun, Eisai brought Zen to Kamakura, where he established the third Zen monastery, the Jūfukuji, and from that time dates the close relationship between Zen and the military caste.

If compromise characterizes Eisai's Zen, that of Dōgen (1200–1253), who introduced the Sōtō (Ts'ao-tung) sect, is typified by its intransigent and uncompromising attitude toward all that is not Zen.

DŌGEN

Dōgen belonged to an aristocratic family; his father was Kuga Michichika (d. 1202), a high functionary (i.e., *naidaijin*), and his mother a Fujiwara. His education was in keeping with his estate. He was early versed in Chinese poetry and classics, yet apparently with little influence on his later writings. By seven, he had lost both father and mother and had gone to live with an uncle at the foot of Mount Hiei. It is not surprising that he entered the Tendai sect in 1212, and he was ordained in the following year. For some time, Dōgen studied Tendai Buddhism on Mount Hiei, and it is here that his interest in the relation of Buddha-nature and Enlightenment awakened. During his period of work on Mount Hiei, Dōgen visited the well-known monk Kōin (1145–1216) at the Miidera.

Kōin had changed from Tendai to Amidism in his search for the Truth. He directed Dōgen to Eisai, who, having returned from China, was teaching a doctrine of direct approach to Enlightenment. A meeting between Dōgen and Eisai may have taken place around 1214.

Dōgen entered the Kenninji under Myōzen. In this temple, Zen was mixed with Tendai and Shingon, and Myōzen taught the so-called three religions of the Exoteric, Esoteric, and the spirit, that is, knowledge of the sūtras, Tantric rites, and Zen. Already on Mount Hiei Dōgen had learned the Esoteric practices, but here in the Kenninji, Zen (of the Rinzai type) was new to him. Dōgen, however, was not satisfied with what he was able to learn under Myōzen, and in 1223 he departed for China, hoping to supplement his knowledge.

One of the things that struck Dōgen profoundly was the stress which the Chinese Zen discipline laid upon daily work. Since Hung-jen (601–674) and Po-chang (749–814), Chinese Zen (Ch'an) had, along with zazen and sūtra reading, emphasized the importance of regulated daily life, with daily work as an integral part of the religious life. This was amply apparent to Dōgen at the Tien-t'ung monastery, where he participated in community life along with some five hundred other followers of Wu-chi. Despite his sincerity, however, Dōgen did not win the "seal of Enlightenment" which he sought. As a result, he set out on a life of wandering, acquainting himself with the various Chinese sects and their teachings. On his return to the Tien-t'ung-ssu, he learned of the death of Wu-chi. The temple had been taken over by Ju-ching (1163–1268), and in 1225 Dōgen became his disciple. Ju-ching was a severe master, given to liberal use of the punishing stick. Life under his rule was in contrast to the five years Dōgen had spent drifting from monastery to monastery, disappointed at the ease with which he was continually accepted in Zen communities. Finally, from the new head of the Tien-t'ung monastery, Dōgen received the seal of Enlightenment and the cloak of patriarch in the Ts'ao-tung sect.

In 1227, Dōgen returned to Japan, unlike so many of his predecessors without sūtras, without pictures or images, and established himself in the Kenninji. There he composed a short treatise on the practice of meditation, entitled *Fukanza-zengi, General Teaching for Zazen.* By 1230, he had moved on to the small temple of Anyōin at Fukakusa, which fast became a Zen center, visited by many pilgrims from nearby Kyoto. Dōgen taught the realising of one's Buddha-nature by means of practice and discipline, through zazen. His great work, the *Shōbōgenzō, Treasury of Knowledge of the True Law,* was a treatise on Zen practice and doctrines from the standpoint of his own Enlightenment. In 1233, Dōgen was given a large building, the Kannondōrin-in in the temple grounds of the Gokurakuji, and here he was joined by his most famous disciple, Ejō (1198–1280). These quarters were not large enough, and in 1236 he constructed a new temple, the Kōshōhōrinji, complete with Zen hall. The Kōshōhōrinji was the first purely Zen temple in Japan, and in it Dōgen reached the climax of his career. Later, in 1245, he founded the famous Eiheiji, "Temple of Enduring Peace," today the principal training center of the Sōtō sect. Unlike Eisai, Dōgen was uncompromising toward other sects and little disposed to associate his Zen with them as Eisai had done. His attitude earned him the hatred of the Tendai monks on Mount Hiei. As a result, in 1247–48, he was obliged to leave the capital for some time and go into "exile" on the domain of Hatano Yoshishige in Echizen, although he spent the winter in Kama-kura at the behest of the regent Hōjō Tokiyori (1226–1263). Dōgen returned to Echizen, but he interrupted his sojourn there for a final visit (1253) to Kyoto, where with his disciple Ejō he went for medical care and where in the same year he died. He was accorded the honorific titles of Buppō zenji in 1250 and Shōyō daishi in 1800.

Dōgen accepted the validity of both oral and scriptural transmission. He was, however, scrupulous to avoid the over-intellectual excesses characteristic of sects, such as the Tendai, which were based strongly on scriptures. "Stay on top of the *Lotus* (sūtra)," he said; "do not let it get on top of you." Drawn as he was to Hīnayāna sources, Dōgen was more interested in the broad truths of Buddhism than in the correctness of Zen. For him, however, the historical Buddha's method of attaining Enlightenment under the pīpal tree was the "proved" method, and from the beginning of his career in Japan he insisted on the efficacy of zazen. Dōgen opposed the Rinzai use of koan as a focus for concentration, for he felt that the sudden, intuitive enlightenment that the kōan were meant to achieve indicated a preoccupation with momentary experience. This was too self-assertive a method, stressing the attainment of a given state and overemphasising mental perception. Dōgen felt that the "whole man" should participate in the experience of Enlightenment. To this end he minimized the value of the kōan and stressed that of zazen—a discipline of meditation without thought of acquisition or attainment. Through zazen, one arrived at a gradual but lifelong rather than sudden awakening. The Rinzai naturally felt that such a practice was overly passive and led ultimately to emptiness, while the kōan was dynamic introspection. Dōgen's gradual approach to Enlightenment reflects a strongly Chinese ethical element and parallels the gradual advancement of the Chinese civil service. For Dōgen, Buddhahood is not a "sudden understanding" but a state constant throughout life, and so there must be no thought of achieving an "end." Rather, Buddhahood must be realized more and more deeply through constant awareness. Buddhahood grows with each effort; it does not spring, as the Rinzai stated, into sudden, complete being. Life is a work of art which must be experienced completely, and Zen is its flowering.

ZEN AND JAPANESE CULTURE

Zen perhaps more than any other sect has penetrated into and profoundly influenced the secular life of the Japanese. In painting, the *sumie* ink washes with their blank spaces suggest the inexpressible, which the lines delimit much as the kōan delimit a line of thought and lead to a realization of the truth lying beyond the unsaid. In poetry, the *haiku* traces a rapid word sketch that only suggests the ultimate poetic meaning, apprehensible through the awakened intuition of the reader. In aesthetics, Zen favors understatement over the ostentation characteristic of the Esoteric sects. Simplicity is the keynote, coupled with a deep appreciation of nature and of everyday life. Simplicity is also to be seen in the barrenness of the Nō stage and in the economy of the actor's gestures. These gestures were based in some measure on another Zen art, that of swordsmanship, a military pastime which under Zen became the "art of protecting life." Moreover, Zen is responsible for an approach to architecture and gardens that is predominant in modern Japan.

MUSŌ SOSEKI

One of the masters particularly responsible for the penetration of Zen ideals into Japanese life is Musō Soseki (1275–1351), more commonly known as Musō kokushi, "Musō the National Teacher." Musō at last found in Zen what he had long been searching for among the traditional doctrines. He was adviser to several rulers, notably to the emperor Daigo II (1319–1338), who tried to reassert imperial rule. At the suggestion of Musō, in 1325 the first official mission in five centuries was sent to China, to be followed by continued relations with the continent. He was also spiritual adviser to Ashikaga Takauji (1305–1358) and doubtless exercised a deep influence on him. Takauji built for his master the famous Tenryūji monastery, which sent the first commercial ship to China in 1339. Moreover, Musō did much to cement relations between Zen and the ruling class, a movement begun by Eisai.

ZEN AND TEA

Zen masters fostered the growth of the cult of tea. It should be noted, however, that this cult is not associated with Zen alone, for during the Tokugawa period the ceremony was thought to teach the neo-Confucian concept of *li*. Tea had originally been introduced by priests to Japan around 800, but its cultivation had not been continued. In 1191, Eisai, home from his second visit to China, had brought tea plants which he planted on a hillside near Kyoto. Later, Dōgen established a center of pottery production which turned out an improved quality of teacup. Impetus was given to the drinking of the new beverage by Eisai's *Kissa yōjo-ji, Drink Tea to Improve Health and Prolong Life,* a treatise which appeared in 1214 and originally aimed at tempering the alcoholism of the shōgun Minamoto no Sanetomo (1192–1219). A place in which the tea could appropriately be consumed was provided by Musō kokushi, who constructed a simple hut in his garden. Thus were at hand beverage, container, and setting. The tea hut itself, with its simplicity and its garden setting, was to become the model of domestic architecture.

The practice of tea drinking, as well as of frequenting the tea hut, became a formalized ritual presided over by Zen ideas, and it was meant to provide a Zen experience. The drinking of the beverage in surroundings intimately bound up with nature provided the means of perceiving the divine in the common.

*The Ryōanji garden, Kyoto. This fourteenth-century garden
replaces trees and grass by white sand and rocks symbolizing
the open sea.*

The tea hut[24] has three elements: its immediate surroundings, standing for evanescence; the garden, standing for the
selflessness of the dharmas; the interior, standing for nirvāna.
The outside of the hut, which is continually weathering, suggests that life is constant change. Near the entrance, to the
right, is a privy which is a reminder of the continual changes
taking place in the human body, while the arrival and departure of the guests through the gate to the hut signifies the
ceaseless movement inherent in life. Various aspects of the
garden stand for selflessness: the stepping-stones, willing to be
trodden upon; the basin, whose water willingly takes away impurities; in a corner, a stone lantern, whose wick consumes
itself so that there may be light. Within the tea room itself is
absolute peace. Rising incense charms by its odor but recalls

also the aspiration that man should feel toward the celestial. Outside, the dripping water and the wind in the branches again stress the transitoriness of all things. Within, in an alcove, are a painting and a flower arrangement, examples of form and color, which make the observer aware, by contrast, of the vacuum that surrounds him. The tea itself is served in simple, everyday utensils which indicate that religious experience is after all an ordinary thing; just as clay is transformed into the teacup, so man is transformed into a vessel capable of receiving Enlightenment and Buddahood.

Like Amidism, Zen aims to bring salvation into the ken of the common man. While Amidism stressed salvation through others, i.e., through the Buddha Amida, Zen emphasizes salvation within oneself. Every man has the Buddha-nature, and this nature is perceptible through a "realization of self." Hence Zen more than any other sect stresses the qualities of self-understanding and self-reliance as prerequisites for apprehending one's own nature.

NICHIREN

The final significant evolution of Buddhism in Japan came in the form of a singularly polemical sect which took its name from its founder, Nichiren.

NICHIREN'S LIFE

Nichiren (Risshō daishi, 1222–1282), son of a humble fisherman, was born in Kominato in the province of Awa. His original name was Zennichi-maru, but at eleven he was ordained under the religious name of Renchō. He was instructed in the Amidist nembutsu, but from the beginning he doubted the efficacy of this invocation. This doubt led to his decision to unify and expurgate the Buddhism of his day. He spent ten years at Mount Hiei, the great Tendai center, where

Nichiren. Edo period, eighteenth century. Lacquered wood.

he became convinced that true Buddhist teaching lay in the Tendai doctrine, not so much the one then preached, but Tendai as Saichō had propagated it. His desire to return to a pure Tendai caused him to leave Mount Hiei, which by this time had become largely Esotericized. In 1253, he returned to his former monastery at Kiyozumi. There he preached his new doctrine, that the salvation of the degenerate age lay in the *Lotus* sūtra. According to Nichiren, the *Lotus* taught essentially the oneness of the Three Bodies of the Buddha : transformation (*nirmānakāya*), bliss or enjoyment (*sambhogakāya*), and law (*dharmakāya*). The various Buddhist schools of Nichiren's day had stressed one or another aspect of this threefold body to the detriment of others : the Esoteric sects, which stressed the Law or universal body in the form of Vairochana; the Amidists, the bliss body of Amida; Zen and Ritsu, the transformation body (i.e., the historical Buddha), leaving aside the eternal and universal aspects. The truth for Nichiren lay in a return to the full threefold body as set forth in the *Lotus*. Rather than calling on the name of a single Buddha, say Amida, one should call on that of the *Lotus*. He proclaimed a kind of nembutsu of his own: *namu myōhō renge-kyō*, "reverence to the wonderful Law of the *Lotus*," an invocation that is the slogan even today of the Nichiren sect. Besides faith in the *Lotus*, Nichiren preached the importance of one's own efforts and of the Bodhisattva ideal of perseverance and sacrifice.

NICHIREN'S DIVISION OF BUDDHISM

At his monastery in Iwamoto, he wrote his famous *Risshō ankoku-ron, Treatise on Establishing Right and the Peace of the Country,* reaffirming Saichō's belief in the relation between religion and national welfare. Nichiren presented this treatise to the Hōjō regent in 1260. The principle of the close connection of religion and nation was not unknown in Fujiwara times, but it had not then been considered a principle. Nichiren showed the intolerance that characterized both his writings and his activities as a propagandist. For example, he did not consider the killing of heretics as murder; indeed, it is the duty of the government to see that they are put to death. Hōnen especially is censured. Even more than the Chinese monk Zendō, whom he imitated, he is the enemy of all the Buddhas. Nichiren divides Buddhist history into three terms: the *shōbō*, or True Law (Hīnayāna), which lasts a thousand years from the time of the Buddha's death (reckoned according to Chinese fashion as 947 B.C.); the *zōbō*, or Image Law (Mahāyāna); and *mappō*, or End of the Law. Each period lasts roughly a thousand years, the last, according to Nichiren's estimate, beginning around 1050 A.D. It is through the belief in the *Lotus* that salvation is to be attained in this end period of the Law.

NICHIREN AS BODHISATTVA

Nichiren was drawn particularly to passages in the *Lotus* concerning the saints. Most particularly he identified himself with Vishishtachārita (J. Jōgyō), the Bodhisattva of Superb Action, who had preached the Law after Shākyamuni's death and devoted himself to the spreading of Buddhism. This Bodhisattva, who appears in the *Lotus,* suddenly rose from the earth at the conclusion of one of the Buddha's sermons. Supposedly in ages past a convert of the Buddha, he was believed to come back into the world in its days of degeneration to work for its salvation. Nichiren also admired, for the obvious analogy it offered to his own life, the career of the Bodhisattva Sadāparibhūta (J. Jōfukyō), the "Ever-Abused," who was insulted and reviled because he addressed people as "Bodhisattva," believing that each person had the Buddha-nature within him and would ultimately be saved. Moreover, Nichiren, probably having forewarning of Mongol intentions toward Japan through his connections with Chinese priests, cautioned against foreign invasion. Indeed, according to him, this invasion would take place precisely because of the false religious views held by the Japanese at that time. Political and spiritual salvation lay in the rectification of such views, and he considered Japan to be the country where the revival of true faith would take place. He took the name of Nichiren, "sun-lotus": *nichi* standing not only for the sunlight of true faith but for Japan itself; *ren,* for the *Lotus.*

EXILE

At about thirty, he publicly proclaimed his religion and attacked all other forms of Buddhism. So violent were his polemics and so inflaming his attitude—he even attacked the government—that he was several times mobbed, and at last he was obliged to flee Kamakura. He later returned and continued his attacks, as a result of which, in 1261, he was banished by the government to the peninsula of Izu. During this exile, Nichiren devoted himself to an intensive study of the *Lotus* sūtra, finding therein a description of the antagonism and persecution of the future (i.e., the present) evil age, and coming to see himself alone as the divinely designated teacher of that age. Nichiren was released from Izu in 1263. He immediately resumed his quarrel with the other sects, concentrating on the Amidists. As a result of these attacks he was sentenced to death, the execution to be carried out on the island of Sado in 1271. The facts of this event in his life are uncertain, but the story of his miraculous stay of execution is told and retold by the followers of his sect.

KAIMOKUSHŌ

Nichiren spent three years on Sado (1271–1274), during which time he became convinced that he was the manifestation of the Bodhisattva Jōgyō (Vishishtachārita), chief of the hosts of Bodhisattvas in the *Lotus* who are said by Shākyamuni to have brought him to maturity and whose task is the dissemination of the *Lotus*. In 1272, Nichiren wrote his famous *Kaimokushō, The Eye Opener*. In this work he set forth his so-called three vows: that is, that he would be (1) the pillar of Japan, (2) the eyes of Japan, and (3) the great vessel of Japan—by which he doubtless meant the container of the religious truth that was to revivify the country. In 1274, he was released and recalled to Kamakura, where he settled with a few disciples at Minobu (on the west side of Mount Fuji). It was on the eve of the Mongol invasion, which he had predicted. The final years of Nichiren's life were spent in a continual struggle for the union of Japan and for his sect, until in the end he retired to his hermitage at Ikegami. He died there in 1282, reciting stanzas from the *Lotus*. In 1922, he was given the honorific title of Risshō daishi.

NICHIRENISM AND GOVERNMENT

Nichiren in his attitude resembles the rough, bold warrior type that characterized this age of early feudalism in Japan. He reacted especially against what he felt to be the flaccidity of Amidist doctrine, with its emphasis on salvation through divine help. The period was one of turbulence and warfare, dominated by a militaristic society. Interest turned on the one hand to Zen, stressing direct experience, and on the other to Nichirenism, stressing the crusading spirit. It was natural for feudal warriors to associate religion with government. Nichiren felt that both subjects and rulers should conform to his ideas, and he preached a state welfare dependent on a religious outlook corrected according to his ideas. It is hard indeed not to see here a parallel to Savonarola, who in his diatribes against the easy-living Florentines of the fifteenth century thundered: "Any who fight against this government fight against Christ!" Indeed, Nichiren's writing frequently bore on this relationship of state and religion: *A Treatise on the Protection of the State* (*Shugo kokka-ron*); *A Memorial on the Remedy for Calamities* (*Sainan taiji*); *Establishment of Righteousness and the Safety of the Country* (*Risshō ankoku-ron*). Of course, these writings were devoted to exposing the errors of other sects, especially the Amidist and Zen, and later the Shingon and Ritsu. In fact, adverse criticism of these four branches became an integral part of Nichirenism.

NICHIREN AND TENDAI

In substance, Nichirenism is little more than a variation of

Tendai teaching, that is, the type of Tendai which Nichiren imagined it to have been under Saichō.

Nichiren's religion was national, a fact that has no parallel in other Buddhist countries. Moreover, it is a religion which depends on one "book." In this, parallels are to be seen with both Christianity and Islam, in contrast to other Buddhist sects which depended on a voluminous canon. This text was the Chinese translation of the *Lotus, Saddharmapundarīkasūtra* (*J. Hokkekyō*), to which the *Muryōgikyō* (T. 276) and the *Fugengyō* (T. 277) are respectively accepted as the introduction and the conclusion.

Nichiren follows the Tendai theory of the Five Periods (*see* Tendai, above), accepting the three classes—Auditors (*shrāvakas*), or simple hearers; pratyeka-Buddhas, or Buddhas who gain enlightenment for themselves (these two classes form the Hīnayāna); and bodhisattvas (Mahāyāna). Actually, in the *Lotus* the Buddha declares himself to be the saving Buddha, hence the above three are really but three aspects of a single unity, that is, the historical Buddha. The Buddha does not really live and die. He is eternal. Hence, since the Buddha-nature is innate in everyone, all, being him, are eternal too. For Nichiren, other systems than his own presented aspects of the truth, half-truths, as it were, that themselves are a blindness typical of the period. In *The Eye Opener* (*Kaimokushō*) Nichiren claims that until men's eyes are wide open they cannot see the whole truth. This state of blindness corresponds to the period called mappō (End of the Law), according to the *Lotus* (chap. XIII), where it is described as "the last five hundred years when the true Law shall be in a state of decay." In fact, the career of Buddhism was contained in the three periods mentioned above, of which mappō is the last, a time to be illuminated by the doctrine of the *Lotus*.

THE FIVE PRINCIPLES

During his stay in Izu (c. 1261), Nichiren formulated the five principal bases of his teaching : (1) The *Lotus* is the perfect scripture which provides in this degenerate (mappō) age the basis for (2) a simple creed. Moreover, (3) this mappō period was the time to proclaim the doctrine, and (4) Japan was the country where it should be taught and from whence it would spread. Finally, (5) all other systems, having done their work, should yield to the *Lotus*. To these five fundamental ideas corresponded Five Principles : sūtra, method, time, country, and sequence of dissemination. Nichiren felt himself to be the instrument for the realization of the foregoing, and as such he considered that he should become the leader of the nation. Nichiren was deeply convinced of this right to leadership. The crystallization of these ideas took definite form during his stay on the isle of Sado. There he formulated the three great secret laws : *honzon, daimoku,* and *kaidan.* The honzon, "original object of worship," referred to the historical Buddha. For the Nichiren sect, the original Buddha is not a nameless entity but the historical Shākyamuni himself, active and benevolent. Because we partake of his nature, we ourselves are him. To represent this idea, Nichiren devised a mandala, in the middle of which was vertically inscribed the invocation *namu myōhō renge-kyō* ("reverence to the wonderful Law of the Lotus"). On the four sides are the names of the four cardinal directions and to the right and left the names of Shākyamuni and Tahō (Prabhūtaratna), the mysterious "extinct" Buddha who appears in the twenty-first chapter of the *Lotus.* The whole mandala represents the universal powers of the Buddha as all-pervading truth. Daimoku, "title," refers to *myōhō renge-kyō,* the title of the *Lotus* sūtra. Although Nichiren hated the nembutsu of the Amidists, his own invocation, which possesses a similar virtue, begins with the Amidist *"namu"* ("honor to . . ."). For Nichiren *renge,* "Lotus," represented the eternal law of causality. This law, being universally true, is a "wonderful Law" (*myōhō*). The daimoku hence stands for the wonderful truth expounded in the *Lotus* sūtra. Kaidan, "ordination altar," stands for the observance of the moral law which *is* the daimoku; the place we receive it (kaidan) is our bodies.

NICHIREN'S SUCCESSORS

Nichiren had three chief successors. The first, Nichiji (1250–?), devoted himself to missionary work. He labored tirelessly among the Ainu in Hokkaidō. He is said to have gone at the end of his life to Siberia, and he was never heard from again. Nichiji accompanied Nichiren into exile at Sado and, being a master of prose, wrote for the Teacher in his old age. Nisshin (1407–1488) carried the Nichiren doctrine to Kyūshū. Later, returning to Kyoto, he became a "street-corner evangelist," calling out the name of the *Lotus.* He summoned the shōgun to suppress all other sects with such vehemence that he was ultimately jailed. Despite torture, he refused to be silent. Overwrought officials jammed a pot over his head with the hope of inducing some moderation of his ideas. He was subsequently known as *nabekaburi,* the "pot wearer." Nichiō (1565–1630) was the leader of the sect known as Fuju-fuse, "accept nothing, give nothing." The slogan referred precisely to nonbelievers and was an admonition to members neither to receive from nor to give to persons not of the Nichiren persuasion. The sect was stubbornly uncompromising in its attitudes toward other schools of Buddhism. Nichiō himself refused the invitations of both Hideyoshi (1536–1598) and later Ieyasu (1542–1616) to appear before them, on the grounds that they were not of the Nichiren sect. As a result of Nichiō's intransigence, Ieyasu banished him for more than ten years, and the Fuju-fuse sect was the object of Tokugawa persecution. It survived, however, and exists today, although not in great numbers.

Post-Nichiren Period
(1300-1600)

THE ASHIKAGA FAMILY ASSUMED the shōgunal power in 1336. Ashikaga Takauji (1305–1358) turned against the emperor Daigo II (1319–1338), who fled Kyoto to Yoshino, in the south. There he established his court, which lasted, in name at least, until 1392 : it was known as the Southern Court. In Kyoto, meanwhile, Takauji set up the emperor Kōmyō (r. 1336–1348, d. 1380). This schism, which lasted until 1392, is known as the Namboku-chō, the period of the Northern and Southern Courts (the Southern Court representing the legitimate dynasty). The time from 1392 to 1568 is called the Muromachi period, after the name of the neighborhood in Kyoto where the Ashikaga lived.

The Ashikaga period was one of great disturbance and at the same time of remarkable artistic production. In a period when war and rebellion were the order of the day, land and wealth were for those who could hold them. Hence it is from this time that the rise of masculine prerogative dates and, in contrast to Fujiwara times, the subordination of women.

SHINSHŪ

Following Nichiren and his reworking of Tendai ideas into a new sect, there was little new religious development in Kyoto and no new sect. Throughout the frequent political upheavals, Hieizan and the other great monasteries suffered in varying degrees. The Zen sect, through its ties with those ruling, came out best. The Shinshū also flourished, and the establishment of a married clergy by Shinran served to bring the priesthood increasingly into touch with secular life. The interesting institution of hereditary abbots arose within this sect, and the Shinshū became a kind of feudal order, erecting fortified temples and protecting its possessions with a truly secular spirit. In 1272, the daughter and the grandson of Shinran erected the Honganji (Temple of the Original Vow) in Kyoto, and Kameyama (r. 1260–1274) accorded it the status of imperial chapel. Its abbacy continued to be held by the direct descendants of Shinran.

Jōdo Sect

The Jōdo-shū was less prominent than either of the foregoing sects, although its leaders worked assiduously to consolidate what gains had been made both in the number of adherents and in worldly possessions. It was never completely suppressed, but it suffered a number of minor persecutions, and Jōdo temples were not infrequently burned. The Hieizan priests, for example, attempted to destroy all Jōdo books; and Shiren (1278–1346), a Zen priest, in his *Biographical History of Buddhism,* called it a "hanger-on sect, because it had no independent domicile."[25] Sansom states the Jōdo situation very nicely. At the death of Hōnen, he says, "Jōdo did not yet really exist as a sect partly because of the persecution which it underwent, partly because of the growth of competitive religious movements, and finally because it was, so to speak, parasitic, and could be practised consistently with other doctrines. This last feature was in fact a source of strength, for it was able to secure adherents without detaching them from other sects, until in the early 17th century it was organized as an independent body."[26] Despite this state of affairs, the Jōdo sect was the only one to produce any innovations at all. The seventh patriarch, Ryōyo Shōgei (1341–1420), taught that in the Jōdo sense rebirth in the Pure Land does not mean rebirth in another land. "Rebirth" is a metaphor for the transformation of the psychic processes of the individual within himself, because the Pure Land is everywhere, if one is only able to apprehend it. It is a condition of the mind, attainable through faith in Amida.

ZEN

Under the Kamakura regents (1200–1333) there had been two centuries of peace; under the Ashikaga shōguns (1336–1568) the political picture was one of constant dissension. Yoshimitsu (1358–1408), the third shōgun, was a fervent Zenist. At the age of thirty-six, he retired to the Golden Pavilion (Kinkakuji), in the manner of the emperors, and from there continued to rule his government. Zen priests active in commercial activities with China imported the Sung black and white techniques in painting, while literary activity was mainly in the hands of ecclesiastics, and Chinese learning flourished in the five Zen monasteries (*gozan*: Enkakuji, Kenchōji, and Jūfukuji in Kamakura and Kenninji and Tōfukuji in Kyoto). By 1336, there were Ten Great Monasteries, five in Kamakura and five in Kyoto, headed by the Nanzenji (Kyoto). Being closely allied to the rulers, Zen priests exerted influence on politics, as well as on the arts. Zen monks were used as government clerks, for their knowledge of Chinese was invaluable in the shipping and other commercial enterprises of the Ashikaga. In 1342, Takauji sent Musō kokushi to China on the ship "Tenryūji," named after the temple with which it was associated. This inaugural venture was an unqualified success, so much so that trading ships to China became known by the generic name of *tenryūji-bune*, "tenryūji ships." By 1452, there was a fleet of ten such vessels managed by Zen monks. Besides their commercial cargoes, these ships brought untold cultural wealth to Japan.

The sixteenth century brought a period of political unrest. Mount Hiei and other great monasteries were in financial straits, while Zen fortunes waxed. Soseki (Musō kokushi) urged that a Zen temple (*ankokuji*) be built in each province, and Zen became virtually a state religion. This does not mean that other sects received no consideration. The shōguns extended their help, in some cases by relieving taxes, in others allocating transit dues to particular temples. The Kōfukuji, for example, received the customs income from the port of Hyōgo (Kobe).

RENNYO : FRANTIC UPRISINGS

The Buddhism of this period is strongly marked by the personalities of certain ardent priests, of which there were various types. The warrior monks of Mount Hiei were under arms on several occasions (1435, 1499), though they were ultimately suppressed. There was a kind of free-lance priest known as *komusō*, who, somewhat like the warrior monk of Mount Hiei, carried a sword and showed a tendency toward dispute. More frequent, however, was the itinerant priest, who, traveling throughout the provinces, did much toward spreading the religion among the common classes. Such a one was the well-known Ikkyū (1394–1481), an eccentric wanderer, belonging to the Daitokuji at Kyoto, about whom the anecdotes are legion.

Another was Rennyo shōnin (1415–1499), the eighth abbot of the Honganji, who is called the second founder of the Shinshū and who enjoyed the favor of the emperor Hanazono II (r. 1429–1465). His prestige so excited the jealousy of the Mount Hiei monks that they burned the Honganji in 1465. By 1471, he had settled in Echizen, where he began to write his famous *O-fumi* (*Letters*). He continued his wandering life, however, and his preaching greatly strengthened the Shinshū in the provinces. Rennyo became something more than a missionary, in fact, and to him no little political power accrued. By the turn of the century, the priests of the Shin sect had gained substantial power, enough at least to wage war with certain lords (*daimyō*), whose estates they seized. In 1576, they were finally suppressed by Nobunaga (1534–1582). These outbreaks were known collectively as the *Ikkō no ran,* the "Ikkō Rebellion." The name of the sect, Ikkō, as applied to Rennyo's Amidism, means "one direction" or "single minded," referring to the devotion to Amida expected of the adherents. Rennyo's frequent phrase was *ikkō isshin,* "one direction, one heart." The uprisings of the Ikkō sect are also known as *Ikkō ikki,* "Frantic Uprisings."

Rennyō's *O-fumi,* still venerated today by the Shin sect, were posthumously arranged in five parts. They place great stress on moral obligations, good citizenship, and the idea that simple belief in Amida's power is not in itself sufficient but must be supplemented by positive unselfishness. In the *O-fumi,* there is thus a discernible ethical current not notable in Shinran. Moreover, Dual Shintō concepts are manifest, for the native gods are accepted as Buddhas; and, since all the Buddhas are, in the last analysis, Amida, the worship of this divinity was encompassed in the worship of the national divinities as well. Nevertheless, Amida is the only Buddha or deity whose image is permitted on Shin altars.

SHINZEI

An extension of the Amidist nembutsu was introduced by Shinzei (1443–1495), who founded a new sect bearing his name. It is a subdivision of Tendai, for it holds that repetition of the nembutsu should be combined with ordinary Buddhist practices and that belief in Amida and meditation on him, coupled with the invocation of his name, assured the observance of the Esoteric mysteries of body, speech, and mind. Shinzei had begun studying on Mount Hiei at the age of thirteen. Seven years later he had a vision, in which he was presented with an Amidist treatise. Thereafter he was devoted to Amida, but within the framework of Mahāyāna Tendai precepts. The fundamental text is Genshin's *Ōjōyōshū*. The sect bearing his name was founded only after his death. Independent until 1872, it then merged with Tendai. Today it has again become independent, though associated.

In the early 1540's, three Portuguese, who had taken passage on a Chinese junk, were driven by a typhoon to Japan. They landed on the island of Tanegashima off the coast of Ōsumi. Their arrival marked the discovery of Japan by Europe. Soon traders followed, and Jesuit priests from Macao and Goa. In 1549, Francis Xavier landed at Kagoshima, and with two companion priests began to preach. "It says a great deal for the tolerance of the Japanese that a stranger, preaching a strange doctrine, was not molested but was even encouraged by all classes, including a number of Buddhist priests who listened respectfully to such expositions of the Catholic faith as the Portuguese were able to give."[27]

The early success of the Jesuit teachings was striking. This was due in part to the fact that the converts considered Christianity a form of Buddhism, a confusion rendered all the more acute by the use of Buddhist and Shintō terms to apply to Christian concepts. Christianity, of course, accompanied trade, and in order to gain this latter some barons went so far as to encourage mass conversions and to persecute Buddhism in their domains. The expected commercial contacts were not always forthcoming, however, and reversion to Buddhism quickly followed. "They were not always without justification for this sudden change of mind, for the Jesuits did not study the feelings of others, and their zeal easily took the form of an aggressive bigotry, though it must be granted that they displayed a splendid courage which undoubtedly gained them the respect of the military class. Xavier himself was in 1550 ordered to leave Satsuma, then a home of devout Buddhism, largely because his intolerance at length offended the Buddhist monks; and in Yamaguchi, the capital of the Ōuchi domains, he made the bad mistake of insisting that all the dead who had not been Christians during their lifetime would burn for ever. To a people who had never believed seriously in the flames of hell, and who paid to the memory of their ancestors a most reverent devotion, this was revolting doctrine; and it is not surprising that his disputations caused an uproar in a city where many learned monks resided, and that Christianity was proscribed in the Ōuchi domains." [28]

The end of the fifteenth century and the beginning of the sixteenth was a period of confusion. Nobunaga (1532–1582), for political motives, favored Christianity over Buddhism. He feared (doubtless justly) the considerable clerical power of Buddhism, and he strove to check it. Hideyoshi (1536–1598) at first felt the same way but was later to turn against Christianity, fearing that the rise of Christian power would mean corresponding political encroachment by foreign nations. It was Ieyasu finally who suppressed the early Christian movement in Japan.

TEMPORAL FALL OF BUDDHISM

In the late sixteenth century, Buddhism had, surprisingly enough, become an important political and military force. The great monasteries were often comparable to the great baronies, both in possessions and in ambitions. Their policies, however, were to be the cause of their ultimate downfall. Mount Hiei, said to have had some three thousand monasteries under its aegis, made the fatal mistake of joining the enemies of Nobunaga, with the result that the sect was almost annihilated. Although it was rebuilt by Ieyasu, it never regained its old power. It was for Hideyoshi to castigate Shingon. Kakuban's branch of the Esoteric sect in Kii, founded like Mount Hiei in 1130, had waxed more and more powerful; it is said to have had over two thousand temples and multitudes of warrior monks. In 1561–62, Kii resisted the shōgun's forces with notable success, and in 1584 a great army of Kii monks from Negoro, said to number fifteen thousand, marched against Osaka. The adventure was to prove their undoing, for they were defeated, and the next year the order was reduced almost to extinction by Hideyoshi. He threatened, but ultimately spared, the great Shingon center at Mount Kōya.

The Nichiren sect, displaced from Yamashina near Kyoto in 1532, grew gradually but steadily stronger in the provinces. The Nichiren had had a fortified temple at Kanazawa in 1475 and, in 1532, built a great castle at Osaka from which its priests defied Nobunaga for about ten years, and although they ultimately surrendered the fortress, the Nichiren were never really beaten.

The latter part of the sixteenth century, then, was a period during which the Buddhist church held great temporal sway and on more than one occasion vied with the government. It was a period in which Buddhism was continually in ferment, as much in secular as in religious areas. Ultimately it was this period that saw the final breaking of the temporal power of Buddhism at the hands of Nobunaga, Hideyoshi, and Ieyasu, in compliance with the centralized government in Edo (modern Tokyo).

Tokugawa Period
(1600-1868)

IN 1600, THE GREAT BATTLE OF SEKIGAHARA was fought. After this date, Japan was ruled by the Tokugawa family for almost three centuries. It is a period of stability, in contrast to the almost continual disturbances that marked the decline of Ashikaga power in the sixteenth century. The Tokugawa were, of course, interested in maintaining the status quo. This they did by carefully limiting the power of the daimyō, "feudal lords." In the seventeenth century they moved the capital of their shōgunate to Edo, a small swamp town—hence this period is also known as the Edo period—far away from the demoralizing court influence of Kyoto, where the imperial family reigned under Tokugawa sponsorship, though it was entirely divested of its power and existed only for its ceremonial function.

Edo

Edo grew with amazing rapidity. By the early nineteenth century, it was among the largest cities in the world (the name Tokyo was adopted in 1868, when it became the Imperial capital). Its culture was dominated by the merchant class (*chōnin*), in whose hands wealth became more and more concentrated. Life in Edo was lusty and animated. Although the merchants as a class were traditionally looked down upon, they were ultimately powerful enough to impose their authority.

Theaters, both kabuki and puppet, sprang up in both Edo and Osaka, and the "gay quarters" provided *divertissement* for townsmen and samurai alike. The high point of this urban culture was reached in the Genroku era. (Actually, Genroku is the name of the period 1688–1703, but this designation is much more widely used to indicate that cultural phase which was at its apogee at the turn of the century.)

TOKUGAWA BUDDHISM

The almost total seclusion of the Japanese nation that marks the political aspect of the Tokugawa period was both salutary and detrimental for Buddhism. After the confusion and warfare of the later sixteenth century, the long era of peace initiated by Ieyasu's victory provided an excellent opportunity for the Buddhist church to re-establish itself, repair the damage to its temples, and devote itself more fully to its adherents. All monasteries were now under Tokugawa rule; their area of activity, like that of society in general, was strictly prescribed. However, the long period of uneventful existence, of status quo, the absence of new ideas or challenges from abroad, were ultimately to sap the vitality of Buddhist institutions until, by the end of the Tokugawa period, their condition can at best be called apathetic.

JŌDO

The Tokugawas were of the Jōdo sect, and Ieyasu was said to have practiced the nembutsu. The Jōdo was hence officially recognized as a sect from the time of Ieyasu, and during the Tokugawa era its fortunes rose. Great numbers of Jōdo temples were built, the head being at the Chion-in in Kyoto. It is doubtless unjust to say that the Tokugawa faith was opportunistic, but it cannot be denied that both Ieyasu and his second successor, Iemitsu (r. 1622–1651), used Buddhism to further their governmental policy. The abbots of the great Edo monasteries were frequently relatives of the emperor, and, since they were under the surveillance of the shōgunal authorities, they were kept from marrying and founding new and possibly inimical houses. In fact, they were virtually hostages until, under Ienobu (1709–1712), the rule was relaxed. Furthermore, the establishment was kept busy building new temples, the construction of which served to keep the coffers in an appropriate state of depletion.

Ieyasu also saw to it that the strength of the Shinshū was divided. In 1591, the great temple, the western Honganji, had been rebuilt, and Ieyasu promoted the building of another, the eastern Honganji, thus dividing the financial and administrative functions that had originally been under a single roof.

ORDINANCES

Tokugawa Buddhism was "set" in a code known as *Various Ordinances Regarding Sects and Temples* which appeared in parts from 1610 to 1615. Actually the code was a collection of generalizations based on decisions in individual cases brought before the government. These decisions embody a number of principles, the most important of which are the following. The power of the main temples was strengthened through a closer control exerted over their dependent temples. This measure also facilitated government sway over all temples concerned. Learning was encouraged, a policy deriving doubtless from Ieyasu's love of scholarship and serving to promote both cultural and social stability. It also served, typically, to keep the priests busy with religious affairs and out of politics. Moreover, the measure assured a certain amount of government control over the clergy, since appointments and promotions were often contingent on the duration of the periods of study engaged in. Finally, the government assumed authority over those temples directly connected with the court. All these measures served the obvious purpose of subordinating the entire Buddhist organization to the shōgunal authority.

IEMITSU

The third Tokugawa shōgun, Iemitsu (1603–1651), was a champion of Buddhism. He proscribed Christianity and did much to advance the building of temples, but he also encouraged Confucianism and the Nichiren branch known as the Fuju-fuse ("neither taking nor giving"), which had been founded by Nichiō in 1595. Suspended in 1624, the sect was re-established in 1868. The fifth shōgun, Tsunayoshi (r. 1680–1709), was an even more fanatical Buddhist. One instance of the extremity to which he carried his faith was the lavish ceremonies designed to provide him with a male heir. They were in vain, it may be observed, for the ostensible reason that he had been guilty of bloodshed during a previous existence. In order to expiate these deeds, he performed extreme acts of kindness. Since he had been born (according to the Chinese system) in the year of the dog, he considered it a personal obligation to protect this animal. He was known as the Dog Shōgun.

BUDDHISM AND SOCIETY

The *Various Ordinances* referred to above, which was also anti-Christian in aim, established the position of Buddhism for the next two and a half centuries. It identified Shintō with Buddhism and gave approval to the Chinese yin and yang concept, as well as to the *Dainichikyō*. Believers were exhorted to attend the Buddhist temple of their home region, regardless of its sect. The temple, for its part, was to keep a register of its members and to issue certificates of adherence. Certain days were set for obligatory attendance. This decree established the Buddhist church in a relation with its members and with the government, for any failure to observe organized church meant a civil misdemeanor. The result was that Buddhism, while it enjoyed an official patronage of sorts, found itself the tool of the government. Such a situation acted as a preservative but scarcely as a stimulant of religious life, and it encouraged the torpor increasingly apparent in religious circles. Buddhism was indeed the "established church"; yet, while used by the government and enjoying the prosperity of the times, it should not be considered a political entity.

HAKUIN

The growing stultification afflicted most sects, with the notable exception of Zen. Hakuin (1685–1768), known as the second founder of the Rinzai Zen sect and after Dōgen perhaps the best known Zen master, is the subject of many anecdotes. He probably represents the strongest religious element in the Tokugawa period. Born in the village of Hara (Suruga), he was the youngest of five children in a family belonging to the Nichiren sect. He was early impressed by the *Lotus* sūtra and the magical powers of the formulas, though he ultimately found them of little value. At fifteen he studied at the Zen temple of his village, where he received the name of Ekaku. Subsequently, he spent many years wandering from place to place, finally establishing himself in the Myōshinji, where he received the name of Hakuin and where great numbers of disciples flocked. Besides commenting on numerous sūtras, Hakuin was a painter and a poet, but most of all he was a tireless worker among the people. He organized and revivified kōan Zen. He was interested in the mystic aspect of Zen, but he was particularly devoted to making his kind of Buddhism

Hakuin's portrait, by one of his disciples, with an inscription by Hakuin. Early eighteenth century.

understandable to the common man.

One of the popular anecdotes told about him concerns his complete Enlightenment. "One day when begging, according to custom, in the village he stopped in front of the house of an old woman who refused to give him any rice. Hakuin, however, being immersed in meditation, remained immobile while the old woman continued sweeping the front of the house. Irritated at his apparent importunity she at last gave him a severe blow with her broom, which knocked him down, the sort of treatment to which he must have been accustomed by now. But this time it had a magical effect. He picked himself up fully enlightened as to the whole truth of Zen, and his first act was to run to the house of his old master to whom he now felt most grateful. Shōju saw him coming and called out 'What is the good news that you are bringing? Come in quick.' When he heard the story he said, 'There, you have it now,' patted him on the back and treated him with the utmost affection ever afterwards." [29]

Present-day Rinzai Zen has divided into two currents: Inzan, named from its founder Inzan Ien (1754–1817), and Takujū, also named from its founder Takujū Kosen (1760–1833). Both trace their lineage back to Hakuin. Inzan was keen and vigorous, Takujū quiet and punctilious. Their respective approaches emphasize the dynamic kōan and its detailed handling.

ŌBAKU SECT

Actually the only new sect to be introduced during this period was a Zen sect known as the Ōbaku (Ch. Hwang-po) branch, introduced by the Chinese priest Yin-yüan (J. Ingen, 1592–1673). Ingen arrived in Japan in 1654 with a retinue of some twenty followers, about half of whom subsequently returned to their homeland. Given land at Uji, to the south-

west of Kyoto, Ingen erected the Mampukuji, recalling the
Chinese style of the Ming period (1368–1644). Soon after
Ingen came another Chinese priest, Mu-an (J. Mokuan, d.
1684), who received the seal of the sect from Ingen. Both he
and, after him, Tetsugen (1630–32) did much to spread the
sect. The architecture and the appointments of the sect are
Chinese in appearance, as are the vestments. In practice, however, Ōbaku has much in common with the Rinzai branch.
Both zazen and the kōan are considered the best approaches
to *satori*, "Enlightenment," but the nembutsu, or invocation
of the name of Amida, is also esteemed. Amida is honored,
not indeed as a transcendental Buddha but as the Buddha-
spirit in daily life. The Pure Land lies in one's heart only. The
Ōbaku believes in the "unity of scriptures and Zen" (*kyōzen
itchi*), and the *Sūtras* have their place in the transmission of
Zen teachings. Reflecting the Chinese nature of the sect, the
Sūtras are read in the Ming pronunciation of the characters,
and Chinese musical instruments accompany the ceremonies.
Mealtime etiquette is Chinese, and the monks use a common
bowl from which they remove their portions with individual
chopsticks. The Ōbaku sect tended to be favored in high
places, for it fitted in with Tokugawa respect for Chinese
studies, but on the whole the introduction of the Ōbaku
branch remains a mere incident in the history of Zen, and the
Manpukuji and its dependent temples represent a kind of
Chinese enclave in Japan.

CONFUCIANISM AND SHINTŌ

From the seventeenth century on, both Confucianism and
Shintō rise in importance, rather to the detriment of Buddhism. Even the fanatical Dog Shōgun (Tsunayoshi) was a
great admirer of Confucius, and at his request lectures on

Confucian subjects were given at the shōgunal court. While Confucianism enjoyed official patronage, however, it never usurped Buddhism in the purely religious field, for it never became a religion in the sense that Buddhism was. Interest in Shintō (to be declared the state religion in 1868) began to grow under the direction of the Mito branch of the Tokugawas. Mitsukuni (1628–1700) compiled a *History of Japan* (*Dainihon-shi*), which was published in the early eighteenth century and, while not anti-Confucian, showed a definite preference for whatever was Japanese. In order to demonstrate his views, Mitsukuni ordered a thousand Buddhist temples destroyed on his estates. The Shintō movement spread in the eighteenth and nineteenth centuries and concurrently assumed an increasingly political character. Scholars were urged to turn to the study of things Japanese, and such men as Kamo Mabuchi (1697–1769) and Motoori Norinaga (1730–1801) are famous for their researches in Japanese studies. Motoori undertook an investigation of the *Kojiki* (712), which contained the first written account of Japanese myths. In his Commentary, he stressed the Japanese elements that hitherto had been neglected through the reverenceing of everything Chinese. Motoori advocated a "pure" Shintō—that is, the native beliefs free from Buddhist or Confucian elements. From his time on, scholarly opinion tended against Buddhism.

Meiji Period
(1868-1912)

DURING THE EIGHTEENTH AND NINETEENTH CENTURIES, Buddhist scholarship continued, though, unlike Confucianism and Shintō, no champion arose to defend the faith; and although, with its governmental support, Buddhism remained unperturbed, it was neither a vigorous nor a strong religion during this period. Indeed, at the beginning of the Meiji era, Buddhism was at its weakest. The years of stultification under Tokugawa control had terminated in the identification of the religion with the shōgunal power. When that power passed from the scene, Buddhism—so it was considered—passed with it. Such, at least, was the attitude of the government; on the popular level the religion went on more or less undisturbed. By many, at least among the intellectual class, Buddhism was identified with the old order, and in the early years of the twentieth century Japan was wholeheartedly involved in creating a new order. In 1854, Commodore Perry, the American naval officer, opened Japan to trade with the West. In 1867, the shōgunate collapsed, and the next year Buddhism was disestablished and largely disendowed. Its emblems were removed from the imperial palace, and Buddhist images were removed from Dual Shintō altars.

DISESTABLISHMENT

The disestablishment of Buddhism was accompanied by the establishment of the governmental department of Shintō and soon after by the so-called Separation Edict, through which official ties between Buddhism and Shintō were severed. This edict opened a period characterized by actual violence against the Buddhist organization. Most of this opposition was Shintō-inspired; Shintō priests, backed by the popular anti-Buddhist feeling that accompanied the fall of the shōgunal power, destroyed Buddhist images and emblems. In some cases, Buddhist temples were turned into Shintō shrines. It must be recognized, of course, that such violence was directed at the tangible and material assets of the religion, for Dual Shintō ideas had been established too firmly and for too long a period for them to be abolished in a matter of months simply by edict.

Exterminating Buddhas and Abandoning Scriptures

This general reaction against Buddhism culminated in the movement known as *haibutsu kishaku,* "exterminate the Buddhas and abandon the scriptures." The climax came in 1871; after that, the spirit which moved it subsided quite rapidly. The new Meiji government had not evolved any sequential policy concerning the treatment of Buddhism. It had, however, generally discriminated against it through disestablishment. In any case, the implementation of "exterminating the Buddhas and abandoning the scriptures" was largely left to the discretion of those immediately involved. This meant that haibutsu kishaku was variously interpreted in different localities. The activities against Buddhism ranged from the destruction of temples and images to the wholesale secularization of priests. The movement defeated itself, however, for the more repugnant acts of violence provoked a general popular criticism of the policy that was soon to temper it.

The haibutsu kishaku policy was a heavy blow to Buddhism, though a temporary one. One of the positive results of the movement was to break the two-hundred-fifty-year apathy that had characterized the Buddhist organization under the Tokugawa. Moreover, the secularization of many priests did much to weed out the parasitic elements that had accumulated over the centuries and to destroy the worldly power that the Buddhist church had come to think it natural due. The result of all this was a reawakening of faith to meet the challenges of a revolutionized society. One of these challenges came from without : Christianity. The impetus to Buddhist reform that this foreign import engendered should not be underestimated, for Christianity rode in on the wave of popular interest in everything Western, with the result that Buddhists found themselves pitted against the whole modernist tendency in their reaction against the new religion. Their efforts, almost of necessity, tended toward a return to the spiritual values of the past and curiously enough toward a re-establishing of ties with the native Shintō through Dual Shintō ideas.

GREAT DOCTRINE

The government proclaimed the adoption of Shintō as the national religion in 1870 under the name of Daikyō, or "Great Doctrine." A strong propagandist movement was initiated, and missionaries were sent throughout the land, whose duty it was to refute Confucianism and Buddhism and defend the concepts of Shintō. This movement was especially active from 1869 to 1871. In the latter year was created the State Department of Religion and Education, which granted to Buddhism a position, although a subordinate one, in the national picture.

The Daikyō-in, "College of the Great Doctrine," began its functions in 1873. Created theoretically for religion in general, it was supposedly a seminary where Shintō and Buddhism were equal, but in reality this was not the case. Shintō was stressed; only Shintō images and cult implements were present. Buddhist priests were obliged to make offerings to Shintō gods. It was a kind of Dual Shintō in which, contrary to the tradition, Shintō predominated. Many large temples in the provinces were placed under the Daikyō-in, a situation which marked the further subordination of the Buddhist organization. In 1875, however, four branches of the Shin sect were permitted to leave the Daikyō-in, and in the same year it was completely abolished, after which time there was no further interference with Buddhism.

MEIJI REFORM

The essential problems for Buddhism under the Meiji reform were recovery from the effects of the haibutsu kishaku and the revitalization of the faith in order to meet the challenge of other religions, notably Christianity. Like their opposite numbers in the political realm, Buddhist leaders tried to institute changes and to bring about a religious modernization. Most active were the east and west Honganji. In 1873, a mission traveled to Europe, and some of its numbers returned to Japan via America. Its aim was to study Western ecclesiastical organization. The Shin sect went so far as to declare its doctrines not inconsistent with those of Christianity, though superior to them. The Buddha Amida was explained as being monotheistic in nature, his role being not unlike that of Jesus in Christianity. Most of all, in an age of growing technological interest, it was claimed that Buddhism was actually closer than Christianity to the spirit of science, because, unlike Christianity, Buddhism did not claim for its divinities the power to change the intricate cause-and-effect relationships that make up nature; indeed, like science, Buddhism recognized the vast interdependence of all things. In order to be quite thorough, however, in 1875 the West Honganji sent a student to the University of Pennsylvania to study Christianity with a view to helping Buddhism by a better understanding of the causes of Christian success.

WESTERN CONTACTS

All Buddhists who had the opportunity of traveling abroad in these early years were struck by the degree of religious freedom they found both in Europe and America. Shimaji Mokurai (in 1872) especially voiced a cautious but straightforward criticism of his government's policy concerning the Daikyō-in. He urged a separation of patriotic elements (Shintō) from purely religious ones (Buddhism), and it was largely due to him that the Daikyō-in was ultimately abolished. Although all felt the necessity of some kind of religious improvement to match the sweeping political reforms that were everywhere taking place, the leaders were not fully supported by their sects, who through indifference or traditionalism were content to let things be as they were. A notable exception was perhaps the west Honganji, which, after its investigations of Western practice, adopted a representative system of organization.

The Buddhist revival of 1877–1889 took its greatest inspiration from the reaction to Christianity, a revival that was ultimately to fail, for anti-Christian attitudes allied Buddhism to nationalism rather than to a basic renewal of Buddhist doctrines. By 1887, there was a strong nationalistic reaction, and in 1889 the new Constitution assured freedom of all religions. Buddhism was now, in theory at least, equal to Christianity and Shintō. In general, Buddhists fell in with the nationalistic tendency and attacked "foreign" Christianity with slogans like *haja kenshō,* "reject the wicked (Christianity) and clarify the right (Buddhism)." This alliance with the government, along with a dependency on state assistance, meant nothing more than a return to the old state of affairs.

Apologetics stressed both the dangers of Christianity and the harmony of Buddhism with Shintō and to a lesser degree with Confucianism.

During the Meiji period, Buddhism, like all of Japanese culture, was obliged to adjust to the rapid pace of change that was prevalent in the country. That it was firmly linked with the old order, and in varying ways continued to be, mediated at first against it. Its strength lay in its being an integral part of Japanese culture—its penetration of all classes. Under the Tokugawa shōgunate, it had become formalized, tradition-alized, to a large extent, apathetic. The new challenges of the Meiji period in the form of Christianity and the persecutions of the haibutsu kishaku movement did much to remove that apathy. But forms are easier to change than ideas, and their success was limited. Perhaps a telling reason was the lack of deep religious feeling, at least as it is understood in the West, that seems to characterize Japanese religious life.

Survey of Japanese Buddhism

WHAT MOST SIGNIFICANTLY MARKS THE CAREER of Buddhism in Japan is the close relationship between the religious and the national life of the Japanese. Buddhism, if not in the realm of its philosophy, at least in the secular domain, has always reflected both political and social movements, a tendency doubtless heightened by long periods of relative seclusion. As in art, religion in Japan is a kind of storehouse where movements and schools, on the continent long since purely academic, are preserved and studied, while remaining a part of the living religion.

The Japanese are not at heart a philosophically minded people, and their interest in this imported religion was, if one may use the term, of a practical nature; at least, the religion was first used for practical ends. Rather than developing the basic philosophic ideas that had been imported from the continent, Japanese Buddhism shows the genius of adaptability, exemplified by the Dual Shintō concepts, in which Buddhism made place for native beliefs, and by the so-called *shingaku,* or "heart learning," in which Buddhism, Shintō, and Confucianism were fused into a kind of composite ethical religion.

EARLY BELIEFS

The religious beliefs of the Japanese in the pre-Buddhist period, that is, until the middle of the sixth century, were chiefly of an animistic type, in which defilement, purity, and fertility were of the utmost importance. These beliefs were not "purely Japanese," for they doubtless did not originate in the Japanese islands but were carried from the mainland with the arrival of the first inhabitants. These beliefs show an undeniable relationship with northern Asiatic (Siberian) shamanism. Another current ascertainable in the mythological accounts of the *Kojiki* and the *Nihongi* shows striking similarities to the mythologies of the South Seas. Generally speaking, the pre-Buddhist beliefs are based on the vague concept of deity called *kami*. "The things of nature, like human beings were considered animated by, or imbued with, a vital spirit; they had a kind of personal vitality. This vitality in whatever departs from the ordinary through shape or color or in any other way was felt to be 'superior.' It was hence characterized by the word kami, the fundamental sense of which is 'above,' 'upper,' 'superior.' "[30] The early beliefs set forth no moral code or discipline.

INTRODUCTION OF BUDDHISM

From the sixth century on, Buddhism profoundly changed the religious aspects of Japanese life, dominating the simpler "native" beliefs with its highly developed metaphysical and philosophical systems, as well as it moral disciplines. More than that, it was the vehicle of importation for continental culture, bringing new concepts in such varied fields as art, medicine, music, and dance. During the seventh and eighth centuries, Japan imported Chinese schools. They studied form over continent. It was a period of little innovation. Buddhism was restricted largely to monkish and intellectual circles, and these groups were responsible for the preservation of the concepts of a nonpopular nature that characterized the religion of this period.

HEIAN PERIOD

The Heian period, ninth to twelfth centuries, saw the spread of Buddhism and its penetration of Japanese civilization. During this period, the Japanese were still importing new forms of Buddhism, but they had begun to be concerned with their own ideas within the context of the imported concepts. Buddhism was still principally an aristocratic belief practiced by restricted groups. But it had become popular to the extent that the magnificent ceremonies presented on public occasions drew the people into at least visual contact with the religion. As such, Buddhism became available to the masses, even though there was little interest in or understanding of the finer points of its metaphysics.

THIRTEENTH TO NINETEENTH CENTURIES

From the thirteenth to the seventeenth centuries, Buddhism penetrated even more deeply into the lives of the common people. It became a truly popular religion, appealing to the masses through easy ways of salvation and promises of an intriguing paradise. New sects reflecting essentially Japanese life arose, and, despite the unrest and confusion that characterized the political picture of the times, Buddhism was a vital, growing faith.

This vitality is in contrast to the Buddhism of the Tokugawa period (seventeenth to nineteenth centuries), which, like the society, maintained a kind of status quo, neither troubled by persecutions nor marked by important innovations. Tokugawa Japan was mainly concerned with the moral-ethical teachings of neo-Confucianism, upon which the government relied to maintain society as changeless as possible. The apathetic religious climate, while not directly adverse to Buddhism, was largely responsible for the stunted growth of the religion in this period.

Meiji Period

Since the Meiji restoration in 1868 and the disestablishment of the religion, Buddhism suddenly has had to face a new world. First, it has been obliged overnight to deal with the intricacies of modern technology, whereas other religions have been able to evolve this relationship more gradually. Second, it has had to meet the challenge of a proselytizing Christianity. In a sense, these challenges have strengthened Buddhism, for they have forced a re-evaluation of its ideals and its organization. Modern Buddhism has been working to break the apathy of recent generations; that its leaders have not been completely successful is a statement that will be open to constant revision. Undeniably, a certain dissatisfaction, on a popular and often untutored level, with Buddhism as an organized religion is indicated by the rise of a number of new syncretistic sects or religions, based on ideas drawn indiscriminately from Christianity, Shintō, and Buddhism.

New Religions

It is hard to know exactly where to begin a definition of the so-called New Sects. The very expression is subject to widely variant usage by the Japanese themselves. *Shinkō shūkyō,* or "Newly Established Religions," in its widest sense refers to sects formed as far back as the beginning of the nineteenth century, while in its more restricted meaning it designates only the twentieth century sects, most particularly those that sprang into being around World War II. However widely in time the term may be understood to extend, the various religions that fall under it do indeed have a number of points in common.

At the time of the Meiji restoration, the degeneration of Buddhism, identified to its detriment, after stultifying years under the Tokugawa, with the downfall of the "old order," as well as the rather false revitalization of Shintō by the new government and the as yet weak Christian influence created a kind of religious vacuum that, although acutely felt by the end of the nineteenth century, had begun to be manifest much earlier. It was inevitable that this vacuum should be filled, and the new religions attempted to do just this, that is, they attempted to supply some of the spiritual needs created by the disaffection of the people with traditional Shintō and Buddhism.

These new religions have in common a number of features that seem to spring from the common need they sought to fill. Generally, the new religions do not recognize a formal hierarchy, that is, at least not in a traditional sense. They rather tend to avoid distinct divisions between secular believers and priests. Everyone is equal, and all are equally permitted to conduct services. The services vary from the elaborate to the simple, but it is characteristic that all are taken very seriously by the faithful. Most of the new religions, particularly those that have been active since 1945, utilize for their propaganda modern media of mass communication : radio, television, and, of course, masses of free literature. Moreover, practically all of the sects require only minimal monthly fees, frequently as low as ten yen a month. They do, however, accept donations, especially contributions from the grateful in the faith-healing sects, and a number of these sects show surprising affluence.

None of the new religions claim an exclusive corner on the truth but rather accept each other on a basis of equality. The degree of tolerance, with few exceptions, is very high, a situation, it might be added, that demonstrates an historical sequence with the high degree of tolerance that characterized the relations between Shintō, Buddhism, and Confucianism throughout the course of Japanese history. In 1952, for example, a League of New Religions (*shinshūkyō remmei*) was founded to provide mutual assistance in the propagation of the various doctrines. The League further published a newspaper, the *Shinshūkyō Shimbun,* which was open to all members alike.

Some of the new religions confine their activities to, or rather concentrate on, Japan. Typical of these are the Shintō groups that exhibit the ancient Shintō preoccupation with pollution and purity and that use Shintō magical and ritual practices. But not all are by any means so provincial in their outlook. Some of the new religions have begun international missionary work. Such work is frequently directed toward converting only the Japanese living abroad, but some are much wider and claim varying degrees of universality for their doctrines.

One may well ponder the causes of the pullulation of new religions in Japan. Their very quantity demands the attention of the student of religion, and their varied doctrines furnish a rich ground for the student of comparative religions and the folklorist. What are some of their common characteristics? First of all, it is interesting to note that almost one half of all the new religions began in one way or another with a revelation. These revelations took place under different circumstances. Typical of the Buddhist sects are revelations that occur through a Buddhist divinity, frequently Amida, who commands the founder to start a given religious movement. Again, the founder or foundress is taken possession of by a spirit, the founder being a kind of medium through which the divinity gives directions for the founding of the new sect. Or again, the revelation occurs in a dream.

A second point in common to a number of the new religions is the working of miracles. Generally, miracles are performed as a result of a power given to the founder through divine intercourse with the gods or a god. Frequently this power can be transmitted to believers, and the transmission is a drawing card for new believers with hopes of gaining material assets : health, success, happiness, and so forth. Sometimes the miracle power is considered as being the central purpose of the religion, at others it is believed to be secondary to ultimate salvation. Yet another group believes that miracles constitute a sort of proof of the existence of the spirit world, a world of power above man. There is no doubt about the strong effect of miracles on the masses and their popular appeal.

Thirdly, the new religions were all originally characterized by the simplicity of their doctrines, which appeals most to people of modest intellectual attainment. These doctrines are usually presented in uncomplicated language and are without the Chinese flourishes of Buddhism and Confucianism or the archaisims of traditional Shintō. Moreover, as has been noted before, the new religions are essentially lay organizations, with no complex hierachy and with extremely easy conditions for entry. The new believer, for example, is often neither requested not expected to give up his traditional religion. The minimal financial requirements pose no problem for those of modest means, and, indeed, new believers are encouraged to join the order by the frequent reference to material rewards in the propaganda. Most of all, the new religions establish a direct contact between leader and believer. In many cases the founder or foundress is still alive, and his or her personal influence exercises great influence on the members. The founder or leader brings to the faithful the example of his personal life, a living example of the doctrines of the religion at work.

The number of new religions—171 by an official estimate—precludes giving any detailed account of them. The following have been chosen because they seem to represent the main themes sketched above and because in number of adherents and in the organization of their doctrine they appear to be among the most important of the new sects.

If the term "newly established religions" is extended to include the nineteenth century, two sects immediately come to mind : the Tenri-kyō, "Religion of Divine Wisdom," and the Konkō-kyō, "Religion of Golden Light."

Tenri-kyō

The foundress of the Tenri-kyō, Nakayama Miki, was born in the year 1789 in the province of Yamato. The first daughter of Maekawa Hanshichi Masanobu, she gave up her father's name upon marrying into the Nakayama family. This family belonged to the Jōdo sect of Buddhism, and, doubtless under familial influence, Miki was soon known for her assiduous

*Tenrikyō dance, a sacred dance performed in front of a
Tenrikyō altar.*

belief in Pure Land doctrines. She especially appears to have
put great faith in the practice of the nembutsu, and one can
see subsequent influence of this practice in Tenri liturgy. Her
biographers praise her filial piety toward her parents-in-law
and the constant respect she bore her husband, despite a
philandering spirit that caused her much anguish.

Foundress's Life

In 1821, Miki bore a son, Shūji, and subsequently two
daughters, Masa and Yasu. When the boy was around twenty,
he was seized with an illness. An itinerant priest (*yamabushi*)
was called, and Miki acted as medium for the magical ritual
of the healer. It is at this time that she is said to have been
possessed by a "heavenly general" (*ten no shōgun*), who,
through her, declared himself to be the "original and true

god." He also declared Miki to be the "dwelling place of the
sun and the moon" (*tsuki hi no yashiro*). It is from this year,
1838, then that the sect claims to have come into being. Miki
was later possessed by some "ten deities" (*tōhashira no kami*)
of the Shintō pantheon and the place of the happening became
the center of Tenri worship. It is marked by an eight-foot
column (*kanrōdai*), and it is difficult not to see an analogy
between it and the heavenly column of traditional Shintō
mythology. This latter column, whose phallic symbolism seems
apparent, is the place where the divinities Izanami and
Izanagi were united in marriage.

Miki's subsequent life was completely changed. She practiced a sort of dramatic charity, giving away all her possessions.
She considered, indeed, that her life must be a "pattern"
(*hinagata*) for all the faithful to follow. In 1863, her husband
died and from that time on she devoted herself ever more
completely to the god. In the beginning, her faith was proclaimed at Osaka on street corners in the simplest fashion. This
is called in Tenri parlance "pouring on of the perfume"
(*nioigake*). Miki herself engaged in faith healing numerous
times, becoming known especially for her ability to grant
painless childbirth (*obiya-yurushi*). Indeed, early Tenri doctrine, as she seems to have understood it, was a curious mixture
of physical healing and spiritual salvation. These powers of
healing were granted to others (*sazuke*), and in one instance
the "granting of the power of the voice" (*koe no sazuke*) was
directed to a farmer for the purpose of making particularly
potent fertilizer.

By 1865, Tenri had gained the disapproval of the traditional
Buddhist setcs, but Miki managed to obtain official recognition
as a Shintō sect and thus some degree of protection. This
recognition entailed the change of the god's name from "Great
Sovereign God of Divine Wisdom" (Tenri ō no mi-kami) to

"Luminous Divinity of Divine Wisdom" (Tenri ō myōjin), which designated a deity of especially high rank.

Religious Practice

Until 1866, the simple nembutsu-like formula of *namu Tenri ō no mikoto* ("Glory to the Sovereign God of Divine Wisdom") was used. After this date the formula was expanded to "Sweep away evil and help us, Sovereign God of Divine Wisdom" (*ashiki wo harōte, tasuke tamae, Tenri ō no mikoto*). And in 1867 the *mi-kagura-uta*, or "sacred dance-song," was conceived, although it was to be several years until it attained its complete form. Later, gestures and music, which bear the influence of popular songs and dances, were added, and by 1868 the so-called "dancing service" (*kagura zutome*), which is now the principal liturgical function, came into being.

From 1869 to 1883, Miki wrote in rather a rambling, disconnected style the articles of her faith. Set down in a provincial Japanese that is not always clear, they are called her *O-fudesaki, Divine Script,* and are divided into some seventeen volumes, comprising 1,711 verses.

Increasingly people were coming to her to obtain all kinds of material and physical benefits (*goriyaku*) that her power was believed able to bestow. In order that her person as well as her doctrine should not become confused in the popular mind with the simpler folk religions, she ordered the so-called "separate fire, separate vessel" (*bekka betsunabe*), by which she set herself apart from ordinary people, dressing differently and taking special food.

In 1875, while working in her garden, she was suddenly seized with a great weakness. This was felt to be a sign from the god, and the place where she stood is considered a holy place (*jiba*).

Miki died in 1886 under conditions that are described in a manner strangely like those of the historical Buddha. On

becoming aware that the end of life was near, the foundress
surveyed her past existence and all the happenings in it, lay
down with her head to the north and her face toward the west,
the direction of the Pure Land (*Jōdo*) paradise in which she
had been so interested in her youth, and so, in her ninetieth
year of age, expired.

Doctrine

The Divine Wisdom doctrine seems to be inextricably
involved with the Tenri genesis of the universe. This genesis
shows undeniable parallels with traditional Shintō mythology.
The original state of the world is a sea of mud (*doro-umi*), or
chaos, into which God the Parent looked down from above
and resolved to create man in order to enjoy his cheerful
living. As in many other new religions, the character of the
central divinity is shadowy indeed. Who is this God the
Parent? Sometimes he is referred to as kami, the traditional
Shintō word for divinity, sometimes as *tsuki-hi* ("moon-sun"),
sometimes, later, as *oya* ("parent"), sometimes, although less
frequently, as Tenri ō no mikoto ("Sovereign God of Divine
Wisdom"), and finally as *oyagami* ("Parent God"). It is difficult to ascertain whether this god—he uses eight other gods
as his tools—is really a monotheistic or a polytheistic concept.

First Divinities

The first two divinities that were created from this sea
of mud are, as in the mythological accounts, Izanagi and
Izanami, the male and female principles respectively, the
model for the human couple. The male was provided with a
male organ in the form of a dolphin and the female a female
organ in the form of a tortoise. A meeting was arranged and
the human race conceived—the spot being marked again by
the kanrōdai mentioned above. The gestative period and the

delivery of the race are studded with fantasy. Those born in Yamato remained where they were, to become Japanese, while those born in the provinces became, when the earth took its final shape, members of other countries. The account is obviously proud that the Japanese are the oldest of all the races and the most favored.

Kashimono Karimono

One of the central themes of Tenri teaching is the disclaiming of personal property, known as *kashimono karimono* ("Things lent, things borrowed"). All possessions even to the human body are things that have been lent to man by God, and it is necessary to realize that all must be returned to him with gratitude. While the body is a thing borrowed, however, the mind can be disposed of freely, and its wrong use sullies, piles dust (*hokori*), on the soul. It is hence important in Tenri to cleanse the mind of this dust which has eight properties: stinginess (*oshii*), greed (*hoshii*), hatred (*nikui*), partiality (*kawai*), animosity (*urami*), anger (*haradachi*), covetousness (*yoku*), and arrogance (*kōman*). A mind cleansed of "dust" brings the favor of long life, specified as being some 115 years.

Although reincarnation is little mentioned in Tenri writings, it is basic to their teaching. Present states are directly related to past acts; but it is necessary to keep in mind that God originally created man to enjoy his cheerfulness, so no matter how dark the present as a result of the karmic chain of events, it is necessary to stress the brightness and joy of living.

Of all the new religions Tenri is doubtless the most influencial. The great center now located in Tenri city is affluent indeed, boasting, besides places for the cult, a library, hospital, and school. Stress is placed on social activity and the training of missionaries and teachers. The sect counts over a million and a half believers.

KONKŌ-KYŌ

Another sect which sprang into existence during the nineteenth century was the Konkō-kyō, or "Religion of Golden Light." Founded in 1859 by a simple farmer who had neither education nor religious training, the sect posits that man is the child of God, that is, of the god Tenchi kane no kami, "God of Heavenly and Terrestrial Brightness." This god is seen as a kind of parent, a father, dependence on whom makes it possible to avoid the distresses of karma.

The god Tenchi kane no kami, or Parent God of the Universe, as the sect choses to interpret the name, is infinitely merciful. Through his grace man is born, and by his love and kindness man may enjoy the happiness of life. Everything in the universe is the creation of this god, and all is given to man, his children. Suffering and calamities occur when man forgets his relation to the god and his love. The god wills to save mankind but cannot if man remains ignorant of His desire. The founder is believed to act as mediator between the god and man. Hence the god revealed to man his love through the founder. What is distress to man is distress to his parent god, just as parent and child share the same prosperity, the same salvation.

Founder

The founder, styled Konkō daijin, was born in 1814 in Konkō, near Okayama. As a farmer he was always concerned with the fertility and abundance of nature, which he believed to be manifestations of the love of the gods for man. His vague attitude toward the gods in general was finally focused on the Parent God of the Universe (Tenchi kane no kami), who revealed himself to him. This was on November 15, 1869, and Konkō daijin was called to the sacred mission of saving men and revealing the ultimate purpose of the god.

The founder died at the age of sixty-nine in 1883. He was succeeded by his son and later his grandson, who carried on the work of mediator between the god and man. The theme of their teachings is that all men shall enjoy happiness and prosperity, happiness and prosperity indeed being coeval with the god himself. The realization of this ideal is to be attained by leading life to the fullest. The scriptures urge prayerful communion with the god, who will grant what is asked of him. Physical health is stressed, and a healthy body is considered the source of the blessings of life. Overeating and overdrinking are to be avoided. Filial piety is emphasized both toward parents and toward God, the Parent, and, finally, a commendable spirit of tolerance condemns disesteem of other religions. Such contempt is narrowmindedness, and the world should be thought of with a broad mind, for in the final analysis the world is this mind.

Activities of Sect

There are at present over 1,500 "churches," mostly in Japan, but also in Hawaii and America; associated with them are over 3,500 ministers. Believers number over 600,000. Since Konkō belief stresses the rationality of creation, and hence the rationality of God, an important place is accorded to educational and research activities. These activities are carried out by various schools, as well as an institute for advanced studies. Social services include a hospital, a public library, and two associations for providing scholarships, while missionary work in prisons and among the sick helps to extend the field of service.

TWENTIETH-CENTURY SECTS

The new religions of the twentieth century tend to divorce themselves, although not completely, from the Shintō influences that mark the sects discussed above. Coming into existence after, during, or shortly before the Second World War, they show a more cosmopolitan approach to religion and reflect the increasing influence of non-Shintō beliefs among the masses. The founders (*kyōso*) of these new religions all claim revelation from a kind of world spirit, in the course of which (1) they receive the new doctrine they will proclaim and (2) they begin a new community. These founders occupy a special position among the believers. They are even called "divinities" (kami) sometimes, and their word is taken as absolute truth even when, as is not infrequently the case, it goes against the proofs of science. Most of the sects recognize a supreme being, whose character is often vague and shadowy, never really defined by the faithful nor indeed by the scriptures themselves. The supreme being seems to be a mixture of monotheistic, polytheistic, and pantheistic traits. The Tenshō kōtai jingū-kyō, or "Doctrine of the Heavenly Resplendent Divinity Dwelling," is an example.

Tenshō kōtai jingū-kyō

The Tenshō kōtai jingū doctrine posits a supreme being, defined as omniscient and omnipotent, an absolute god, not unlike the Buddha or the Christ. This god is not only the first principle of all things but one that rules and creates eternally.

Foundress

The sect was founded in 1945 by the wife of a farmer, Kitamura Sayo, who lived in the village of Tabuse in Yamaguchi prefecture in southern Japan. Like Miki of the Tenri sect, after a three-year period of religious austerity, she began to preach her doctrine in the streets. Her sermons were kinds of extemporaneous hymns. One of her themes was that the recent war was the will of God and a means by which he, through her, could bring souls to salvation by making them realize the folly of the degraded human world. Playing on the national pessimism of the time, her movement quickly gained considerable popular support in the countryside. Later in the same year she transferred her teaching to her house. She announced that she was the savior and that her mission was the establishment of God's Kingdom. She was called "Great Divinity" (*ōgami-sama*).

Doctrine

The sect holds that God entrusted his kingdom to mankind and that ultimately he will take it back. The kingdom of man is a shadowy world, but it will be ultimately saved, for the God in heaven is not merciless no matter how corrupt his world has become. Idols, temples, property and professional religionists are signs of this corruption. God's world is characterized by a great abundance of all things, but man in his ignorance never discovers the cache.

Religious Practice

Human life should therefore be a life of religious practice. The main object of life is the polishing of the soul to make it worthy of the divine kingdom. Carnal love, fortune, and success deter one from this goal, and only daily religious routine leads to it. The first step in religious practice is to purge the "six roots of evil": regret, desire, hatred, fondness, love, and being loved. The erasing of these six roots of evil and their resultant "sins" is made possible through reflection and confession. Confession is made to God, who keeps a kind of record book and rewards sincere religious practice.

Three things are necessary in religious practice: courage— to give everything to God; sincerity—to perform all action with a true heart; and prayer—the saying of the specific catechistic prayer of the sect, which calls on God for world peace and for purging the six roots of evil and which ends with a chanting of the name of the *Lotus* sūtra.

Selflessness

Essential to religious practice is the state of selflessness. By selflessness the sect means obedient to God's will, doing the will of God. Ego implies doing the will of one's self. Those who arrive at non-ego enter the kingdom of God and enjoy a life of bliss, for their conduct is in accord with the will of God. This selfless state of union with God is demonstrated in a particular dance called the Dance of Selflessness (*muga no odori*), which is performed at religious services and for the purpose of proselytizing. From this practice comes the popular name for the sect, the "Dancing Religion" (*odoru shūkyō*).

The sect was formally registered with the government in 1947, and the headquarters were designated as being the home of the foundress. Branches were soon established in other communities. The foundress subsequently traveled to Hawaii and later to America, where her success was at best restricted.

A special feature of new religions is their syncretism, which in many ways reflects the spiritual interests of the founder. Typical of such tendencies are the Ananai-kyō, "Doctrine of the Three and the Five," and the Seichō no Ie Kyōdan, "Brotherhood of the House of Growth."

ANANAI-KYŌ

The Ananai-kyō was founded by Nakano Yonosuke, who had begun as a believer in the Ōmoto-kyō, "Religion of the Great Foundation." The Ōmoto sect had been founded in 1892, suppressed in 1937, and refounded in 1946. Highly syncretic, it stresses spiritist elements. God is the main all-pervading spirit, who urges man to work for universal brotherhood. Nakano had been deeply impressed by the spiritism of the Ōmoto, and he believed himself to be the medium between the spirit world and the world of man. He considered himself ordered by the spirit world to contact the Hung-wan-tzu-hui, "Society of the Red Swastika," a Taoist organization, as well as Persian Bahaism. He believed that there was but one universal religion and that the multitude of organized sects were but branches of it. He called this, his universal religion, the Ananai-kyō.

The aim of the Ananai is to bind man to God. It stresses union with the great spirit of the universe through "god-possession" (*kamigakari*) and "tranquillizing the soul" (*chin-kon*). Ananai is a mixture of Christian and Shintō ideas. The name itself designates the hempen cord that hangs before Shintō shrines. It is thought to bind the believer to the world of the gods when he strikes the gong over which it is suspended. The Ananai, however, is not chiefly Shintō. The word itself is written with the characters for three and five and pretends thereby to indicate the universality of the system. Three stands for the three religions that the founder felt had most influenced him : Ōmoto-kyō, Hung-wan-tzu-hui, and Bahaism. The five refers to the five great religions of the world : Christianity, Islam, Confucianism, Buddhism, and Taoism. The sect believes in the coming of a savior and in the magical power of the heavens, this latter item accounting for the rather large number of observatories that the sect maintains throughout Japan. Its believers number around 100,000.

Seichō no Ie

The Seichō no Ie, or "House of Growth" (i.e., the macrocosm), is a kind of mental science, highly syncretistic in nature. It was revealed to the founder, Taniguchi Masaharu, in 1928 that there is only one True Being (*jisō*), that all else is nothing but the figment of the mind. This True Being may be designated in many ways: as the Shintō kami, as the Buddhist Buddha (most specifically Amida), or the Christian Christ. In the beginning Taniguchi permitted the True Being of his revelation to be worshiped in any of these traditional forms and only later devised a special liturgy for his religion. Formerly connected with the Ōmoto-kyō, the House of Growth shows a number of influences from this sect.

Articles of Faith

All men are thought to be the sons of God. Realization of this leads to limitless possibilities. The seven articles of faith set forth the main concepts of the doctrine. Man stands as it were above sectarianism and worships life itself and the rules of life. Belief is in eternal growth, all things are constantly in a process of growth, and indeed life in man knows no death. Love is the basis and the nourishment of life, while prayer, words of love, and praise constitute the creative power of the Word and serve to actualize life. Since life is growth, the sect stresses an essentially optimistic view of things and feels that looking on the bright side of existence will bring about a kind of transformation in man. It is the aim of the sect to spread this ideal among the men of the world. It is but a step from such a viewpoint to the emphasis on suppression of all that makes life disagreable, specifically diseases and anguish. Consequently an extensive use of faith healing typifies the practice of the religion.

The House of Growth is one of the most influential of the new religions and in its propaganda uses all the modern means of mass communication. Members number about one and a half million.

SEKAI MESHIYA-KYŌ

Almost all the new religions are concerned with faith healing to some extent. Such preoccupations demonstrate the longevity of shamanistic ideas starting with the original native cult and continuing down to the present. One new religion particularly stresses faith healing. It is the Sekai Meshiya (or kyūsei)-kyō, "World Messianic Doctrine." Its founder was Okada Mokichi, who believed himself to be possessed of the wonder-working power of the Bodhisattva Kannon (Skt. Avalokiteshvara). This power is said to be a pearl some two inches in size, which the founder carried in his abdomen. From the pearl radiated a kind of light-energy that had the power to kill bacteria. The energy was brought into play by the founder when he moved his hand over the afflicted. The power could be brought to effect nonhuman subjects, and the founder was believed capable of causing agricultural fertility as well. This power could be transmitted to others by presenting to them a kind of talisman, a piece of paper on which was written the character for "light" (*hikari*).

Okada, however, claimed a higher purpose for his religion than the simple healings of the human body. He claimed that, almost on a universal plane, he was able to remove the great evils of sickness, poverty, and war and so establish an earthly paradise.

Okada had been a member of the Ōmoto sect and his teaching reflects its influence on him. It numbers around 400,000.

REIYŪ-KAI

Another sect that shows considerable shamanistic influence, but which is chiefly Buddhist, is the Reiyū-kai, or "Society of Friendship with Souls." Founded in 1925 by Kubo Kakutarō and others, the sect derives largely from Nichiren Buddhism. It is based on the *Lotus* sūtra and stresses filial piety and duty toward ancestors. The basic text, taken largely from the *Lotus* and called the *Blue Sūtra,* has three sections : (1) *Muryōgikyō, Sūtra of Limitless Meaning* (T. 276); (2) the *Lotus;* and (3) the *Kanfugengyō, Sūtra of Meditation of Fugen* (T. 277).

Doctrine

Reiyū teaching maintains that through constant transmigration all human beings are related as friends. This oneness of humanity extends to ancestors. The acts of the ancestors have formed men as they are now, but also the deeds of the descendants are thought capable of modifying the status of the ancestors. Hence, one of the main religious activities of the sect is the offering of memorial services to the dead. General social welfare is of primary importance to all and consequently there is great stress on social activities on the part of the membership. Such belief in social welfare is based on the Mahā-yāna concept of Charity (Skt. *dāna*). The sect believes that social benefits to others mean in reality self-help. In short, it is a sect which has made a selection of a few basic Mahāyāna principles, in the observance of which one may discern a trace of Christian influence, most particularly in the emphasis on the social aspect of religion. Membership is said to stand at around three and a half million.

RISSHŌ KŌSEI-KAI

Also based on the *Lotus* sūtra is the Risshō kōsei-kai, "Society for the Establishment of Righteous and Friendly Relations." The Risshō sect separated from the Reiyū-kai and was founded in 1838 by Niwano Shikazō and (Mrs.) Numa Myōkō. It is now one of the more active of the new religions. It maintains that actual physical evil stems from moral evil, which produces evil acts and thus the karmic sequence. Freedom is repentance of sins, which breaks the karmic chain. In order to accomplish this freedom, it is necessary to understand the invisible world of the gods and the Buddhas, that is, the world of the spirits (*myō*). It is also necessary to comprehend the phenomenal world, which is actually the world of the spirits realized in the "world about us" (*tai*). Also necessary is an understanding of *furi*, that is, the action which brought the realization of this world about us. Furi, then, is faith which unites man with the gods and the Buddhas. Moreover, to escape the bonds of the karmic chain, one must be aware of one's own karma, one must know just exactly what it is. This knowledge may be obtained through divination, most especially onomancy (*seimei handan*), or divination by names. Great importance is accorded to the Nichiren mandala. The sect claims almost one and a half million members.

SŌKA GAKKAI

Another sect based on the *Lotus* sūtra, and specifically on the Nichiren Shōshū ("Nichiren's True Sect") branch of the Nichiren sect, is the Sōka Gakkai, or "Value Creating Study Group."

The Sōka Gakkai was started in 1930 by Makiguchi Tsunezaburō, only to be suppressed during the war years. It was revived in 1947. A sect of somewhat fanatical ideas, its doctrine is that happiness has three values: profit, goodness, and beauty. These values must be understood by detailed study of them, and hence the sect terms itself a "study group." Actually, it aims at preparing the world for the time when the Nichiren Shōshū branch of Nichirenism will become the state religion of Japan. Its activities in some cases recall the intolerance displayed by Nichiren himself. The main growth of the sect has taken place since the early 1950's. It claims more than a million households and its role in politics has become increasingly important. It counts several of its members in the Diet.

A number of the new religions, concerned with world peace as well as the propagation of their doctrine, have begun international missionary work. Those sects which show the greatest activity in this area are the Seichō no Ie, "House of Growth," and the PL-kyōdan, or "Brotherhood of Perfect Liberty."

PL-KYŌDAN

The PL sect is the postwar form of the old Hito no Michi ("Man's Path"). Man's Path was founded in 1926 by Miki Tokuharu and shows the strong influence of sectarian Shintō.

Miki Tokuharu was born on the island of Shikoku in 1867. A Buddhist since childhood, he became the chief priest of the Anjōji, a temple of the Ōbaku (Zen) sect. At the age of forty-five, he met a Christian minister, Kanda, in Osaka and was so profoundly impressed by his teaching that he gave up his post as Buddhist priest and in 1916 became the disciple of Kanda. Kanda died in 1919, and Miki erected a *himorogi,* a primitive form of Shintō shrine, where he had died and worshiped there for five years. During the course of this worship, he received three revelations, as a result of which he established the Hito no Michi. The movement was suppressed in 1937, and it was only in 1946 that it was revived by Miki Tokuchiku under the new and improbable name of PL. The sect worships the supreme being of the universe, while ancestral spirits and their importance in the lives of the believers are given considerable attention. The ancestral spirits are believed through their acts to have an active role in determining the lives of their descendants.

Twenty-one Rules of Life

The motto of the sect is Life is Art, which is in fact the first item in the so-called Twenty-one Rules of Life (*shosei-kun*), the rest of which define this motto and set the aims of the sect.

Man's life is the expression of his personality, and this personality in turn is the expression of God. The godhead is called "Great Parent Spirit" (*Mi-oya-ōkami*), and, by expressing himself, he becomes man and all things. He is the first artist, and man should imitate his artistic work. No true expression causes distress; it is only by losing control of oneself, by submitting to one's feelings that one's expression is falsified. This is the reason for the existence of evil (*gashō,* "manifesting of self"). That is, if man does not imitate God or if he gives in to his feelings, he becomes "inartistic," and evil occurs.

The Twenty-one Rules (6–21) include a number of practical hints for the daily exercise of the artistic life, the life of Perfect Liberty. All things are relative, and men are to be considered equal. One is to respect oneself and his neighbor as well, for the "selfless man knows his neighbor." Each thing has its own "Way." The Way of man and the Way of women differ, but just as there can be harmony between the two, so should there be harmony between all things and universal peace. In order to lead the good life, one must stand at the crossroads of good and evil; one must grasp the mean. But most of all one should live according to one's inner light (*satori*), which one receives at the time of conversion to the beliefs of the PL sect. After this point, the believer knows the meaning of life, and his acts are in accordance with his awareness.

There is considerable stress on social action on the part of the members, and the great PL center (*habikino*) near Osaka is impressive with its golf course, pottery kiln, school, hospital, and athletic center, besides the halls of worship and the various shrines. Membership is over a million.

What these new religions point up in Japan today is a general religious foment rather than an organized evolution of Buddhism or Shintō doctrine. Religious thought is often disorganized, and the indiscriminate borrowings from Buddhism (especially Nichirenism and the *Lotus* sūtra), Christianity, and Shintō show a dissatisfaction with the place each of these three religions occupies in the spiritual life of the nation. In many cases, however, this dissatisfaction stems from a misunderstanding of the existing religions—or perhaps a boredom with them. The choice of imperfectly understood concepts, particularly those of Christianity, shows a desire for exoticism. Frequently the founders are simple people whose formal knowledge of any religion is slight and intuitive rather than intellectual. Almost always the trend in modern religious movements in Japan has been toward simplification, toward bringing religion into the ken of the common man.

Notes

See Bibliography for complete entries.

1. Filliozat, *L'Inde classique,* p. 469.
2. *Ibid.,* p. 346.
3. Murti, *The Central Philosophy of Buddhism,* p. 32.
4. Govinda, *Foundations of Tibetan Mysticism,* p. 96.
5. Tucci, *The Theory and Prictice of the Mandala,* p. vii.
6. Kitagawa, *Religions of the East,* p. 209.
7. *Ibid.,* pp. 195–196.
8. Wright, *Buddhism in Chinese History,* p. 36.
9. Kitagawa, *op. cit.,* p. 209.
10. Sansom, *Japan,* p. 108.
11. Takakusu, *Essentials of Buddhist Philosophy,* pp. 64–65.
12. Conze, *Buddhism,* pp. 106ff.
13. *Ibid.,* p. 136.
14. *Ibid.,* p. 163.
15. Eliot, *Japanese Buddhism,* p. 174.
16. Conze, *op. cit.,* p. 164.
17. Tsunoda, *Sources of the Japanese Tradition,* p. 138.
18. Eliot, *op. cit.,* p. 337
19. Saunders, *Mudrā,* p. 19.
20. *Ibid.,* p. 23.
21. Sansom, *op. cit.,* p. 228.
22. Skt. Vaishravana. See glossary.
23. Cf. Fung Yu-lan, *History of Chinese Philosophy,* pp. 270ff.
24. The remarks on the tea house are based on Tsunoda, *Sources of the Japanese Traditions,* pp. 263–266.
25. Coats and Ishizuka, *Honen, the Buddhist Saint,* p. 60.
26. Sansom, *Japan,* p. 330.
27. *Ibid.,* pp. 414–415.
28. *Ibid.,* p. 415.
29. Eliot, *op. cit.,* p. 495.
30. Saunders, "Japanese Mythology," p. 412.

A Selected Bibliography

INDIAN BUDDHISM

General

Basham, A. L. *The Wonder That Was India: A Survey of the Indian Sub-Continent before the Coming of the Muslims.* New York : Grove, 1954.

Conze, Edward. *Buddhism, Its Essence and Development.* New York : Philosophical Library, 1951.

Eliot, Sir Charles. *Hinduism and Buddhism.* London : Arnold, 1921.

Filliozat, Jean, and Louis Renou, *et al. L'Inde classique: manuel des études indiennes.* Tome II. Paris : Imprimerie Nationale, 1953.

Kitagawa, Joseph M. *Religions of the East.* Philadelphia : Westminster, 1960.

Lamotte, Etienne. *Histoire du bouddhisme indien; des origines à l'ère Śaka.* Louvain : Institut Orientaliste, 1958.

Morgan, Kenneth W. *The Path of the Buddha.* New York : Ronald, 1956.

Zimmer, Heinrich. *Philosophies of India.* New York : Bollingen, 1951.

Background

Eliot, Sir Charles. *Japanese Buddhism.* London : Arnold, 1935. "Buddhism in India," pp. 62–98.

Murti, T. R. V. *The Central Philosophy of Buddhism.* London : Allen and Unwin, 1955. "The Two Traditions in Indian Philosophy," pp. 3–35.

Zimmer, Heinrich. *Philosophies of India:* "Brahmanism," pp. 333–463. "Sānkhya and Yoga," pp. 280–332.

Life of the Buddha

Foucher, Alfred. *La Vie du Bouddha.* Paris : Payot, 1949.
Herold, Ferdinand. *The Life of the Buddha.* Tokyo : Tuttle, 1954.
Thomas, Edward J. *The Life of the Buddha as Legend and History.* London : Routledge and Kegan Paul, 1956.

The Canon

Conze, Edward, ed. *Buddhist Texts throughout the Ages.* New York : Philosophical Library, 1954.
De Bary, William T., et al., eds. *Sources of Indian Tradition.* New York : Columbia, 1958. Theravāda, pp. 93–153; Mahāyāna, pp. 154–189; Tantrism, pp. 190–202.
Eliot, Sir Charles. *Japanese Buddhism.* London : Arnold, 1935. Pp. 3–29.
Suzuki, D. T. *Studies in the Lankavatara Sutra.* London : Routledge and Kegan Paul, 1957.

The Councils

Bareau, André. *Les Premiers Conciles bouddhiques.* Annales du Musée Guimet, No. LX. Paris : Presses Universitaires, 1955.

Tantrism

Bhattacharyya, B. *An Introduction to Buddhist Esoterism.* London : Oxford University Press, 1932.
Das Gupta, S. B. *An Introduction to Tantric Buddhism.* Calcutta : University of Calcutta, 1950.
Eliade, Mircea. *Yoga: Immortality and Freedom.* New York: Bollingen, 1958.
Tucci, Giuseppe. *The Theory and Practice of The Mandala;*

with special reference to the modern psychology of the sub-conscious. London : Rider, 1961.

Comparisons

Bouquet, A. C. *Comparative Religion.* Penguin, 1956.

Lubac, Henri de. *Aspects du bouddhisme.* Paris : Edn. du Seuil, 1951.

Smith, H. W. *Man and His Gods.* New York : Grosset, 1952.

CHINESE BUDDHISM

General

De Bary, Wm. T., et al., eds. *Sources of Chinese Tradition.* New York : Columbia, 1960.

Dumoulin, H. *Zen, Geschichte und Gestalt.* Bern : Francke, 1959.

Eliot, Sir Charles. *Japanese Buddhism.* London : Arnold, 1935. "Buddhism in China," pp. 142–176.

Fung Yu-lan. *A History of Chinese Philosophy.* Tr. by Derk Bodde. 2 vols. Princeton: Princeton University Press, 1952-1953.

Morgan, Kenneth W. *The Path of the Buddha; Buddhism Interpreted by Buddhists.* New York : Ronald, 1956.

Reischauer, Edwin O. *Ennin's Travels in T'ang China.* New York : Ronald, 1955.

Wright, Arthur F. *Buddhism in Chinese History.* Stanford : Stanford University Press, 1959.

Yang, C. K. *Religion in Chinese Society: a Study of Contemporary Social Functions of Religion and Some of Their Historical Factors.* Berkeley : University of California Press, 1961.

Zürcher, E. *The Buddhist Conquest of China.* Leiden : Brill, 1959.

TIBETAN BUDDHISM

General

Bell, Sir Charles. *The Religion of Tibet.* Oxford : Oxford University Press, 1931.

Demiéville, Paul. *Le Concile de Lhasa: une controverse sur le quiétisme entre bouddhistes de l'Inde et de la Chine au VIIIe siècle de l'ère chrétienne,* tome 1. Paris : Imprimerie Nationale, 1952.

Eliade, Mircea. *Le Chamanisme et les techniques archaïques de l'extase.* Paris : Payot, 1951.

Govinda, Anagarika. *Foundations of Tibetan Mysticism.* London : Rider, 1959.

Maraini, Fosco. *Secret Tibet.* New York : Viking, 1952.

Waddell, L. A. *The Buddhism of Tibet or Lamaism.* Cambridge : Heffner, 1943.

JAPANESE BUDDHISM

Bibliographies

Borton, Hugh, et al., comps. *A Selected List of Books and Articles on Japan, in English, French, and German.* Cambridge : Harvard, 1954.

General Works

Bunce, William K., ed. *Religions in Japan—Buddhism, Shintō, Christianity: from the report prepared by the Religions and Cultural Resources Division, Civil Information and Education Section, General Headquarters of the Supreme Commander for the Allied Powers, Tokyo, March, 1948.* Tokyo : Tuttle, 1955.

Eliot, Sir Charles. *Japanese Buddhism.* London : Arnold, 1935.

Kishimoto, Hideo, comp. and ed. *Japanese Religion in the Meiji Era.* Tokyo : Ōbunsha, 1956.

Sansom, Sir George B. *Japan: A Short Cultural History.* New York : Appleton-Century-Crofts, 1943.

Takakusu, Junjirō. *The Essentials of Buddhist Philosophy.* Honolulu : University of Hawaii Press, 1947.

Tsunoda, R., et al., eds. *Sources of the Japanese Tradition.* New York : Columbia, 1958.

Shintō

Holtom, Daniel C. *National Faith of Japan: A Study in Modern Shintō.* London : Routledge and Kegan Paul, 1938.

Saunders, E. Dale. "Japanese Mythology," in S. N. Kramer, ed., *Mythologies of the Ancient World.* New York : Doubleday, 1960.

Early Buddhism

Anesaki, Masaharu. "The Foundation of Buddhist Culture in Japan : The Buddhist Ideals as conceived and carried out by the Prince Regent Shōtoku," *Monumenta Nipponica,* VI (1943), 1–12.

De Visser, M. W. *Ancient Buddhism in Japan: Sūtras and Ceremonies in Use in the Seventh and Eighth Centuries A.D., and their History in Later Times.* Leiden : Brill, 1935.

Esotericism

Glasenapp, Henri de. *Mystères bouddhistes.* Paris : Payot, 1944.

Saunders, E. Dale. *Mudrā: A Study of Symbolic Gestures in Japanese Buddhist Sculpture.* New York : Bollingen, 1960.

Amidism

Coates, Harper H., and Ishizuka, Ryugaku, tr. *Hōnen the Buddhist Saint, his Life and Teaching.* Kyoto : Chion-in, 1949.

Lubac, Henri de. *Amida.* Paris : Editions du Seuil, 1955.

Nichiren

Anesaki, Masaharu. *Nichiren the Buddhist Prophet.* London : Oxford University Press, 1916.

Renondeau, Gaston. *La Doctrine de Nichiren: suivie de la traduction annotée de six de ses ouvrages.* Paris : Presses Universitaires, 1953.

Zen

Blyth, R. H. *Zen in English Literature and Oriental Classics.* Tokyo : Hokuseido, 1942.

Herrigel, Eugen. *Zen in the Art of Archery.* New York : Pantheon, 1956.

Humphreys, C. *Zen Buddhism.* London : Allen and Unwin, 1957.

Suzuki, D. T., Fromm, E., and DeMartino, R. *Zen Buddhism and Psychoanalysis.* New York : Harper, 1960.

New Religions

Bairy, Maurice A. *Japans Neue Religionen in der Nachkriegszeit.* Bonn : Röhrscheid, 1959.

Hammer, Raymond. *Japan's Religious Ferment.* New York : Oxford University Press, 1962.

Offner, Clark B. and Henry van Straelen. *Modern Japanese Religions: With special emphasis upon their doctrines of healing.* New York : Twayne, 1963.

Schiffer, Wilhelm. "New Religions in Postwar Japan," *Monumenta Nipponica,* XI, 1 (1955), 1–14.

Thomsen, Harry. *The New Religions of Japan.* Rutland, Vt.: Tuttle, 1963.

van Straelen, Henry. *The Religion of Divine Wisdom: Japan's most Powerful Religious Movement.* Kyoto : Veritas, 1957.

Watanabe, Baiyū. "Modern Japanese Religions; Their Success Explained," *MN,* XIII, 1–2 (1957), 253–262.

Texts

Ch'an, Chu, tr. *The Sūtra of 42 Sections: and two other scriptures of the Mahayana school.* London : The Buddhist Society, 1947.

Conze, Edward, ed. *Buddhist Scriptures.* London : Penguin, 1959.

──────. *Buddhist Texts through the Ages.* New York : Philosophical Library, 1954.

Kern, H. *The Saddharma-pundarīka, or The Lotus of the True Law.* Oxford : Clarendon, 1909.

La Vallée Poussin, Louis de, tr. *L'Abhidharmakosa de Vasubandhu.* 6 vols. Paris : Geuthner, 1923–1931.

Price, A. F. *The Diamond Sutra; or the Jewel of Transcendental Wisdom.* London : The Buddhist Society, 1955.

Suzuki, Daisetz Teitaro. *Studies in the Lankavatara Sutra. One of the most important texts of Mahayana Buddhism, in which almost all its principal tenets are presented, including the teaching of Zen.* London : Routledge and Kegan Paul, 1957.

Tajima, Ryūjun. *Etude sur le Mahāvairocana-Sūtra (Dainichikyō); avec la traduction commentée du premier chapitre.* Paris : Maisonneuve, 1936.

Statistics on Religions

These statistics are based on Shinshō Hanayama, *A History of Japanese Buddhism* (Tokyo: CIIB, 1960). The statistics on the New Religions are based on Watanabe Baiyū (consult bibliography), W. K. Bunce, *Religions in Japan,* and Harry Thomsen, *The New Religions of Japan* (Tokyo : Tuttle, 1963). Figures are at best approximative.

Sect	Headquarters	Temples	Priests	Followers
TENDAI	Enryakuji (Mt. Hiei)	3435	4246	720,086
Jimon	Onjōji (Otsu)	222	1058	32,299
Shinzei	Saikyōji (Otsu)	424	550	27,706
SHINGON				
Kōya-san	Kongōbuji (Mt. Kōya)	3552	4381	887,062
Tōji	Kyōōgokokuji (Kyoto)	358	325	102,497
Daigo	Daigoji (Kyoto)	946	3510	767,871
Omuro	Ninnaji (Kyoto)	795	903	132,437
Chizan	Chishakuin (Kyoto)	2989	5207	818,223
Buzan	Hasedera (Nara)	2859	2376	324,653
JŌDO	Zōjōji (Tokyo)	5173	6116	3,193,762
Seizan	Kōmyōji (Kyoto)	578	661	219,360
Seizan-Zenrinji	Zenrinji (Kyoto)	65	480	129,740
ZEN				
Rinzai	Kenninji (Kyoto)	72	67	28,856
	Tōfukuji (Kyoto)	384	535	28,814

Sect	Headquarters	Temples	Priests	Followers
	Kenchōji (Kamakura)	412	285	34,240
	Engakuji (Kamakura)	210	157	32,180
	Daitokuji (Kyoto)	205	286	73,015
	Myōshinji (Kyoto)	3510	3580	1,846,091
	Tenryūji (Kyoto)	109	95	245,800
	Shōkokuji (Kyoto)	126	122	73,470
Sōtō	Eiheiji (Fukui) and			
	Sōjiji (Tsurumi)	14,914	15,836	6,758,818
Ōbaku	Mampukuji (Uji)	547	712	111,604

JŌDO SHIN

Honganji	Nishi-Honganji			
	(Kyoto)	10,641	14,921	7,060,761
Otani	Higashi-Honganji			
	(Kyoto)	9306	15,638	6,402,544
Takata	Senjūji (Mie)	625	1200	300,330
Bukkōji	Bukkōji (Kyoto)	370	706	172,998
Izumoji	Goshōji (Fukui)	56	167	31,900
Kōshōji	Kōshōji (Kyoto)	501	798	120,115
Kibe	Kinshokuji (Shiga)	224	414	112,756
Yamamoto	Shōjōji (Fukui)	24	45	3040
Jōshōji	Jōshōji (Fukui)	56	63	90,135
Sammonto	Senshōji (Fukui)	56	86	13,005
NICHIREN	Kuonji (Yamanashi)	4489	4918	1,399,202
Shōshū	Daisekiji (Shizuoka)	117	132	116,710
Kemponhokke	Myōanji (Kyoto)	196	176	46,592
Hokke	Honjōji (Niigata)	718	1789	534,570
Hommonbu-	Honryūji (Kyoto) and			
tsuryū	Yuseiji (Kyoto)	167	444	61,718
Nichiren				
honshū	Yoboji (Kyoto)	38	59	18,160
Nakayama				
myōshū	Hokkyōji (Chiba)	16	59	103,234

Sect	Headquarters	Temples	Priests	Followers
Hossō	Yakushiji (Nara)	21	649	44,685
Shōtoku	Hōryūji (Nara)	22	25	7795
KEGON	Tōdaiji (Nara)	51	512	53,800
RITSU	Tōshōdaiji (Nara)	23	47	33,204
JISHŪ	Shōjōkōji (Kanazawa)	424	590	43,799
YŪZUNEMBUTSU	Dainembutsuji (Osaka)	354	318	60,000
NEW RELIGIONS				
Ōmoto	Kyoto	618	335	203,888
Ananai	Shizuoka	65	510	104,436
Seichō no Ie Kyōdan	Tokyo	33	5,300	1,469,844
Sekai kyūsei-kyō	Atami	95	2,201	385,664
Reiyūkai	Tokyo	5	593	3,465,688
Risshō kōsei-kai	Tokyo	84	4,650	2,000,000
Tenri-kyō	Tenri	15,162	102,000	2,021,600
Tenshō kōtai jingū	Tabuse	136	221	110,124
Konkō-kyō	Konkō chō (Okayama)	1,621	3,569	634,303
Sōka gakkai	Tokyo			10,000,000
PL Kyōdan	Tondabayashi	203	631	605,213

Chronologies

India

B.C. 558–478	Siddhārtha Gautama, the Buddha.
c. 542–490	Bimbisāra, King of Magadha.
c. 480	First Buddhist Council at Rājagriha.
327–325	Invasion by Alexander of Macedon.
c. 273–237	Ashoka; Buddhist missions.
c. 200–200 A.D.	Period of greatest Buddhist influence in India.
c. 200	Buddhism penetrates Ceylon.
c. 190	Greek kingdoms in northwest India.
c. 170–165	Yüeh-chih (Iranians) invade India.
c. 150	Milanda (Gk. Menander), greatest of Indo-Greek kings.
c. 90	Shakas invade northwest India.
c. 80	Pāli canon.
A.D. c. 100–200	Rise of Mahāyāna Buddhism; prominence of Nāgārjuna's Mādhyamika school until the fifth century. Buddhism spreads to Funan, Champa, Sumatra.
c. 300	Buddhism spreads to Java and Borneo.
c. 400–500	Asanga and Vasubandhu, Mādhyamika philosophers. Founding of Buddhist monastery at Nālandā. Buddhism spreads to Cambodia.
c. 500–1000	Prominence of Yogāchāra school; Buddhism spreads to Burma.
c. 600–700	Buddhist Tantrism systematized.
c. 600–800	Buddhism spreads to Nepal and Tibet.

c. 1200   Muslims defeat Hindus (1192) and organized
               Buddhism disappears.

CHINA

B.C. 200–200 A.D. Han Dynasty.
A.D. 65   First reference to Buddhism in China.
220–280   Three Kingdoms (Wei, Shu, Wu).
280–420   Chin dynasty.
317   North China abandoned to barbarians.
399–414   Pilgrimage of Fa-hsien to central Asia and
               India.
405   Kumārajīva (344–413).
d. 527   Bodhidharma, first Chinese Ch'an patriarch.
542   T'an-luan (476–542), patriarch of Pure
               Land sect.
575   T'ien-t'ai school of Buddhism founded by
               Chih-k'ai (531–597).
589–618   Sui dynasty.
618–906   T'ang dynasty.
623   Chi-tsang (549–623) exponent of Mādhy-
               amika school and commentator on the
               Three Treatises (Ch. San-lun; J. Sanron).
629–645   Hsüan-tsang (596–664) travels to India.
641   Chinese Buddhist princess marries king of
               Tibet.
645   Death of Tao-ch'o, patriarch of Pure Land
               sect.
671   I-ching begins pilgrimage to India.
693   Empress Wu (r. 684–705) adopts Buddhist
               title of "Divine Empress Who Rules the
               Universe" (*chakravartin deva Empress*).
713   Hui-nêng (638–713), sixth Ch'an patriarch.
845   Official repression of Buddhism.
867   I-hsüan (d. 867), founder of Lin-chi (Rin-
               zai) school of Ch'an Buddhism.
868   Printing of Diamond Sūtra.

869	Liang-chieh (807–869), founder of Ts'ao-tung (Sōtō) school of Ch'an Buddhism.
972	Printing of Buddhist canon begins.
907–960	Five Dynasties.
960–1279	Sung Dynasty.
1260–1368	Yüan Dynasty.
1368–1644	Ming Dynasty.
1644–1911	Ch'ing Dynasty.
1911–	Republic.

TIBET

A.D. 617–698	Srong-tsan-gampo; introduction of Buddhism to Tibet.
641	Treaty with China.
c. 747	Padmasambhava establishes Buddhism.
791	Buddhism proclaimed state religion.
838	Persecution of Buddhism.
1050	Atīsha's (b. 982) reforms.
1261	Conversion of Kublai Khan to Lāmaism.
c. 1400	Tsonkhapa (1357–1419) establishes Gelukpa tradition.
1647	Tibet united politically.

KOREA

The Three Kingdoms

B.C. c. 57–935 A.D.	Silla.
B.C. c. 18–663 A.D.	Paikche.
B.C. c. 37–668 A.D.	Koguryo.
A.D. 918–1257	Koryo.
1259–1356	Mongol domination.
1392–1910	First dynasty.
1910–1945	Japanese domination.
1945–	Divided independence.

JAPAN

B.C. c. 2500–c. 200   Jōmon culture.
B.C. c. 200–
   c. 200 A.D.   Yayoi culture.
   c. 200–645   Clan period.
   552   Introduction of Buddhism to Japan.
   592–628   Reign of Suiko. Shōtoku regent.
   594   Buddhism proclaimed state religion.
   604   Shōtoku's "Constitution."

NARA PERIOD (710–784)

   710   First permanent capital at Nara.
   712   Kojiki.
   720   Nihongi.
   752   Dedication of Great Buddha at Tōdaiji (Nara).
   754   Ganjin establishes ordination platform at Nara.
   764–770   Dōkyō's rule.
   788   Saichō founds temple (Enryakuji) on Mount Hiei.

HEIAN PERIOD (794–1185)

   794   Capital changed to Heian-kyō (Kyoto).
   805   Saichō (767–822) returns from study in China.
   806   Kūkai (774–835) returns from study in China.
   816   Kūkai founds monastery on Mount Kōya.
   818   Saichō codifies rules for monks at Mount Hiei.
   838–847   Ennin studies in China and returns to introduce Esotericism into Tendai.
   858   Enchin returns from China and founds center at Miidera.

933	Beginning of strife between Miidera and Hiei factions of Tendai.
972	Kūya (903–972), Amidist popularizer.

FUJIWARA (980–1185)

1017	Genshin (942–1017), author of *Essentials of Salvation*.
1095	Sōhei, militant monks, make first raid on capital from Mount Hiei.
1132	Ryōnin (1071–1132), forerunner of Pure Land sect.

TAIRA (1159–1185)

KAMAKURA PERIOD (1185–1333)

1191	Eisai (1141–1215) introduces tea and Rinzai sect of Zen.
1192	Yoritomo becomes first shōgun.
1206	Hōnen (133–1212) exiled.
1222	Dōgen (1200–1253), Japanese founder of Sōtō sect of Zen, goes to China.
1260	Nichiren (1222–1282) predicts invasion.
1262	Shinran (1173–1262), founder of Shin sect.
1268	Nichiren warns of Mongol invasion.
1271	Nichiren escapes death sentence and is banished.
1274	First Mongol invasion.
1281	Second Mongol invasion.
1289	Ippen (1238–1289), Amidist popularizer.

ASHIKAGA PERIOD (1333–1568)

c. 1350	Musō Soseki (1275–1351), exponent of the tea cult and Zen.
1488	Nisshin (1407–1488), of Nichiren sect.
1499	Rennyo (1415–1499), of Pure Land sect.

1542   First Europeans, Portuguese merchants land
              on Kyūshū.
1549   St. Francis Xavier arrives in Japan.
1565   Nichio (1565–1630), leader of Fuju-fuse
              sect.
1576   Ikkō rebellions suppressed.
1587   First persecution of Christians.

TOKUGAWA PERIOD (1600–1868)

1600   Victory of Tokugawa at Sekigahara.
1610–1615   *Various Ordinances Regarding Sects and
              Temples.*
1617   Persecutions of Christians.
1654   Introduction of Ōbaku sect of Zen by Yin-
              yüan (1592–1673).
1688–1703   Genroku period.
c. 1700   Hakuin (1685–1768), second founder of
              Rinzai Zen.

MEIJI PERIOD (1868–1912)

1854   Perry "opens" Japan.
1868   Tokugawa house falls; Emperor restored;
              Buddhism disestablished.
1871   Climax of "exterminate the Buddhas and
              abandon the scriptures" movement.
1870   Shintō becomes state religion.
1873–1875   "College of the Great Doctrine" functions.
1873   Buddhist missions to Europe and America
              for study.

Glossary of Indian Terms
with Their Japanese Equivalents

A

ABHĀVA (J. MU)—Nonexistence.

ABHAYA (J. MUI)—Fearlessness.

ABHIDHARMA (J. ABIDAMMA)—Third "Basket," or part, of the canon, treating in detail the technical elements of the Law.

ABHISAMBODHANA (J. ABISAMBODAI)—The final and complete act of Awakening.

ABHISHEKA (J. KANJŌ)—Consecration by anointment.

ACHALA (J. FUDŌ)—Immobile.

ĀCHĀRYA (J. AJARI)—Master.

ADVAYA (J. MUNI)—Nonduality.

ĀGAMA (J. AGON)—"References." See NIKĀYA. General name for Hīnayāna scriptures.

AHIMSĀ (J. FUGAI)—Nonviolence.

ĀNANDA (J. ANAN)—Favorite disciple of the Buddha.

ANĀTMAN (J. MUGA)—"Absence of Self," by which Buddhism means that the personality has no existence in and by itself. The individual exists as an aggregate of psychic phenomena, not as an independent being.

ANGUTTARANIKĀYA (J. ZŌICHI AGON)—See NIKĀYA.

ANITYA (J. MUJŌ)—Impermanence.

APSARAS (J. TENNYO)—Divine females, nymphs.

ARHANT, ARHAT (J. RAKAN)—Saint, "worthy." One of the numerous epithets of the Buddha. The term also signifies one who has fully realized in himself the essence of the Buddhist Law.

ARŪPA (J. MUSHIKI)—Formless.

ĀRYA (J. SHŌ)—Saint.

ĀRYASATYA (J. SHŌTAI)—The Four Noble Truths : (1) suffering; (2) origin of suffering; (3) the stopping of suffering; (4) the way leading to the stopping. First set forth by the Buddha in his first sermon at Benāres.

ASANGA (J. MUJAKU)—Founder of the mystic Mahāyāna school called Yogachāra or Vijnānavāda.

ASAMSKRITA (J. MUI)—Uncompounded.

ASHOKA (J. AIKU)—Indian emperor converted to Buddhism. Grandson of the founder of the Maurya dynasty, he encouraged the dissemination of Buddhism.

ASHVAGHOSHA (J. MEMYŌ)—Famous Mahāyānist writer and councilor of Kanishka (c. 100 A.D.).

ASHVATTHA (J. ASHUBATA)—Pipal tree (*ficus religiosa*), under which the Buddha attained Enlightenment.

ASURA (J. ASHURA)—Demons, titans, rivals of the gods.

ĀTMAN (J. GA)—In Brāhmanism, a permanent Self, partaking of the great All. Denied by Buddhism in its theory of non-self (*anātman*).

AVALOKITESHVARA (J. KANNON)—Bodhisattva of Compassion. Chinese : *kuan-yin*.

AVATĀRA (J. GONGEN)—An historical incarnation.

AVIDYĀ (J. MUMYŌ)—Ignorance.

B

BHADRAVARGĪYA (J. GO-BUSSHI)—"Those of the Happy Group," disciples of the Buddha.

BHAGAVAT (J. SESON)—The Blessed One (i.e., the Buddha).

BHAVA (J. U)—Existence; type of "desire."

BHIKSHU (J. BIKU)—Monk.

BHIKSHUNĪ (J. BIKUNI)—Nun.

BHŪTA (J. JITSU)—Reality, actuality.

BĪJA (J. SHUJI)—Seed.

BODHI (J. BODAI, KAKU)—Awakening, Enlightenment, i.e., the supreme knowledge which enables one to see all previous existences and to recognize the cause of suffering.

BODHISATTVA (J. BOSATSU)—"Being to be Enlightened," i.e.,

those who are on the way to Enlightenment and to becoming Buddha.

BRAHMĀ (J. BON-TEN)—Supreme god of Brāhmanism, who with Indra often appears in the Buddhist legend; stands for Brahman, *q.v.*

BRAHMAN (J. BON)—According to Brāhmanism, the Absolute, essence of the All.

BRĀHMAN—A member of the priestly cast.

BUDDHA (J. BUTSU, HOTOKE)—"He who is Awakened," that is, he who has realized the true state of things. One who has attained BODHI.

BUDDHAGHOSA (J. BUTSUMYŌ)—Famous Theravāda writer; second half of fourth century A.D.

BUDDHATĀ (J. BUSSHIN)—State of Buddhahood.

C

CHAITYA (J. SEITEI)—A sacred spot, a shrine.

CHAKRA (J. RIN, HŌRIN)—The Wheel, symbol of Buddhist Law. The Buddha puts in motion the Wheel of the Law (DHARMA-CHAKRA) when he makes his first sermon at Benāres.

CHAKRAVARTIN (J. RINNŌ, TENRINNŌ)—"Wheel King," or universal monarch, an epithet of the Buddha.

CHETANĀ (J. I)—Volition, willing.

CHITTA (J. SHIN)—Spirit, mind.

D

DAGOBA—*See* STŪPA.

DĀNA (J. SE)—Charity, giving. One of the six virtues of a Bodhisattva.

DĀNAPATI (J. SESHU)—Donor.

DEVA (J. -TEN)—Gods, "one who shines." Not a creative divinity, nor one who is omniscient or omnipotent, but rather simply an inhabitant of the heavens.

DEVADATTA (J. DAIBADATTA)—Cousin of the Buddha, who after being converted betrays the Buddha.

DEVARĀJA (J. TENNŌ)—God-king.

DhāranĪ (J. darani)—Magic formulas in Tantric Buddhism. By extension, Mahāyānist works treating these formulas.

Dharma (J. ho)—(1) The final Reality; (2) correctness, order, virtue; (3) order of things; (4) by extension, the universal Order, the Law; (5) perceptions grasped through the intellect (manas).

Dharmachakra (J. hōrin)—The Wheel of the Law, symbol of the Buddha's Enlightenment. See chakra.

Dharmachakrapravartana (J. tembōrin)—Turning the Wheel of the Law. See chakra.

Dharmadhātu (J. hokkai)—(1) The domain of the Buddhist Law (*dharma*); (2) the universe as being comprised of things and beings.

Dharmapāla (J. Gohō)—Guardian of the Law; name of a philosopher.

Dharmashūnyatā (J. hōkū)—The non-reality of the phenomenal world. See shūnyatā.

Dhātu (J. kai)—Domain, world, the four elements, as in rūpa-dhātu, "form world," etc.

Dhātugarbha (Skt.)—"Relic container," see stūpa.

Dhritarāshtra (J. jikoku-ten)—Guardian king, east.

Dhyāna (J. zen)—One of the six virtues of a Bodhisattva. The four d. represent four stages of meditation leading to the awakening of knowledge.

Dīghanikāya (J. chō agon)—See nikāya.

Duhkha (J. ku)—Suffering, see āryasatya.

G

Garbha (J. tai, taizō)—Matrix.

Gāthā (J. gata)—Song, versified stanza in Pāli or Sanskrit.

Gati (J. shu)—Destination.

Gautama—Name of the family line of the historical Buddha.

Guhya (J. mitsu)—Mystery.

Guna (J. toku, kudoku)—Merit.

H

HĪNAYĀNA (J. SHŌJŌ)—"Lesser Vehicle," a term applied to the older schools of Buddhism by those believing in Mahāyāna. Its usage should be replaced by that of Theravāda, "those following the opinions of the Elders."

HOMA (J. GOMA)—Libation.

HSÜAN-TSANG (J. GENJŌ)—A Chinese monk (602–664) who traveled in India.

I

I-CHING (J. ICHIGYŌ)—A Chinese monk (635–713) who traveled in India.

INDRA (J. INDARA, TAISHAKU-TEN)—God of the Vedic and Brāhmanic pantheon, but also appearing in the Buddhist legend.

INDRIYA (J. KON)—Organ, root.

J

JĀTAKA—Collection of accounts concerning the previous existences of the Buddha.

JĀTI (J. SHŌ, HONJŌ)—Birth. *See* JĀTAKA.

JINA (J. SHŌSHA)—"Conqueror," one of the epithets of the Buddha.

JNĀNA (J. CHIE)—Knowledge.

K

KĀLA (J. JI)—Time, conceived of as cyclical.

KALĀJNĀNA—The sixty-four arts.

KALPA (J. KŌ)—Unit of cosmic time.

KĀMA (J. YOKU)—Desire, love.

KAPILAVASTU (J. KABIRABASOTSU)—Capital of Uttarakosala, present-day Rumindeī.

KARMA (J. GŌ)—Act. In Brāhmanism, the ritual act or the psychic act accompanying any action of a conscious being. The psychic act is indelible and determines the course of transmigration.

In Buddhism, the psychic act which according to its goodness or badness brings retribution in the following existence. Karma is intimately connected with the chain of existences. *See* SAMSĀRA.

KARUNĀ (J. HI)—Compassion.

KĀSHAYA (J. KESA)—Monk's stole.

KĀYA (J. SHIN)—Body, *see* TRIKĀYA.

KLESHA (J. BONNŌ)—Passions.

KŌAN (J.)—An irrational theme for Zen meditation.

KRISHNA (J. KIRISHNA)—Hero and god, eighth incarnation of Vishnu.

KSHĀNTI (J. NIN)—Patience.

KSHATRIYA—Warrior class, second of the four traditional classes in India, to which the Buddha belonged.

KUMĀRA (J. DŌJI)—Child (m.).

L

LAKSHANA (J. SŌ)—Sign.

LOKA (J. SEKAI, SEKEN)—World.

LOKAPĀLA (J. SHI-TENNŌ)—The four Guardian Kings of the world : Dhritarāshtra (east), Virūdhaka (south), Virūpāksha (west), Vaishravana (north).

LUMBINĪ—Garden located near the city of Kapilavastu, place of birth of the historical Buddha.

M

MĀDHYAMIKA (J. CHŪDŌ)—Middle Path.

MAGADHA—Indian province located in the Ganges basin between Benāres and Bengal, the present Bihar.

MAHĀBHINISHKRAMANA—"The Great Departure" of the Buddha from his palace to begin a life of austerities.

MAHĀBODHI (J. DAI BODAI)—Great Awakening.

MAHĀKĀSHYAPA (J. KASHŌ)—Disciple of the Buddha who called the first council at Rājagriha.

MAHĀPARINIRVĀNA (J. DAI-HATSU NEHAN)—"Great total extinction" of the Buddha.

MAHĀPRAJĀPATĪ GAUTAMĪ (J. AIDŌ)—Second wife of Shuddhodana, father of the Buddha, and sister of Māyā, the Buddha's
mother; the adoptive mother of the Buddha and the first
woman to be admitted into the Community.

MAHĀPURUSHA—"Great Man," having, like the Buddha, the
thirty-two signs. *See* PURUSHA.

MAHĀSĀNGHIKA (J. DAISHUBU)—Those of the "Great Assembly"
who, opposing the "Elders," or *thera,* caused the schism which
was ultimately to lead to the division of Buddhism into the so-
called Greater and Lesser Vehicles.

MAHĀYĀNA (J. DAIJŌ)—"Great Vehicle," or means of advancement toward salvation. Opposed to Hīnayāna, or "Lesser
Vehicle," *q.v.* A term invented by later, northern Buddhism.

MAITRĪ (J. JI)—Goodness.

MĀDHYANIKĀYA (P. MAJJHIMANIKĀYA; J. CHŪ AGON)—*See* NIKĀYA.

MĀLĀ (J. NENJU)—Rosary.

MANAS (J. I)—Intellect, considered as a sixth sense; organ of perceiving and of mental functions.

MANDALA (J. MANDARA)—Magic circle containing the power of
the divinities contained in it. In Tantrism, the mandala is used
as an object of meditation.

MANTRA (J. SHINGON)—Formula, spell.

MĀRA (J. MA)—The spirit of evil or of death.

MĀRGA (J. DŌ)—The Way, i.e., the fourth Noble Truth, or the
way which leads to the stopping of suffering.

MĀYĀ—First wife of Shuddhodana and mother of the Buddha.

MILINDA (J. MIRAN)—Indianized name of the Indo-Greek king
Menandros, or Menander, who was converted to Buddhism.
Ruled over the Panjāb c. 166–145 A.D. His discussions with
Nāgasena on Buddhism are contained in the famous *Milin-
dapanha,* or *Question of Milinda.*

MOKSHA (J. GEDATSU)—Liberation from the chain of births and
deaths.

MUCHILINDA (J. MOKUSHIRINDA[-RYŪ])—Serpent which protected
the Buddha during his meditation after the Awakening. Also a
lake (J. MUCHILINDA RYŪCHI).

MUDRĀ (J. IN, INGEI, INSŌ, MUDARA)—Seal, hand gesture.

MUNI (J. MUNI)—Wiseman; whence the epithet of the Buddha, Shākyamuni, "wiseman of the Shākyas."

N

NĀGA (J. RYŪ)—Mythical serpents who inhabit the water.

NĀLANDĀ (J. NARANDA)—Buddhist monastery and university.

NĀMA (J. MYŌ)—"Name," generally associated with "form" (RŪPA) in Buddhist thought.

NĀMARŪPA (J. MYŌSHIKI)—"Name and Form," notion comprising the whole of the psychic and physical individual.

NARAKA (J. JIGOKU)—Hells, of which there are eight cold and eight hot.

NIDĀNA (J. INNEN)—Cause. The chain of twelve causes explains the inevitable concatenation of death and rebirth.

NIKĀYA (J. ĀGAMA, *q.v.*)—The four general categories into which the *Sūtras* are divided : DĪGHA—long; MAJJHIMA—medium; SAMYUTTA—"gathered"; ANGUTTARA—"numbered." Combined they are called ĀGAMA, "references."

NIRMĀNA (J. KE, HENGE)—Metamorphosis.

NIRODHA (J. METSU)—Extinction; the third Noble Truth on the stopping of suffering.

NIRVĀNA (J. NEHAN)—Extinction or destruction of thirst or desire; supreme state of Void, goal of Buddhism, consisting of the escape from the chain of births and deaths and the liberation from all effects of karma. Also the real world as opposed to the illusory world of SAMSĀRA.

P

PADMA (J. RENGE)—Lotus.

PĀLI—Sacred language of Theravāda Buddhism.

PANCHASKANDHA (J. GOUN)—The Five Aggregates : matter, sensation, perception, psychic functions, thought.

PARAMĀRTHA-SATYA (J. SHINDAI)—Absolute Truth.

PĀRAMITĀ (J. DO)—The six virtues of a Bodhisattva : charity, observance of monastic rules, patience, energy, meditation, intelligence. An additional four are often added to the list : skill in using means of helping beings toward salvation, vow, strength, knowledge. The Theravāda list differs in part.

PĀTALIPUTRA—Present-day Patna, on the Ganges, site of the third Buddhist council around 241 B.C.

PĪPAL (J. HITSUHARA)—Tree under which the historical Bodhisattva attained Awakening; *ficus religiosa.* Also AJAPĀLA.

PITAKA (J. ZŌ)—"Basket," or collection of sacred scriptures. The "Three Baskets" form the Tripitaka, the whole of the Buddhist canon.

PRABHŪTARATNA (J. TAHŌ)—Bodhisattva of "Abundant Treasures," long in nirvāna. He appears to hear the Buddha preach the *Lotus* sūtra and so demonstrates that nirvāna is not annihilation.

PRAJNĀ (J. E, HANNYA)—Intelligence, knowledge, Wisdom. The third principle which governs Buddhist discipline. One of the Six Virtues (PĀRAMITĀ).

PRAJNĀPĀRAMITĀ (J. HANNYA HARAMITSU)—The perfection of intelligence or Wisdom given only to Bodhisattvas or Buddhas. A class of canonical works.

PRAKRITI (J. JISHŌ)—Matter.

PRANIDHĀNA (J. GAN)—Determination, or vow of the Bodhisattva to become Buddha.

PRĀTIMOKSHA (J. KAIHON)—Fundamental text comprising the list of disciplinary rules and, in case of infringement, sanctions.

PRATĪTYASAMUTPĀDA (J. JŪNI INNEN)—Chain of causality, having a double series of terms, one positive, one negative; suffering is caused by ignorance, and the suppression of ignorance means the suppression of suffering.

PRATYEKABUDDHA (J. ENGAKU)—Buddha-for-self.

PRETA (J. GAKI)—Hungry ghosts.

PUDGALASHŪNYATĀ (J. FUTOGARA-KŪ)—The nonexistence of The "person."

PŪJĀ (J. KUYŌ)—Prayer, act of faith.

PURUSHA (J. JŌBU)—Male, the male prototype, of which Vishnu, Buddha, Christ, etc., may be considered as examples.

R

Rāhula (J. Karakora)—Name of the son of the Buddha who became one of his disciples.

Rākshasa (J. arakasetsuba)—Canabalistic demons capable of assuming human form.

Rāma (J. Rama)—Hero and incarnation of Vishnu.

Ratna (J. hō)—Jewel.

Rishi (J. sen)—Ascetic, hermit, an immortal.

Rūpa (J. shiki)—Form. *See* nāma.

Rūpaskandha (J. shiki-un)—First Aggregate. That which may be experienced, the whole of appearances, all that is material in the universe. It includes the four elements (earth, water, fire, wind); the six sense organs (eye, ear, nose, tongue, body, heart) and their objects (form, sound, odor, taste, the tangible).

S

Sadāparibhūta (J. Jōfukyō)—A former incarnation of the Buddha. Nichiren identified himself with this manifestation.

Saddharma (J. myōhō)—True Law.

Sādhana—"Real-izing."

Samādhi (J. sammaji, jō)—Profound meditation in which the psyche becomes "fixed."

Samgīti (J. sōgyata)—Assembly or council called in order to codify and edit the oral teachings of the Buddha.

Samjnā (J. sō)—Perceptions, the third Aggregate.

Samjnāskandha (J. sō-un)—The perceptions as forming the third Aggregate.

Sāmkhya (J. sū)—Number; a system of classification and enumeration.

Samsāra (J. shōji)—The unending cycle of births and deaths; also the phenomenal, illusory world as opposed to nirvāna, the "real" world.

Samskāra (J. sōsokukara, gyō)—Formations, dispositions, or tendencies of the psyche which determine future existence.

Samskāraskandha (J. sosokukara-un)—Voluntary mental activity as forming the fourth Aggregate.

SAMSKRITA (J. UI)—Compounded. *See* ASAMSKRITA.

SAMUDAYA (J. SAMMUDAYA)—Second Noble Truth on the origin of suffering.

SAMVRITI (J. SANBUTSURITEI)—World of appearances.

SAMYAKSAMBUDDHA (J. SHŌTŌBUTSU)—Perfectly and completely Enlightened one.

SAMYUTTANIKĀYA (J. ZŌ AGON)—*See* NIKĀYA.

SANGHA (J. SŌ)—Community. With the Buddha and the dharma, the Community form the Three Jewels (TRIRATNA) of Buddhism.

SARVA-JNATĀ (J. ISSAI-CHI)—Omniscience.

SATTVA (J. UJŌ)—A being, a sentient being.

SATYA (J. TAI)—Truth.

SHAKTI (J. KŪNŌ)—Energy, the feminine counterpart of a god.

SHĀKYA—Clan to which the Buddha belonged.

SHĀKYAMUNI (J. SHAKA)—"Wise man of the Shākyas," one of the epithets of the Buddha.

SHĀLA (J. SHARA)—Tree under which Māyā is delivered.

SHĀNTIDEVA—Famous author, c. seventh century A.D.

SHĀRIPUTRA (J. SHARIHOTSU)—A disciple of the Buddha, head of the first Sangha.

SHARĪRA (J. SHARI)—Relic.

SHĪLA (J. KAI)—Rules, morality. The first principle governing the Buddhist discipline; one of the Six Virtues of a Bodhisattva.

SHLOKA (J. SHURU)—Sanskrit stanza composed of two verses divided into four hemistiches. The versification is based on the length of the syllables.

SHRAMANA (J. SHAMON)—Buddhist monk.

SHRAMANERA/SĀMANERA (J. SHAMI/SHAMINI)—Novice.

SHRAVAKA (J. SHARABAKA)—"Hearers," those who listen to the Buddha's words.

SHROTĀPANNA—According to the Theravāda tradition, "he who has entered the current," i.e., the wiseman who understands the final goal and who is on the way to attaining it.

SHUDDHODANA (J. EDDODAN)—Father of the Buddha, of the

Brāhmanic line of the Gautamas, head of the warrior clan of the Shākyas.

SHŪNYA (J. KŪ)—Void, emptiness, that which is without substance.

SHŪNYATĀ—*See* SHŪNYA.

SIDDHĀRTHA (J. SHITTATA)—"Goal Reached," name given to the historical Buddha after his birth.

SKANDHA (J. KENDO, SOKUKENDA, KENDA, UN)—Aggregates, or groups of elements, which compose the physical and mental being comprising : body, perception, form, knowledge.

SMRITI (J. NEN)—Memory, presence of mind.

STHAVIRA (J. SHITTABEIRA)—"Elders," those who represent the early Buddhist tradition; most commonly used in the Pāli form THERA.

STŪPA (J. TŌ, SOTOBA)—Reliquary, commemorative monument.

SUJĀTĀ (J. SHUJATA)—Woman who made the first offering to the Buddha after his six years of ascetic practices.

SUKHĀVATĪ (J. GOKURAKU SEKAI, JŌDO)—Heaven of the Satisfied, located in the west, presided over by Amitābha.

SŪTRA (J. KYŌ)—"Thread." Works supposedly containing the discourses of the Buddha or his immediate disciples; one of the Three Baskets (TRIPITAKA).

T

TANHĀ (Skt. TRISHNĀ; J. AI)—Desire; caused by the three impurities (KLESHA) : attachment (RĀGA), hate (DVESHA), and stupidity (MOHA).

TATHĀGATA (J. NYORAI)—"He who has thus come (or gone)," that is, he who has come like the Buddhas before him; one of the epithets of the Buddha.

TATHATĀ (J SHINNYO)—"Thusness," the reality of things.

THERA—"Elders." Originally designating those who followed the earlier form of Buddhism as opposed to the Mahāsānghikas, or followers of the Great Assembly. THERAVĀDA—doctrine based on the Pāli scriptures (Ceylon, Burma, Thailand, Cambodia, Laos).

Tope—*See* stūpa.

Trikāya (J. sanshin)—The Three Bodies of the Buddha : Law body (dharmakāya), Enjoyment body (sambhogakāya), and Transformation body (nirmānakāya). In Japanese these bodies are respectively : hosshin, hōjin or juyūshin, and ōjin or kashin.

Tripitaka (J. sanzō)—The Three Baskets, or parts, forming the Buddhist canon : Sūtra, Vinaya, and Abhidharma.

Triratna (J. sambō)—The Three Jewels : Buddha, dharma, and sangha, i.e., the Buddha, his Law, and the Community of monks.

Trishiksha—The three principles of Buddhist discipline : precepts (shīla), meditation (samādhi), and Wisdom (prajnā).

Trishnā—*See* tanhā.

Tushita (J. tosotsu)—Heaven of the Satisfied.

U

Upāsaka/upāsikā (J. ubasoku/ubai)—A lay member of the Community.

Upāya (J. hōben)—"Means" of progress toward salvation, or of helping toward salvation.

Uttarakosala—Confederation of; headed by the Shākya clan.

V

Vaishālī (J. bishari)—City, site of one of the Buddhist councils.

Vaishravana (J. bishamon or tamon-ten)—Guardian King, north.

Vajra (J. kongō)—Diamond, thunder, symbol of strength, power.

Varsha (J. ango)—Retreat.

Vasubandhu (J. Seshin)—Brother of Asanga, author of Mahāyānist metaphysical works and commentaries on the Sūtras.

Vedanā (J. jū)—Sensations.

Vedanāskandha (J. jū-un)—Sensations, as forming the second Aggregate.

Vibhava (J. mu-u)—Nonexistence; type of desire.

VIBHAVATANHĀ—Desire of annihilation.

VIDYĀ (J. MYŌ)—Knowledge.

VIDYĀRĀJA (J. MYŌŌ)—Knowledge King.

VIHĀRA (J. JŪ)—Monastery, residence.

VIJNĀNA (J. SHIKI)—Discerning, understanding, knowing.

VIJNĀNAVĀDIN—Mahāyānist sect based on the theory that all of the exterior world is only mental action.

VIJNĀSKANDHA (J. SHIKI-UN)—Knowing, as forming the fifth Aggregate.

VINAYA (J. RITSU)—Discipline, rules; one of the Three Baskets of the Buddhist canon.

VIRŪDHAKA (J. ZŌCHŌ-TEN)—Guardian King, south.

VIRŪPĀKSHA (J. KŌMOKU-TEN)—Guardian King, west.

VĪRYA (J. SHŌJIN)—Energy, one of the six Virtues of the Bodhisattva.

VISHISHTACHĀRITA (J. JŌGYŌ)—The Bodhisattva in the *Lotus* sūtra, who in ages past had been converted by the Buddha. Nichiren identified himself with V.

VISHNU (J. BISHICHU)—God, with solar characteristics, connected in part with the sacrifice.

VITARKA (J. JIN)—Reasoning, exposition.

Y

YAKSHA (J. YAKISHA)—Malevolent or benign spirits inhabiting trees.

YĀNA (J. JŌ)—Vehicle, means of transportation, as in Mahāyāna, "Greater Vehicle."

YOGA (J. YAKU, YUGA)—Yoke.

Index

Names of persons are printed in small capitals. Titles of works are printed in italics.

Abhidharma, 34, 36–37, 68, 106–111
Abhidharma school, 106
Abhidharmakosha, 105–111, 295
Absolute, nature of, 119–120, 215–216
Aggregates (of compounded "things"), 56–57
Aizen, 176
"All exists," 68, 107–109; *see also* Sarvāstivāda
America, contacts with, 258–260
Amida and Amidism, 145, 160, 168–170, 174, 187–203, 207, 222, 228, 229, 233, 240, 241–243, 253, 258, 293; origins of cult of, 187–192
Amida sūtras, 43
Amitābha; *see* Amida
Ananai, 278–279, 299
Antecedents of Buddhism; *see* Origins of Buddhism
Art, 162–164; *see also* Images and and Iconography
Asceticism of the Bodhisattva, 25
Ashikaga period (1333–1568), 237–245, 263, 305–306
Ashoka, 31, 46, 82–83
Atoms, theory of, 58, 107–109
Avadānasātaka, 39

Avatamsaka-sūtra, 118–119, 127–128, 131, 204–205
Awakening, 211; *see also* Enlightenment
Awakening of the Bodhisattva, 26

Being, categories of, 59
Bodhidharma, 205, 207–209
Bodhisattvas, 19–27, 41–43, 60–61, 70, 144, 172–176, 231, 232, 234
Brahmā, 52
Brahman, 15, 60
Brāhmanism, 15–17, 50–52, 60
Branches of Buddhism; *see* Schools
Buddha, The, 18–30, 50, 71, 165–166, 170, 234–235, 290
Buddhas, 60–61, 70–71, 144, 165–172, 194
Buddhists in contemporary Japan, statistical tabulation of, 297–299
Burmese Buddhism, 82–83, 84, 253

Canon, 34–37, 39–40, 40–43, 45, 290
Cause and effect, 61–63, 73, 110, 113, 121–122, 123–124
Celibacy and marriage, 119, 200, 239

Central Asia, Buddhism in, 47–48, 85

Ceylonese Buddhism, 33, 37–39, 47, 83–84

Ch'an; *see* Zen

Chinese Buddhism, 85–87, 106–107, 112, 116, 120–121, 124–125, 127–128, 138–139, 152–155, 188–189, 206–218, 220, 222–223, 291, 302–303

Chinzei, 196–203

Christianity, 243–244, 249, 258–260

"Church and state"; *see* State and religion

Classifications of Buddhist doctrine; *see* Divisions or stages of Buddhism

Commentaries, Pāli, 37–38

Conception and nativity of the Buddha, 19–22

Conduct, psychic; *see* Meditation; Training

Confucianism, 86–87, 96–97, 103, 150–151, 179, 249, 253–254

Consciousness, 119–120

Constitution of Seventeen Articles, 96–97

Cosmology, 57–58

Councils, Indian, 34, 37, 45–46, 48, 106, 290

Dai-butsu, 103

Dainichi; *see* Vairochana

Dainichikyō, 153, 154, 161, 249

Death of the Buddha, 29

Decline of Buddhism, periods or places of, 48–50, 75, 244–245, 247, 255–258; *see also* Meiji period

Deities; *see* Divinities

Dharma, 15; *see also* Element

Diamond sūtra, 295

Discipline; *see* Meditation; Training

Disestablishment, 255–258

Divine wisdom, Tenri doctrine of, 272; *see also* Tenri

Divinities, 57–58, 59–61, 76–77, 161, 166–176, 183–184, 242, 272–273; *see also* Brahmā; Brahman; Buddha; Vairochana

Division of Chinese Zen (into northern and southern schools), 210–211

Divisions or stages of Buddhism, according to: Kegon, 130–131; Tendai, 142–144; Shingon, 179–180; Nichiren, 230; New Sects, 272–273, 277, 280, 282, 284–285

Doctrine; *see* Canon; Divisions or stages of Buddhism; Schools; Sects; Texts

Dōgen, 221–225, 226

Dōshin; *see* Tao-hsin

Dual Shintō, 136–137, 183–184, 242, 255–256, 257, 258

Edo period, 246–254

Eight Doctrines, 142–144

Eightfold Negation, 117, 118–119

Eightfold Path, 54–55, 203–204

Eisai, 216, 218, 220–221, 222, 226

Eka; *see* Hui-k'o

Elements, 56, 58, 71, 107–111, 112–114, 122–123, 130, 131–132

Enchin, 146

Enlightenment, 203–204, 206–207, 211–212, 214, 216–218, 224, 252, 253; *see also* Awakening; Illumination; Meditation

Ennin, 145–146

Enō; *see* Hui-nêng

Eon; *see* Hui-yüan

Esoteric Buddhism; *see* Tantrism; *see also* Shingon

Esoteric Nembutsu, 189–190
Esoteric sects; *see* Shingon; Tendai
Esotericism, 136–137, 145–147, 176–184, 229, 293; *see also* Shingon; Tantrism
Essentials of Salvation, 137, 191
"Establishment" of Buddhism, 98, 102–103, 248–250
Establishment of Shintō, 255, 257–258
Europe and America, contacts with, 258–260
Exercises; *see* Meditation; Training
Exile of NICHIREN, 231–235
Exoteric, the, 176
Extensions of Buddhism ; *see* Growth or revival of Buddhism
"Exterminate the Buddhas and abandon the scriptures," 256–257
Eye Opener, The; see Kaimokushō

Five Aspects, 130–131
Five Houses (of Chinese Zen), 214–218
Five Periods, 142–143, 234
Five principles of NICHIREN, 235–236
Four Meetings of the Bodhisattva, 23–24
Four Noble Truths, 23–24, 26–27, 52–55, 64–65
"Frantic uprisings," or Ikkō Rebellion, 242
Fudō, 176
Fujiwara period (980–1185), 147–148, 160, 180–181, 190–195, 304
Fujū-fuse, 236–237, 249

Gautama the Buddha; *see* Buddha, The
GENJŌ; *see* HSÜAN-TSANG

Genroku period (1688–1703), 246–247
GENSHIN, 137, 191, 202
GIGEN; *see* I-HSÜAN
Gods; *see* Divinities
Great Departure of the Bodhisattva, 24
"Great Divinity" (KITAMURA SAYO), 276–277
Great Doctrine, College of, 257–258, 259
Growth or revival of Buddhism, periods of, 46–48, 74, 82–88, 91–93, 104–105, 134–136, 186–187, 218–221, 247, 257, 259–260; *see also* Heian period

HAKUIN, 250–252
Heian period (794–1185), 134–184, 263, 304–305
HIDEYOSHI, 244–245
Hiei, Mt., 135–140, 146–147, 190, 192–193, 198, 221, 228–229, 238, 239, 241, 242, 244, 297
Hīnayāna, 49–50, 111–112, 118, 125, 130, 131, 143, 179, 203–204, 224, 230, 234; *see also* Pāli canon; Theravāda
Hindu culture; *see* Brāhmanism
HŌNEN, 180, 192–196, 202–203, 230
HŌNEN, disciples of, 196–200
Honganji, 239, 241, 248, 258, 259, 298
Hossō, 119–124, 127, 130, 131, 133, 180, 218, 299
HSÜAN-TSANG, 218
HUI-K'O, 205, 209
HUI-KUO, 153–155, 161
HUI-NÊNG, 211–212
HUI-YÜAN, 207
HYAKUJŌ; *see* PO-CHANG

Ideation, 119, 121–124, 128–130

IEMITSU, 248, 249
IEYASU, 247–248
I-HSÜAN, 216
Ikkō, 201, 242
Illumination, 211, 215; see also Enlightenment
Images and iconography, 21, 29, 30, 32–33, 78–80, 91–93, 103–104, 161–176, 235
Indian Buddhism, 15–88, 114–116, 187–188, 203–208, 289–291, 301–302
Indications to the Teachings of the Three Religions, 150–152
Indra's Net, 129, 131, 204–205
INGEN; see YIN-YÜAN
Inscriptions, early Indian, 33
Introduction of Buddhism to Japan, 262
IPPEN, 200–201

Japanese Buddhism, survey of, 261–264; chronology, 304–306
Jina (the five Buddhas), 166–172
Jiriki and tariki, 193, 194
Jizō, 174–176
Jōdo (doctrine); see Amidism
Jōdo (school), 192–197, 199, 202–203, 239–240, 247–248, 297; see also Chinzei
Jōdo Shin, 194–202, 238–239, 241–242, 248, 258, 298
Jōjitsu, 111–114, 127, 132–133

Kaimokushō, 232, 234
KAKUBAN, 160, 190–191, 202, 245
Kamakura period (1185–1333), 184–237, 263, 305
Kannon, 172–174
Kashimono karimono ("things lent, things borrowed"), 273
Kashmir, council of, 48
Kegon, 127–132, 133, 180, 187, 191–192, 202, 218, 299

Kenninji, 221, 222, 223, 240
KŌAN, 206, 212–213, 216–218, 250, 252, 253
Kongōchōgyō, 161
KONKŌ DAIJIN, 274–275
Konkō, 274–275
Korean Buddhism, 91–92, 303
KŌSAI, 197, 203
Kōya, Mt., 148, 157–158, 159, 245, 297
KŪKAI, 136, 140–141, 149–159, 179–180, 184
KŪKAI, successors of, 160
KUMĀRAJĪVA, 115–116
Kusha, 105–111, 127, 130, 132
KUSHĀNA, 47–48
KŪYA, 137, 201

Lāmaism; see Tibetan Buddhism
LANKĀVATĀRA-SŪTRA, 43, 205–206, 209, 295
LIN-CHI (I-HSÜAN), 216–218
Lin-chi (sect); see Rinzai
Lotus of the Good Law, Sūtra of the, 41–43, 99–100, 119, 138, 142, 144, 172, 191–192, 201, 224, 229–236, 281, 282, 283, 294

Mādhyamika, 43, 88, 114–119; see also Middle Path
Magical practices and formulas, 44, 49, 75–76, 77, 79–80, 99, 159–160, 177–179
Mahāvairochana-sūtra, 161, 295
Mahāvastu, 40
Mahāyāna, 40–43, 49–50, 70–74, 75–81, 83–85, 118, 119, 125, 130, 143, 165, 179, 180, 204–206, 230, 234, 242–243, 282, 294–295
Maitrakanyaka, 39–40
Mandala, 79–80, 162–163, 166–

172, 180–181, 235; worlds of, 162–163

Man's Path, 284

Mantrayāna, 160–161

Mappō, 137, 185–186, 230–231, 234, 235

Marriage; *see* Celibacy and Marriage

Matter, 56–58, 109–111

Mean, 206

Meditation and psychic discipline, 55, 65–67, 79–80, 144–145, 163, 177–179, 188–189, 203–204, 206–207, 211–212, 214–216, 223–225

Meiji period (1868–1912), 255–260, 264–266, 306

Middle Path, 43, 72–74, 77–78, 88, 114–119, 123–124, 133, 144

Middle Way, 206

Miidera, 146–147, 221

Miki, 268–272

Miroku, 172

Monju, 174, 205

Moral and social aspects of doctrine, 65, 67

Mudrā, 165–176, 178

Musō, 225–226, 240, 241

Nan-ch'üan, 212

Nansen; *see* Nan-ch'üan

Nara period (710–784), 101–133, 304

Nara sects; *see* Hossō; Jōjitsu; Kegon; Kusha; Ritsu; Sanron

Native religion, 92–93, 98–100, 181–184, 261–262; *see also* Shintō

Negativism in Jōjitsu, 111, 112–113

Nembutsu, 145, 189–193, 195–197, 202–203, 228, 242–243, 247, 253

New Sects, 265–286, 294, 299

Nichiō, 236–237

Nichiren, 228–237

Nichiren (sect), 228–237, 245, 249, 293, 298

Nichiren, successors to, 236–237

Nirvāna, 36, 55–56, 66–67, 122, 138, 206

Nisshin, 236

Nobunaga, 244–245

Northern sect of Chinese Zen, 210–211

Ōbaku, 252–253, 298

Ōmoto, 278–279

Opposition to Buddhism in India, 87

Ordinances of Tokugawa, 248–249, 249–250

Ordination, 125, 135, 141

Origins of Buddhism, 15–17, 31–44, 45–52, 165; in Japan, 91–100, 262, 293

Painting and sculpture; *see* Art

Pāli canon, 34–37, 51–69

Pāli commentaries, 37–38

Pantheism, Tantric, 161, 166–176, 183–184

Phenomena, reality of, 54–56, 72–74, 78, 107, 113, 115–116, 119, 121–124, 128

Pillars of Ashoka, 31

PL, 284–286

Po-chang, 213–214, 222

Post-Nichiren period (1300–1600), 238–245, 305–306

Practices, religious, 44, 45–46, 48–49, 65, 67, 76, 77, 78–81, 101–103, 124–127, 144–145, 148, 159–160, 162–163, 177–178, 200, 209–210, 213–214, 248–249, 271–272, 277–278; *see also* Training; Vinaya

PRAJNA, 154–155
PRAJNĀPĀRAMITĀ, 78
Prajñāpāramitā-sūtras, 43, 143, 204, 207, 211
Pre-Nara period (to 710 A.D.), 91–100, 304
Pronunciation of Indian and Japanese words, 8–9
Pure Land, 188, 194–195; *see also* Amidism
Pure Land sects; *see* Jōdo; Jōdo Shin

Rājagriha, council of, 34, 37, 45–46
Reiyū-kai, 281–282, 299
RENNYO, 201–202, 241–242
Rinzai, 206, 213, 214, 216–218, 220–221, 250–252, 297–298
Risshō kōseikai, 282–283, 299
Ritsu, 124–127, 133, 148, 187, 218, 229, 233, 299
Rules; *see* Practices, religious; Ritsu; Vinaya
RYŌNIN, 191–192, 202
Ryūkan, 196, 203

Saddharma-pundarīka-sūtra; see Lotus of the Good Law
SAICHŌ, 135–136, 140–142, 153, 184, 220
Salvation, 186, 228; *see also* Amidism; New Sects
Sankhya, 15–16
Sanron, 112, 114–119, 130, 131, 133, 152, 180; *see also* Jōjitsu
Sanskrit, 39–43
Sarvāstivāda, 88, 106–109, 111
Sātyasiddhishāstra, 111–114
Sautrāntika, 111–112
Schools or branches of Buddhism; *see* Abhidharma; Amidism; Chinzei; Dual Shintō; Hīna-

yāna; Hossō; Jōdo; Jōdo Shin; Jōjitsu; Kusha; Mādhyamika; Mahāyāna; Pure Land; Ritsu; Sanron; Sarvāstivāda; Seizan; Tachikawa; Tantrism; Tendai; Theravāda; Vajrayāna; Vijnā-vadin; Yogāchāra; Zen
Scriptures; *see* Canon, Texts
Sects; *see* Anani; Chinzei; Fuju-fuse; Hossō; Ikkō; Jōdo; Jōdo Shin; Jōjitsu; Kegon; Konkō; Kusha; New Sects; Nichiren; Ōbaku; Ōmoto; Ōtani; PL; Reiyū; Rinzei; Risshō Kōsei; Ritsu; Sanron; Shingon; Seichō no Ie; Seizan; Sekai no Ie; Sekai Meshiya; Shinzei; Shōshū; Sōka Gakkai; Sōtō; Tachikawa; Tendai; Tenri; Tenshō kōtai jingū; Yūzunembutsu
Secular relations of Buddhism; *see* State and religion
Seichō no Ie, 279–280, 299
Seizan, 196, 203, 297
Sekai Meshiya (Sekai kyūsei-kyō), 280–281, 299
Self, 17, 51, 72, 107, 109, 110–111, 122–123, 212, 215, 278
Sex, 53, 77–78, 80–81, 181
Shākyamuni, 144–145, 170–172, 235
Shingon, 136–137, 148–181, 189, 190–191, 220, 221, 222, 233, 245, 297
SHINRAN, 196–200, 203, 239
Shinshū; *see* Jōdo Shin
Shintō, 103–104, 136–137, 181–184, 201, 243, 249–250, 253–258, 259–260, 265–266, 293; *see also* Tenri
SHINZEI, 242–243
Shinzei (sect), 202, 242–244, 297
SHŌKŌBŌ, 196, 203

Shōshū, 298; *see also* Nichiren sect
Shōtoku, Prince, 94–100
Siddhartha Gautama; *see* Buddha,
    The
Six Nara Sects, 102, 104–133
Social beliefs, 65–66
Society, culture, and life, 96–97,
    101–102, 104–105, 185–187,
    225–228, 246–247, 249–250, 260,
    261–264; *see also* State and re-
    ligion
Soga family, 93–100
Sōhei; *see* Warrior monks
Sōka Gakkai, 283
Soshicchijikarakyō, 161
Sōtō, 214–216, 221–225, 298
Sources for early Buddhism, 31–
    44
State and religion, 82, 84, 87, 91–
    100, 102–105, 134–136, 146–
    147, 148, 156–158, 159, 193,
    231–233, 235, 239, 240–241,
    241–242, 244–245, 247–250,
    253–254, 255–256, 257–258,
    259–260
Stūpa, 28, 31–32
Suchness, 71, 73–74, 114–115
Sūtra, 34–36, 41–43, 294
Symbols in representations of
    Buddha; *see* Mudrā
Syncretism; *see* Divisions and
    stages of Buddhism; Dual Shin-
    tō; *Indications to the Teachings
    of the Three Religions;* New
    Sects

Tachikawa, 180–181
Taika reform, 98–99
Taira period (1159–1185), 184
Tantrism, 44, 49–50, 75–81, 83,
    87–88, 148, 153–154, 159–160,
    163–176, 177–178, 180–181, 222,
    290; *see also* Shingon

Tao-hsin, 209–210
Taoism, 86–87, 150, 151, 179, 188,
    206–207
Tārā, 77, 78
Tariki, 194
Tea, 226–228
Temporal power of Buddhism; *see*
    State and religion
*Ten Stages of the Heart, Treatise
    on the,* 179–181
Tendai, 112, 131, 135–148, 159,
    163–164, 172, 180, 189–193,
    202, 220–222, 228–229, 230,
    233–234, 238, 242–243, 297
Tenri, 268–273, 299
Tenshō kōtai jingū, 276–278, 299
Texts, central: Pāli and Sanskrit
    (Theravāda and Mahāyāna), 33–
    44; Kusha, 106–107; Jōjitsu,
    111–112; Sanron, 115–116;
    Yogāchārin and Hossō, 119–
    120; Ritsu, 124–126; Kegon,
    128–129; Tendai, 138; Shingon,
    161; Jōdo Shin, 199; Nichiren,
    232–233; Shinzei, 243; Reiyū,
    281
Thai Buddhism, 82–83, 84
Theravāda, 34, 68–69, 71, 82–83,
    84; *see also* Hīnayāna; Pāli
    canon
Things, character of, 73–74; 122–
    124
Three Bodies, 71–72, 144, 229–
    230
Three Mysteries, 166, 176–179
Three Religions, 222
Three States of Mind, 195
Three Treatises; *see* Sanron
Tibetan Buddhism, 87–88, 291–
    292, 303
T'ien-t'ai; *see* Tendai
Time, 58–59, 108–109, 113–114
Tōji, 157–158, 297

Tokugawa period (1600–1868), 246–254, 263–264, 306
Training, 65–67, 125–127, 212–213, 214–218; *see also* Meditation and psychic discipline
Transmigration, 63–65
Trapusha and Bhallika, offering of, 27
Treasury of Analyses of the Laws; see Abhidharmakosha
Treatise on the Completion of the Truth; see Sātyasiddhishāstra
Tripitaka; *see* Pāli canon
Triple Truth of Tendai, 139
True Pure Land sect; *see* Jōdo Shin
Ts'ao-tung; *see* Sōtō
Tung-shan, 214
Twentieth century, new sects in, 275–286
Twenty-one Rules of Life, of PL, 284–285
Twofold truth, Sanron, 117–118
Twofold truth, Jōdo Shinshū, 200

Vairochana, 144–145, 159, 161–163, 167, 168, 176, 180, 229; *see also* Shingon
Vairochana-sūtra; see Dainichikyō
Vaishālī, council of, 46

Vajrayāna, 76–81
Vijnānavādin, 73–74
Vimalakīrtinirdesha, 205
Vinaya, 34, 37, 40, 46, 62, 124–127; *see also* Ritsu
Void, 71–72, 77–78, 109, 112–114, 114–115, 117–118, 132–133, 139, 204, 206, 213

Warrior monks, 146–148, 241, 245
Western contacts, 259–260
Western Paradise; *see* Pure Land
Wheel of the Law, 28
Wisdom Kings, 176
Wisdom sūtras; *see Prajnāpāramitrā-sūtras*

Xavier, St. Francis, 243–244

Yakushi, 172
Yin and yang, 180–181, 249
Yin-yüan, 252–253
Yoga, 15–16, 24, 51, 65, 67, 77, 79–80, 119, 177
Yogachārin, 118–121
Yōkan, 190–191, 202

Zen, 129, 130, 145, 196, 203–228, 229, 233, 238–239, 240–241, 250–253, 294, 297–298